Prentice Hall

LITERATURE
Timeless Voices, Timeless Themes

Open-Book Tests

THE BRITISH TRADITION

Prentice
Hall

Upper Saddle River, New Jersey
Glenview, Illinois
Needham, Massachusetts

ISBN 0-13-058396-0

3 4 5 6 7 8 9 10   05 04 03

CONTENTS

UNIT 1: FROM LEGEND TO HISTORY (449–1485)

UNIT 2: CELEBRATING HUMANITY (1485–1625)

Part 3: Focus on Literary Forms: Drama

UNIT 3: A TURBULENT TIME (1625–1798)

Part 1: The War Against Time

Part 2: The Story of Britain: A Nation Divided

Part 3: The Ties That Bind

Part 4: Focus on Literary Forms: The Essay

UNIT 4: REBELS AND DREAMERS (1798–1832)

Part 1: Fantasy and Reality

Part 2: Focus on Literary Forms: Lyric Poetry

Part 3: The Story of Britain: The Reaction to Society's Ills

UNIT 5: PROGRESS AND DECLINE (1833–1901)

Part 1: Relationships

UNIT 6: A TIME OF RAPID CHANGE (1901–PRESENT)

Part 3: Focus on Literary Forms: The Short Story

Part 4: From the National to the Global

Name _____   Date _____

"The Seafarer"
"The Wanderer"
"The Wife's Lament"
Open-Book Test

Multiple Choice and Short Answer

Write your answers to all questions in this section on the lines provided.
For multiple-choice questions, circle the letter of the best answer.

1. Which of the following best describes the author's tone at the beginning of "The Seafarer"? Choose the best answer, and then explain your choice.
   a. glorifying   b. reckless   c. frantic   d. solemn

   _____

   _____

2. In lines 47—51 of "The Seafarer," the speaker says: "And all these admonish that willing mind" (line 50). Select the best definition for *admonish*. Write one quotation that explains what admonishes a seafarer.
   a. indulge   b. pursue   c. warn   d. distract

   _____

   _____

3. Choose the statement that best describes the speaker's attitude toward fate in "The Seafarer." Find one quotation that supports your answer.
   a. Only brave men can endure fate.
   b. Faith in God can change a person's fate.
   c. Everyone fears the uncertainty of fate at some time.
   d. Fate is suffered only by people who believe in it.

   _____

   _____

4. How does your knowledge of historical context help you to understand the following passage from "The Wanderer"?
   > Who bears it, knows what a bitter companion, / Shoulder to shoulder, sorrow can be, / When friends are no more. His fortune is exile, / Not gifts of fine gold;

   _____

   _____

5. The speaker in "The Wanderer" says: "and never again / Shall come the loved counsel of comrade and king" (lines 33–34). How might the speaker feel about this situation? Explain your answer with evidence from the text.

   _____

   _____

6. Explain why "The Wife's Lament" is an elegy. Use specific examples from the poem to illustrate your point.

   _____

   _____

7. Which of the following characteristics shows that "The Wife's Lament" is a fitting example of Anglo-Saxon poetry? Select the best characteristic and explain your answer.
   a. a lyric quality
   b. a heroic battle
   c. a character changing fate
   d. a commoner's rise to glory

   _____

   _____

8. What literary characteristics are used in the following quotation from "The Wife's Lament"? Choose the correct answers. Explain why each of your choices is correct.

   > First my lord went out / away from his people
   > over the wave-tumult. / I grieved each dawn
   > wondered where my lord / my first on earth might be.

   a. caesura   b. metaphor   c. kenning   d. compound predicate

   _____

   _____

9. The speaker in "The Wife's Lament" says

   > May that young man   be sad-minded always
   > hard his heart's thought   while he must wear
   > a blithe bearing   with care in the breast
   > a crowd of sorrows.... (lines 42–45)

   What does the woman feel toward the "young man" in this quotation? Circle the letters of the best answers. Then explain why your choice is appropriate.
   a. rapture   b. fervor   c. rancor   d. compassion

   _____

   _____

10. In the space below, draw a picture of the wall described in lines 89 to 93, of "The Wanderer." Include details from these lines to show you understand the speaker's words. Explain what the wall might symbolize. Use reasons and examples from the poem to support your opinion.

    ```
    [blank box for drawing]
    ```

    _____

    _____

Extended Response

11. In question 10, you suggested what the wall in "The Wanderer" might symbolize. Now expand your thoughts by writing one or two paragraphs in which you explain why that symbolism is appropriate. Use examples from the poem to support your position.

12. In his journeys, the speaker in "The Wanderer" learned many lessons. He talks about one of the lessons in lines 12 to 13, when he says

> I have learned truly / the mark of a man
> Is keeping his counsel / and locking his lips

Why does the speaker believe this, and how has this belief shaped his actions? Answer these questions in a one- to two-paragraph written response. Be sure to support your ideas with evidence from the poem.

13. In lines 55–56 of "The Seafarer," the speaker says, "Who could understand, / In ignorant ease, what we others suffer." Based on evidence from the poem, what do the seafarer and people like him endure? Write one to two paragraphs in which you show that you understand what these seamen experience and why they go through such trouble. Be sure to use reasons and examples from "The Seafarer" to support your opinions.

14. Imagine you are the speaker in "The Seafarer" and another seaman has told you to turn away from God and believe in your own ability to deal with life. How would you respond? Write a short essay in which you explain why you can or cannot take this person's advice. Remember that you are the speaker in the poem and that your reasons and examples should come from the poem.

15. The woman in "The Wife's Lament" lives in an exile imposed upon her by her husband and his deceitful relatives. Why has she accepted this way of life? How has this separation affected her actions and beliefs? Respond to these questions with a short essay in which you provide evidence from the poem to illustrate your points.

Oral Response

16. Choose question 1, 3, 9, 11, or 14 or the question your teacher assigns you. Take a few minutes to look through the poems to prepare an oral response to give in class. If necessary, make notes to be clear about the order in which you want to present your answer.

Rubric for Evaluating Extended Responses

0	1	2	3	4
Blank paper Foreign language Illegible, incoherent Not enough content to score	Incorrect purpose, mode, audience Brief, vague Unelaborated Rambling Lack of language control Poor organization	Correct purpose, mode, audience Some elaboration Some details Gaps in organization Limited language control	Correct purpose, mode, audience Moderately well elaborated Clear, effective language Organized (perhaps with brief digressions)	Correct purpose, mode, audience Effective elaboration Consistent organization Sense of completeness, fluency

Name _____   Date _____

from *Beowulf*, translated by Burton Raffel

Open-Book Test

Multiple Choice and Short Answer

Write your answers to all questions in this section on the lines provided.
For multiple-choice questions, circle the letter of the best answer.

1. Review lines 15–29 of *Beowulf*, and list three reasons why Grendel might have led
    a painful life.

    _____

    _____

2. When Hrothgar's warriors fight Grendel, "No one / waited for reparation from his
    plundering claws" (lines 72–73). Reread lines 67—73 from *Beowulf*, and explain what
    reparation means. Then list at least two reasons from these lines to support your answer.

    _____

    _____

3. Review the Danish guard's speech to Beowulf in lines 158—165 of the text. What is the
    watchman's opinion of Beowulf? What evidence from these lines supports your ideas?

    _____

    _____

4. Which of the following literary terms best describes the underlined words in the following
    quotation from *Beowulf*? Choose the correct answer, and then explain why your choice is
    accurate.

    > That mighty protector of men / Meant to hold the monster till its life/Leaped out
    > (lines 366–369)

    a. caesura   b. kenning   c. appositive phrase   d. compound predicate

    _____

    _____

5. Which phrase best restates the underlined words in this quotation from *Beowulf*?
    Explain why your answer choice is the correct answer.

    > He who had come to them from across the sea, / Bold and strong-minded, had
    > driven affliction / Off, purged Herot clean. (lines 399–401).

    a. had killed Grendel in battle   c. had forced the evil monster from the hall
    b. had rid the land of pain and suffering   d. had successfully repelled fate

    _____

    _____

6. Paraphrase the following quotation from *Beowulf*.

    > Edgetho's / Famous son stared at death, / Unwilling to leave this world, to
    > exchange it / For a dwelling in some distant place (lines 697–701).

    _____

    _____

7. Choose the line from *Beowulf* that contains an example of a ceasura. Then explain why your answer is the best choice.
   a. Was great but all wasted: they could hack at Grendel (line 372)
   b. His miserable hole at the bottom of the marsh (line 395)
   c. Hidden evil before hidden evil (line 423)
   d. She welcomed in her claws, / clutched at him savagely (lines 475–476)

   _____

   _____

8. List two kennings from *Beowulf*, and explain what or whom each example represents. Then explain why writers might include kennings in their work.

   _____

   _____

9. What does Beowulf probably mean when he tells Wiglaf, "You're the last of all our far-flung family" (line 835)? Answer this question, providing one quotation from the text for support.

   _____

   _____

10. Use the following timeline to show the major battles in *Beowulf.* State the battle you think is the most important, and then use reasons and examples from the poem to explain why.

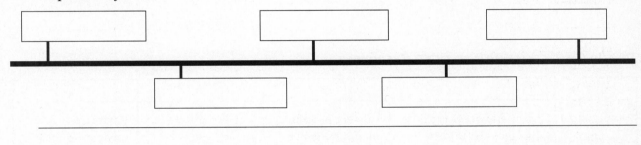

   _____

   _____

Extended Response

11. Beowulf and Wiglaf are formidable warriors who kill the dragon in *Beowulf.* How else do they compare? Find information from the poem, and fill in the following Venn diagram to show the similarities and differences between these two characters. Then write a paragraph in which you answer the question and support your opinion with evidence from your diagram.

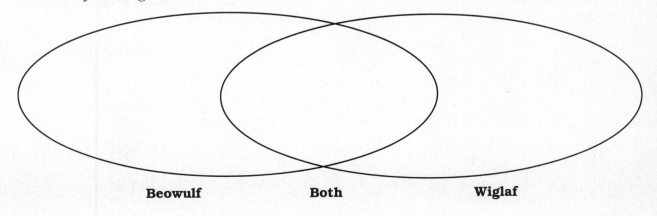

Beowulf   Both   Wiglaf

12. Extend the thoughts you expressed in number 11 above. Write a one-paragraph response in which you use your knowledge of the epic hero and evidence from *Beowulf* to answer this question: Are Beowulf and Wiglaf suitable figures for an epic? Provide additional support for your opinion from the information recorded on your Venn diagram.

13. Imagine that Grendel has escaped unharmed after fighting Beowulf at Herot. Based on what the poem has taught you about the monster, what do you think Grendel will do next in his war against Beowulf and the Danes? Use reasons and examples from *Beowulf* to further explain your opinion.

14. One of the major themes in *Beowulf* is conquest. What lessons can you learn from reading about the battles and accomplishments of the characters in this epic? Answer this question, providing evidence from the text to support your opinion.

15. When Grendel fights Beowulf, the reader learns that the monster's "time had come," and he will soon die. What does this idea say about the Danish belief in fate? Write a short essay in which you show how the belief in destiny influences the thoughts and actions of the characters. Provide several other examples from *Beowulf* to support your position.

Oral Response

16. Choose question 1, 8, 10, 11, or 15 or the question your teacher assigns you. Take a few minutes to look through the epic to prepare an oral response to give in class. If necessary, make notes to be clear about the order in which you want to present your answer.

Rubric for Evaluating Extended Responses

0	1	2	3	4
Blank paper Foreign language Illegible, incoherent Not enough content to score	Incorrect purpose, mode, audience Brief, vague Unelaborated Rambling Lack of language control Poor organization	Correct purpose, mode, audience Some elaboration Some details Gaps in organization Limited language control	Correct purpose, mode, audience Moderately well elaborated Clear, effective language Organized (perhaps with brief digressions)	Correct purpose, mode, audience Effective elaboration Consistent organization Sense of completeness, fluency

from *A History of the English Church and People* by Bede
from *The Anglo-Saxon Chronicle*, translated by Anne Savage

Open-Book Test

Multiple Choice and Short Answer

Write your answers to all questions in this section on the lines provided.
For multiple-choice questions, circle the letter of the best answer.

1. Based on the following line from *A History of the English Church and People*, what does *innumerable* mean?

    > In old times, the country had twenty-eight noble cities, and innumerable castles,
    > all of which were guarded by walls, towers, and barred gates.

    _____

    _____

2. Why might historians hesitate to believe Bede when he tells us in *A History of the English Church and People* that the Scots said, "We can give you good advice. There is another island not far to the east, which we often see in the distance on clear days. Go and settle there if you wish"?

    _____

    _____

    _____

3. What is the main purpose of *The Anglo-Saxon Chronicle?* Explain your reasoning.
   a. to inform people of the events
   b. to entertain the nobility
   c. to describe major battles of the time
   d. to persuade the Church to denounce the enemy

    _____

    _____

    _____

4. Read the following line from *The Anglo-Saxon Chronicle*, and write the definition for *stranded.*

    > They were very awkwardly aground: three were stranded on the same side of the
    > deep water as the Danish ships.

    _____

    _____

5. From his phrase "all are united in their study of God's truth," what can be inferred about Bede's attitude toward the English church? Explain your answer.
   a. He believes in its teachings.   b. He was aware of its influence.
   c. He questioned its sovereignty.   d. He reluctantly obeyed its mandates.

    _____

    _____

6. Read the following quotation from *A History of the English Church and People.* Which sentence best describes the cultural attitude toward women expressed here? Explain your answer choice.

> Having no women with them, these Picts asked wives of the Scots, who consented on condition that, when any dispute arose, they should choose a king from the female royal line rather than the male. This custom continues among the Picts to this day.

a Picts believed Scots women brought a higher social status.

b. Picts held little respect for Scots women.

c. Scots wanted political influence in the Pict royal court.

d. Scots women were eager to marry Pict men.

_____

_____

7. According to the first three paragraphs in *The Anglo-Saxon Chronicle*, why were the English weakened? Explain who the "force" and king are.

_____

_____

8. Bede's account suggests that Britain had which of the following? Cite a few details from the text to support your answer.

a. an ideal climate.   c. abundant natural resources.

b. a powerful navy.   d. a unified government.

_____

_____

9. Complete the timeline below, showing the six most important events given for the year 900 in *The Anglo-Saxon Chronicle.*

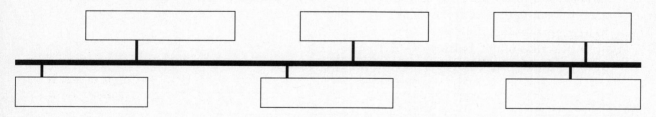

10. List three sources a medieval historian might use in writing a history of the times.

_____

_____

11. *In The Anglo-Saxon Chronicle*, the speaker lists the Danes and Kentish killed in a 903 military battle. He says, "Ealdorman Sigulf was killed there, ealdorman Sighelm . . . Eadwald son of Acca, and many besides them although I have named the most distinguished." Why would historians consider this a prejudiced statement? How might the speaker's attitude affect the history he is recording? If historians use *The Anglo-Saxon Chronicle* as a secondary source for writing history, what might they do to make this chronicle more accurate? Answer these questions in a well-thought-out paragraph.

12. As the British shifted their allegiance from lord and town to king and nation, they experienced a new sense of regional identity. Write an essay in which you show how *A History of the English Church and People* reflects this nationalism. Use examples from Bede's history to support your ideas.

Extended Response

13. When studying history, a reader should distinguish between fact and opinion. Show your ability to do this by completing the following chart on either *A History of the English Church and People* or *The Anglo-Saxon Chronicle*. Write four facts in the right column and four opinions in the left column. Then summarize only the facts in a clear, well-organized paragraph.

Title of the Work:_____	
Facts	Opinions
1.	1.
2.	2.
3.	3.
4.	4.

14. Modern historians use new technological tools such as DNA testing and computers to conduct their research. In a short essay, discuss three modern technological devices that would have helped historians in recording *A History of the English Church and People* and *The Anglo-Saxon Chronicle*. Support your propositions with specific references to the text.

15. The oral tradition preserves the past while entertaining the listeners. Write an essay in which you explain how Bede uses literary techniques, such as imagery, detail, and tone, to hold the people's interest. Use examples from *A History of the English Church and People* to support your opinion.

Oral Response

16. Choose question 3, 5, 9, 11, or 14 or the question your teacher assigns you. Take a few minutes to look through the selections to prepare an oral response to give in class. If necessary, make notes to be clear about the order in which you want to present your answer.

Rubric for Evaluating Extended Responses

0	1	2	3	4
Blank paper	Incorrect purpose, mode, audience	Correct purpose, mode, audience	Correct purpose, mode, audience	Correct purpose, mode, audience
Foreign language	Brief, vague	Some elaboration	Moderately well elaborated	Effective elaboration
Illegible, incoherent	Unelaborated	Some details	Clear, effective language	Consistent organization
Not enough content to score	Rambling	Gaps in organization	Organized (perhaps with brief digressions)	Sense of completeness, fluency
	Lack of language control	Limited language control		
	Poor organization			

The Prologue from *The Canterbury Tales* by Geoffrey Chaucer
Open-Book Test

Multiple Choice and Short Answer

Write your answers to all questions in this section on the lines provided.
For multiple-choice questions, circle the letter of the best answer.

1. Read the following excerpt from *The Canterbury Tales*. Then fill in the chart, using the *who, what, where, when, why,* and *how* questioning strategy.

   > It happened in that season that one day / In Southwark, at The Tabard, as I lay / Ready to go on pilgrimage and start / For Canterbury, most devout of heart,/ At night there came into that hostelry / Some nine and twenty in a company / Of sundry folk happening then to fall / In fellowship, and they were pilgrims all / That towards Canterbury meant to ride (lines 19-27).

Question	Answer
Who?	
What?	
Where?	
When?	
Why?	
How?	

2. In line 343 of the Prologue, Chaucer describes the Franklin as "a sanguine man,   high-colored and benign." Choose the best definition for *sanguine*. Write two   quotations from the text to support your answer.
   a. drunken   b. cheerful   c. feverish   d. mild

   _____

   _____

3. Which phrase describes Chaucer's attitude toward the Nun? Support your answer with specific references to the text.
   a. amused tolerance   c. marked scorn
   b. polite detachment   d. weary reproachfulness

   _____

   _____

4. Which pilgrim would most likely give absolution to a character in *The Canterbury Tales*? Explain your reasoning.
   a. Friar   b. Cook   c. Merchant   d. Wife of Bath

   _____

   _____

5. In describing the Cook, Chaucer says, "But what a pity--so it seemed to me, / That he should have an ulcer on his knee" (lines 395-396). Is this a direct or indirect characterization? Is it both? What do these lines tell you about the Cook?

   _____

   _____

6. Review Chaucer's description of the Oxford clerk in *The Canterbury Tales*. Cite one example of direct characterization and one of indirect characterization that suggest the clerk is a serious student.

   _____

   _____

7. Read the description of the Wife of Bath. Cite two quotations of direct and indirect characterization that imply this woman is not as "worthy," or virtuous, as the speaker first indicates. Explain what a reader might infer about the woman's character.

   _____

   _____

8. Review lines 745–766 of *The Canterbury Tales*. Describe the speaker's tone, and explain what effect he might hope to have on his listeners.

   _____

   _____

9. We learn that the miller is "a great stout fellow big in brawn and bone" (line 562). Provide two images or quotations from the narrator's description that suggest the Miller is large and strong.

   _____

   _____

10. Chaucer's characters represent every level of medieval society, from the nobility to the lower class. Provide evidence for this on the following chart. List three pilgrims from different social classes in *The Canterbury Tales*. Briefly describe each character. Describe the level of society from which each comes. Describe the effect this broad presentation of life in the Middle Ages has on the reader.

	Pilgrim	Description	Social Level
1.			
2.			
3.			

   _____

   _____

Extended Response

11. As the father of English poetry, Chaucer is well known for his "penetrating insight into human character." In an essay, explain how this illuminating view is evident in *The Canterbury Tales.* Use specific examples from the poem to elaborate on your thoughts.

12. Chaucer says the Knight in *The Canterbury Tales* "was a true, a perfect gentle-knight" (line 74). The knight's son was "a fine young Squire/a lover and cadet, a lad of fire" (lines 81–82). Compare and contrast these two noblemen. What have they accomplished? What motivates them? What do they value? Then write an essay in which you use specific examples from the poem to show the similarities and differences between the father and son.

13. Both the Nun and Parson serve their church and its people, but they have two very different personalities. Based on Chaucer's direct and indirect characterizations, which of the two does he most likely consider the more devout Christian? What evidence from *The Canterbury Tales* supports your opinion? Respond to these questions in a thoughtful, well-organized essay.

14. In Chaucer's day, the science of medicine was taught quite differently from the way it is taught today. Chaucer tells us the doctor "was a perfect practicing physician" (line 432). If this is true, how did doctors treat their patients in the 1400s? Write a detailed paragraph describing the physician's art, using examples and quotations from the poem for support.

15. The Monk in *The Canterbury Tales* is an avid hunter who "did not rate that text at a plucked hen / Which says that hunters are not holy men / And that a monk uncloistered is a mere / Fish out of water" (lines 181–184). The Narrator agrees with the Monk. How does the Monk's life reflect this opinion? Discuss these questions in a short essay, using evidence from the poem to illustrate your points.

Oral Response

16. Choose question 7, 8, 10, 11, or 14 or the question your teacher assigns you. Take a few minutes to look through the selection to prepare an oral response to give in class. If necessary, make notes to be clear about the order in which you want to present your answer.

Rubric for Evaluating Extended Responses

0	1	2	3	4
Blank paper	Incorrect purpose, mode, audience	Correct purpose, mode, audience	Correct purpose, mode, audience	Correct purpose, mode, audience
Foreign language	Brief, vague	Some elaboration	Moderately well elaborated	Effective elaboration
Illegible, incoherent	Unelaborated	Some details	Clear, effective language	Consistent organization
Not enough content to score	Rambling	Gaps in organization	Organized (perhaps with brief digressions)	Sense of completeness, fluency
	Lack of language control	Limited language control		
	Poor organization			

"The Nun's Priest's Tale" and "The Pardoner's Tale" from *The Canterbury Tales*
by Geoffrey Chaucer

Open-Book Test

Multiple Choice and Short Answer

Write your answers to all questions in this section on the lines provided.
For multiple-choice questions, circle the letter of the best answer.

1. The narrator of "The Nun's Priest's Tale" says the widow-woman leads "a very patient, simple life" (line 6). After reading your text, briefly describe her lifestyle, and provide two additional quotations from the text for support.

   _____

   _____

2. Choose the words that most closely match the meaning of the word *maxim* in the following excerpt from "The Nun's Priest's Tale." What context clues could a reader use to determine the definition?
   > A rhetorician with a flair for style/Could chronicle this *maxim* in his file / Of Notable Remarks with safe conviction (lines 389-391).
   a. Bible quotation   c. common law
   b. popular saying   d. news article

   _____

3. Write a definition for *timorous* as it appears in the following quotation from "The Nun's Priest's Tale." Then list the context clues that a reader could use in defining this word.
   > You timorous poltroon! / Alas, what cowardice! By God above, You've forfeited my heart and lost my love (lines 88-90).

4. Which word best describes Peretelote's attitude toward Chanticleer when she tells him, "How dare you say for shame, and to your love,/That anything at all was to be feared?/Have you no manly heart to match your beard?" (lines 98–100). Explain your answer.
   a. vain   b. playful   c. derisive   d. thoughtless

   _____

5. Which of the following choices most accurately describes how the narrator of "The Nun's Priest's Tale" portrays himself? Support your answer with a quotation from the text.
   a. dislikes and mistrusts women   c. seeks only to entertain
   b. admires rhetorical skill   d. invents fictional tales

   _____

   _____

6. Identify the reason the old man tells the three rioters in "The Pardoner's Tale," that they can find Death beyond the grove? Expand on the old man's purpose.
   a. He is running from Death himself and needs their protection.
   b. The man hopes to get the gold for himself.
   c. He hopes that the men will kill Death.
   d. He plans that the men will die.

   _____

7. In which of the following ways does an *exemplum* differ from a short story? Explain your answer.
   a. An *exemplum* has a narrator that tells the tale.
   b. The main purpose of an *exemplum* is to give an example to teach a lesson.
   c. A short story uses characters to move the plot forward.
   d. An *exemplum* is only for adults.

   _____

   _____

8. The narrator of "The Pardoner's Tale" says that the three rioters" . . . made their bargain, swore with appetite, / These three, to live and die for one another / As brother-born might swear to his born brother." Briefly describe how the three rioters do and do not fulfill this vow.

   _____

9. Which word best decribes the attitude the three rioters have when they declare, "And we will kill this traitor Death, I say! / Away with him as he has made away / With all our friends. God's dignity! Tonight!" Explain your answer.
   a. hoary
   b. timorous
   c. prating
   d. tarrying

   _____

10. What does "The Pardoner's Tale" suggest about the Pardoner? Explain your answer.
   a. He believes that Death is the greatest enemy.
   b. He admires the bravery of the three rioters.
   c. He believes greed is worse than dying.
   d. He does not hold to any absolute truths.

   _____

   _____

Extended Response

11. Chaucer chooses animals to play Chanticleer and Sir Russel Fox in "The Nun's Priest's Tale." Of all animals, why might he have chosen a rooster and fox? What characteristics do they have that make them appropriate for their roles? In one or two paragraphs, explain your answers, using evidence from the tale for support.

12. Like hero stories and epics, "The Nun's Priest's Tale" reflects a respect for higher learning and authority. For example, Pertelote cites Cato to strengthen her position on dreams. What other examples from the text illustrate this respect? Why might Chaucer use this approach? How does this method reinforce Chaucer's mock-heroic style? Answer these questions in a short essay, using evidence from the tale to support your opinion.

13. In Chaucer's time people believed in higher gods and powers that guided and dictated their daily lives. List the various forces in which characters from "The Nun's Priest's Tale" placed their faith. Then present your findings in an essay in which you also explain what these beliefs suggest about the English culture of this time.

Power, Authority, or Force	Example

14. The Pardoner concludes his tale in lines 235–239 by saying that each of the men received his due. Is that true or not? Do you agree that the men should have died because of their greed? Write an essay answering these questions. Support your opinion with evidence from the text.

15. Dialogue can play an important part in any story. In an essay analyze the dialogue between the young rioters and the other characters in the story. What does the dialogue show about the rioters? What does it say about the other characters?

Oral Response

16. Choose question 4, 7, 10, 11, or 15 or the question your teacher assigns you. Take a few minutes to look through the selection to prepare an oral response to give in class. If necessary, make notes to be clear about the order in which you want to present your answer.

Rubric for Evaluating Extended Responses

0	1	2	3	4
Blank paper Foreign language Illegible, incoherent Not enough content to score	Incorrect purpose, mode, audience Brief, vague Unelaborated Rambling Lack of language control Poor organization	Correct purpose, mode, audience Some elaboration Some details Gaps in organization Limited language control	Correct purpose, mode, audience Moderately well elaborated Clear, effective language Organized (perhaps with brief digressions)	Correct purpose, mode, audience Effective elaboration Consistent organization Sense of completeness, fluency

Open-Book Test

Multiple Choice and Short Answer

Write your answers to all questions in this section on the lines provided.
For multiple-choice questions, circle the letter of the best answer.

1. The speaker of *Sir Gawain and the Green Knight* describes the Green Knight's arrival at King Arthur's court. How does this scene satisfy the medieval reader's interest in realism as well as the supernatural? Give three details from the poem to support your answer.

2. Describe King Arthur's attitude and behavior when he first meets the Green Knight in *Sir Gawain and the Green Knight*.

3. The Green Knight proposes a Christmas game to King Arthur. Explain the game.

4. Sir Gawain tells the Green Knight, "First I ask and adjure you, how you are called / That you tell me true so that trust it I may." Which definition best suits the word *adjure*? Explain what this statement tells you about Sir Gawain's character.
   a. plead   b. mock   c. urge   d. honor

5. Which of the following events from *Sir Gawain and the Green Knight* conveys a sense of the supernatural? Cite a detail from the poem to support your answer choice.
   a. The Green Knight challenges King Arthur's Knights.
   b. Sir Gawain arrives at the Green Castle and finds it hideous.
   c. The Green Knight does not die from Sir Gawain's blow.
   d. The Green Knight only scratches Sir Gawain with his ax.

6. Which word best describes the tone of *Morte d'Arthur*? Explain your reasoning.
   a. entreating   b. self-righteous   c. feigned   d. informative

7. King Arthur and Sir Mordred agree to meet. Choose the sentence that best describes their behavior at the time of this decision. Write one quotation that supports your answer.
   a. King Arthur decides to surrender England to Sir Mordred.
   b. Sir Mordred and King Arthur arrange to meet with their hosts at Camelot.
   c. King Arthur and Sir Mordred mistrust each other.
   d. King Arthur believes Sir Mordred is afraid of meeting him.

_____

_____

8. Select the sentence that best summarizes the paragraph of *Sir Gawain and the Green Knight*, beginning "And thus they fought." Then read the next paragraph, and summarize King Arthur's feelings toward the battle.
   a. A hundred thousand men under King Arthur's command are needed to kill Sir Mordred.
   b. King Arthur and Sir Mordred fight all day and all night until the earth turns cold.
   c. After the battle King Arthur sees Sir Mordred half hidden among the only living survivors.
   d. King Arthur and Sir Mordred fight until only they, Sir Lucan, and Sir Bedivere are left alive.

_____

_____

9. King Arthur gives Sir Bedivere his sword, Excalibur. Considering what you know about medieval romances, explain what Excalibur symbolizes. Support your response with specific examples from *Morte d'Arthur*.

_____

_____

10. Review King Arthur's death in *Morte d'Arthur*. Then fill in the cluster diagram with details showing how the treatment of King Arthur is suitable for a legendary king.

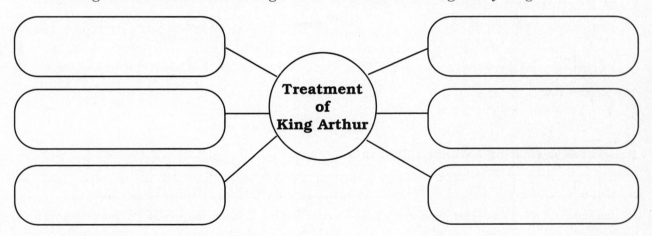

Extended Response

11. People in the Middle Ages were attracted by legends that presented the ideal knight while revealing his more human, vulnerable side. Write an essay in which you show these two sides of Sir Gawain. Support your view with reasonable evidence from *Sir Gawain and the Green Knight*.

12. The medieval heroes of English legend believe in a code of chivalry, principles by which kings and knights live. For example, Sir Gawain believes a noble knight must fight for and protect women in distress. What are some of the other principles a noble knight had to live by? In the chart provided, list three other principles you might infer from *Sir Gawain and the Green Knight* and *Morte d'Arthur*. Include examples to support your opinions. Then present your "code of conduct" in a well-organized, one-page essay.

Principles	Examples
1	
2	
3	

13. Think about the Green Knight's behavior in *Sir Gawain and the Green Knight*. Then write a short essay in which you answer these questions: Does the Green Knight live by the same code of conduct as King Arthur and the knights of the Round Table? If he does not, under what principles does the Green Knight guide his thoughts and actions? What evidence from the legend can you find to defend your position?

14. Authors use foreshadowing to gain the readers' interest and help them predict upcoming events. In one or two paragraphs, explain how Malory foreshadows Arthur's death. Use specific details from the legend to elaborate on your ideas.

15. What can you infer about Sir Gawain's belief in God? What can you conclude about the English medieval belief in God? Answer these questions in one or two paragraphs. Support your opinion with evidence from the legend.

Oral Response

16. Choose question 1, 5 , 8, 9, or 12 or the question your teacher assigns you. Take a few minutes to look through the selection to prepare an oral response to give in class. If necessary, make notes to be clear about the order in which you want to present your answer.

Rubric for Evaluating Extended Responses

0	1	2	3	4
Blank paper	Incorrect purpose, mode, audience	Correct purpose, mode, audience	Correct purpose, mode, audience	Correct purpose, mode, audience
Foreign language	Brief, vague	Some elaboration	Moderately well elaborated	Effective elaboration
Illegible, incoherent	Unelaborated	Some details	Clear, effective language	Consistent organization
Not enough content to score	Rambling	Gaps in organization	Organized (perhaps with brief digressions)	Sense of completeness, fluency
	Lack of language control	Limited language control		
	Poor organization			

Letters of Margaret Paston
"Lord Randall," "The Twa Corbies," "Get Up and Bar the Door,"
and **"Barbara Allan,"** Anonymous

Open-Book Test

Multiple Choice and Short Answer

Write your answers to all questions in this section on the lines provided.
For multiple-choice questions, circle the letter of the best answer.

1. What is the main reason Margaret Paston wrote to her husband on October 17? Give evidence to support your answer.
   a. to convince her husband to ally himself with Heveningham and Wingfield.
   b. to ridicule and demean the Duchess of Suffolk.
   c. to send news of Hellesdon's capture.
   d. to ask pity for her tragic circumstances.

   _____

   _____

2. Write the definition of the word *certify* as it appears in this excerpt from *Letters of Margaret Paston.*
   . . . that they should take and arrest and correct them, and certify to him the names by 8 o'clock on Wednesday.

   _____

3. Which literary device is used in this line from "Lord Randall"? Explain your answer.
   "I hae been to the wild wood; mother, make my bed soon."
   a. stanza   b. repetition   c. direct address   d. indirect address

   _____

   _____

4. Use the reading strategy described in your text to define the word *hussyfskap* as it is used in the fourth stanza of "Get Up and Bar the Door."

   _____

   _____

5. Review the reading strategy and use modern English to rewrite the following quotation from "Get Up and Bar the Door."
   But neer a word wad ane o' them speak (stanza 6)

6. Give two reasons why the dead-bell in the eighth stanza of "Barbara Allan" rings. Consider the bell's symbolic meaning as you write your answer.

   _____

   _____

   _____

7. Identify the literary device used in this line from "Barbara Allan." Then explain your answer.

O haste and come to my master dear, / Gin ye be Barbara Allan.

    a. dialect   b. dialogue   c. Latin root   d. rhyming couplet

_____

_____

8. Which of the following literary elements is absent in "The Twa Corbies"? Explain your answer choice.

    a. stanza   b. rhyme scheme   c. refrain   d. dialogue

_____

_____

9. Like soap operas, historical letters intrigue readers by depicting the drama, romance, and adventure present in everyday life. In the cluster diagram, list examples of details from *The Letters of Margaret Paston* that readers might find fascinating. Then present your ideas in a well-organized paragraph.

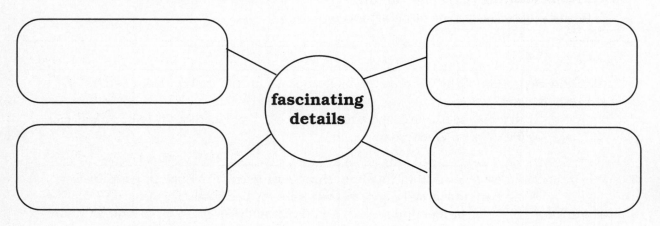

10. Explain why the two ravens in "The Twa Corbies" are unafraid of the hound, the hawk, and the lady.

_____

_____

Extended Response

11. Review the definition of folk ballad in your textbook. In a short essay, explain how "Lord Randall" fits this description, using specific examples from the ballad to support your reasons.

12. Margaret Paston's letters to her husband give a thoughtful reader a sharp insight into the prevailing attitude toward women in the 1400s. In a one-page essay, explain the female role at this time. Before writing, consider how Margaret Paston reacts to the activities around her. How is she treated by her husband, son, the tenants, and the soldiers? What do these people most likely expect of her? What examples can you give from Margaret Paston's letters to illustrate your points?

13. Ballads portraying the comical side of life often convey an underlying cynical message. In a one page-essay, explain how "Get Up and Bar the Door" preserves a humorous tone while presenting a scornful or mocking view of reality. Use details and examples from the ballad to elaborate on your opinions.

14. Sir John Graeme tells people close to him, "Adieu, adieu, my dear friends all./And be kind of Barbara Allan." Does Barbara Allan deserve this kindness? Why or why not? Answer these questions in a well-organized paragraph in which you use information from "Barbara Allan" to support your position.

15. Consider the images created in the fourth stanza of "Lord Randall," and the fourth stanza of "The Twa Corbies." How do these scenes affect the reader? How do these images contribute to each ballad's tone? Respond to these questions in one or two paragraphs and include evidence from the text to back up your opinions.

Oral Response

16. Choose question 6, 9, 11, 12, or 13 or the question your teacher assigns you. Take a few minutes to look through the selection to prepare an oral response to give in class. If necessary, make notes to be clear about the order in which you want to present your answer.

Rubric for Evaluating Extended Responses

0	1	2	3	4
Blank paper Foreign language Illegible, incoherent Not enough content to score	Incorrect purpose, mode, audience Brief, vague Unelaborated Rambling Lack of language control Poor organization	Correct purpose, mode, audience Some elaboration Some details Gaps in organization Limited language control	Correct purpose, mode, audience Moderately well elaborated Clear, effective language Organized (perhaps with brief digressions)	Correct purpose, mode, audience Effective elaboration Consistent organization Sense of completeness, fluency

Name _____ Date _____

Sonnets 1, 35, and 75 by Edmund Spenser
Sonnets 31 and 39 by Sir Philip Sidney

Open-Book Test

Multiple Choice and Short Answer

Write your answers to all questions in this section on the lines provided.
For multiple-choice questions, circle the letter of the best answer.

1. In Spenser's Sonnet 1, to what do the "leaves" in line 1 refer?
   Choose the best answer for this question. Then explain your choice.
   a. the flat green pieces that stick out from the stems of lilies
   b. the departure of the woman that the speaker loves
   c. the departure of the speaker's happiness
   d. the pages of a book held by the woman that the speaker loves

   _____

   _____

2. Paraphrase the last two lines of Spenser's Sonnet 35.

   _____

   _____

3. Why does the speaker in Spenser's Sonnet 35 feel that he is like Narcissus? Choose the
   best answer, and then explain your choice.
   a. Like Narcissus, he loves himself more than anyone else in the world.
   b. He considers Narcissus a wonderful poet.
   c. He thinks of himself as a very handsome young man.
   d. No matter how much he looks at the object of his love, he wants to continue looking.

   _____

   _____

4. Explain the two meanings of "vain" in line 5 of Spenser's Sonnet 75.

   _____

   _____

5. Which of these statements is true for a Spenserian sonnet? Choose the best answer, and
   then explain the reasons for your choice. Your explanation may cite examples from
   Spenser's three sonnets.
   a. The end rhymes in the last two lines rhyme with each other.
   b. The end rhymes follow the pattern *abbaabba cdecde*.
   c. The number of lines in the sonnet may range from ten to fourteen.
   d. There is always a break in meaning between the octave and the sestet.

   _____

   _____

   _____

6. Considering all three poems together, what seems to be Spenser's goal in writing his sonnet sequence? Select the best answer, and then, explain the reasons why your choice is correct and the others are not.
   a. to please and pay tribute to his beloved

   _____

   b. to call upon his Muse

   _____

   c. to win fame and fortune

   _____

   d. to express his anguish at unrequited love

   _____

7. Select the statement that best reflects the speaker's attitude toward love in Sidney's Sonnet 31. Then explain how each answer choice does or does not reflect the speaker's attitude toward love.
   a. He is hopeful that his beloved returns his affections.

   _____

   b. He believes that his down-to-earth love will outlast even the moon.

   _____

   c. He is sad and bitter because his beloved does not return his love.

   _____

   d. He is so happy in his love that he wants to make the moon jealous.

   _____

8. In Sonnet 39, what does the speaker mean when he calls sleep the "balm of woe"?

   _____

9. Which sentence best restates the last lines of Sidney's Sonnet 39? Briefly explain your answer.
   a. If I do not sleep peacefully, do not allow Stella to sleep peacefully either.
   b. If I do not sleep peacefully, I will see Stella's image in my dreams.
   c. It is Stella's right to have a peaceful sleep, even though I do not.
   d. Even though Stella has a heavy grace, she is a lively person in my dream images.

   _____

   _____

10. Which of these statements is true for a Petrarchan sonnet? Choose the best answer, and then explain your reasons.
    a. The end rhymes in the last two lines never rhyme with each other.
    b. It is another term for a Spenserian sonnet.
    c. The number of lines in the sonnet may range from ten to fourteen.
    d. It generally consists of an octave with one set of rhymes and a sestet with another.

    _____

    _____

Extended Response

11. Explore the attitude toward the beloved expressed in these sonnets. In which sonnet does the speaker seem to suffer most from unrequited love? In which one does the speaker simply celebrate his love or pay tribute to his beloved? Write one or two paragraphs in which you cite details from the sonnets to support your response.

12. Spenser's sonnet sequence was dedicated to the woman he was courting, Elizabeth Boyle. How do you think she reacted when she first read the sonnets? In a paragraph or two, describe the reaction that you think she had. Be sure to make specific references to the three sonnets.

13. Rewrite Spenser's Sonnet 75 as a modern conversation between the speaker and his beloved. Express the same ideas, but use contemporary language.

14. Complete this sunburst diagram by listing the images and ideas that Sidney associates with sleep in Sonnet 39. Then, in a paragraph or two, discuss these images and ideas and the overall impression of sleep that they help to convey.

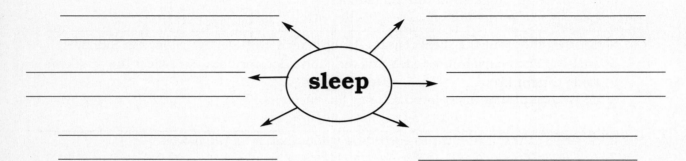

15. Apostrophe is a figure of speech in which the speaker directly addresses an absent person, or object, or idea. For example, the speaker may address an inanimate object as if it were capable of hearing or an absent person as if he or she were present and able to hear the speaker. In a brief essay, discuss the use of apostrophe in Spenser's Sonnet 1 and the two sonnets by Sidney. What is the effect of using apostrophe? Who or what is addressed in each sonnet? Answer these questions in your essay.

Oral Response

16. Go back to question 6, 7, 11, 12, or 15 or one assigned to you by your teacher, and take five to ten minutes to expand your answer and prepare an oral response. Find additional details in the sonnets that will support your points. If necessary, make notes to guide your response.

Rubric for Evaluating Extended Responses

0	1	2	3	4
Blank paper Foreign language Illegible, incoherent Not enough content to score	Incorrect purpose, mode, audience Brief, vague Unelaborated Rambling Lack of language control Poor organization	Correct purpose, mode, audience Some elaboration Some details Gaps in organization Limited language control	Correct purpose, mode, audience Moderately well elaborated Clear, effective language Organized (perhaps with brief digressions)	Correct purpose, mode, audience Effective elaboration Consistent organization Sense of completeness, fluency

Sonnets 29, 106, 116, and **130** by William Shakespeare

Open-Book Test

Multiple Choice and Short Answer

Write your answers to all questions in this section on the lines provided.
For multiple-choice questions, circle the letter of the best answer.

1. Which sentence best describes the speaker's mood or condition in the first nine lines of
   Sonnet 29? Explain your answer.
   a. He is bewildered by the hectic pace of an urban life.
   b. He is filled with shame and self-pity.
   c. He is caught up in love's ecstasy.
   d. He is overjoyed to learn that his love is returned.

   _____

   _____

2. At the end of Sonnet 29, what is the main reason that the speaker does not wish to
   change places with a king? Choose the best answer, and then explain your choice.
   a. He believes in democracy.
   b. He feels that kings are corrupted by their power.
   c. He is one of Europe's richest men, with more money and property than most kings.
   d. He is so happy in his love that he would never want to be anyone else.

   _____

   _____

3. Think about the meaning of *chronicle* and the kinds of events that most chronicles record.
   Then explain what Sonnet 106 might mean by a "chronicle of wasted time." Why would the
   things it records seem liked "wasted time" to the speaker?

   _____

   _____

   _____

4. Why does the speaker in Sonnet 106 think that present-day writers lack the words to
   praise his beloved? Select the best answer, and then explain your reasons.
   a. He thinks that she is so beautiful and wonderful that she is beyond words.
   b. He thinks that she is so cruel and unworthy that no once could praise her.
   c. He thinks that present-day writers lack talent.
   d. He thinks that present-day writers are too timid to express their ideas and opinions.

   _____

   _____

5. Based on the details in Sonnet 116, what seems to be the speaker's definition of love?
   Briefly state the definition and include examples from the poem to support that
   definition.

   _____

6. Which item below would most clearly be an impediment to marriage? Explain your answer, making sure you include a definition of the word *impediments*.

   a. a love letter

   b. a marriage license

   c. a prior marriage still in existence

   d. a member of the clergy with authority to perform marriages

   _____

   _____

7. In general, how does the speaker describe his beloved in Sonnet 130? Write a single sentence that sums up the speaker's descriptions of his beloved.

   _____

   _____

8. Which sentence best expresses the relationship of the final couplet in Sonnet 130 to the rest of the poem? Explain your answer.

   a. It sums up the rest of the poem.

   b. It poses a question about the ideas expressed in the rest of the poem.

   c. It clinches the argument expressed in the rest of the poem.

   d. It contrasts with the ideas expressed in the rest of the poem.

   _____

   _____

9. Choose the sentence that best expresses the theme of Sonnet 130. Explain your choice, citing details from the poem to support your explanation.

   a. Those we love seem special to us, regardless of their actual physical appearance.

   b. Love changes and grows over time.

   c. Physical attraction is the most important element of love, even if it is not the only element.

   d. People often fall in love with those who seem aloof or hard to get.

   _____

   _____

10. Which statement most accurately describes Shakespearean sonnet form? Select the best answer, and then explain your reasons. Your explanations may cite examples from the four sonnets.

    a. It consists of an octave and a sestet.

    b. It may be ten to fourteen lines long.

    c. It always concludes with a rhymed couplet.

    d. Its meter is usually iambic tetrameter, in which there are four iambic feet to a line.

    _____

    _____

Extended Response

11. Choose one sonnet, and write a brief sketch of the speaker based on the details of the poem. Describe his personality, mood, and general outlook toward life and love.

12. Based on these sonnets, what seems to be Shakespeare's attitude toward the passage of time? In a paragraph or two, discuss the role of time in Sonnets 103 and 116. Cite details from the sonnets to support the general points you make.

13. Choose one sonnet, and examine its structure in a brief essay. Consider to what degree Shakespearean sonnet form reflects the poem's content by identifying the main point or points of each quatrain and the clinching point made in the final couplet. Use the chart below to help you organize your ideas.

Main Point(s) of Quatrain 1:

Main Point(s) of Quatrain 2:

Main Point(s) of Quatrain 3:

Clinching Point in Final Couplet:

14. Do you agree with the ideas about love presented in the sonnets? For example, do you agree with the way love is depicted in Sonnet 106? Or the statement "Love is not love/Which alters when it alteration finds" in Sonnet 116? Choose one idea about love that is stated or implied in the sonnets, and write your own personal reaction to it. Use examples and logical arguments to support your opinion.

15. Examine the speaker's methods and reasoning in Sonnet 130. How is the poem different from a typical love poem? Do those differences make the poem more or less effective in conveying the speaker's love? Why? Answer these questions in a brief essay that cites examples from the poem to illustrate or support your main points.

Oral Response

16. Go back to question 1, 4, 5, 7, 12, or 13 or one assigned to you by your teacher, and take five to ten minutes to expand your answer and prepare an oral response. Find additional details in the sonnets that will support your points. If necessary, make notes to guide your response.

Rubric for Evaluating Extended Responses

0	1	2	3	4
Blank paper Foreign language Illegible, incoherent Not enough content to score	Incorrect purpose, mode, audience Brief, vague Unelaborated Rambling Lack of language control Poor organization	Correct purpose, mode, audience Some elaboration Some details Gaps in organization Limited language control	Correct purpose, mode, audience Moderately well elaborated Clear, effective language Organized (perhaps with brief digressions)	Correct purpose, mode, audience Effective elaboration Consistent organization Sense of completeness, fluency

from *Utopia* by Sir Thomas More
Elizabeth's Speech Before Her Troops
by Queen Elizabeth I

Open-Book Test

Multiple Choice and Short Answer

Write your answers to all questions in this section on the lines provided.
For multiple-choice questions, circle the letter of the best answer.

1. What kind of monarch does Thomas More criticize? Explain why your answer is correct, based on the details in the selection.
    a. a monarch who lives comfortably
    b. a monarch who treats his subjects the way a shepherd treats his flock
    c. a monarch who does not try to improve the lot of his subjects
    d. a monarch who gets his nation involved in warfare

    _____
    _____

2. In More's thinking, why did Fabricius say that he would rather govern rich men than be rich himself? Write the most likely reason.

    _____
    _____

3. Which of the following monarchs would be guilty of *sloth?* Select the best choice, and then explain your answer.
    a. one who has trouble making decisions and often changes his or her mind
    b. one who fails to work very hard
    c. one who cares too much about wealth and fine clothing
    d. one who cracks down heavily on dissent

    _____
    _____

4. Write a single sentence that sums up the three questions in the excerpt from *Utopia*.

    _____
    _____

5. Which of these main points does the passage from *Utopia* most clearly make about the monarch as hero? Explain your answer.
    a. The braver the monarch is in battle, the more heroic that monarch will seem.
    b. A monarch governs effectively when his or her rule benefits the governed.
    c. A monarch who is rich can do more for the poor.
    d. It is better for a monarch to focus on his or her own pleasures than to try to improve the lives of his or her subjects.

    _____
    _____

6. What sort of subject is most clearly guilty of *treachery?* Explain your answer.
   a. a rich subject who inherits his or her money instead of working for it
   b. a poor subject who complains about his or her situation
   c. a subject who wins fame and fortune through political connections, not skill or talent
   d. a seemingly loyal subject who is actually a spy for a foreign enemy

   _____

   _____

   _____

7. Write a sentence that sums up the opening sentence of Queen Elizabeth I's speech.

   _____

   _____

   _____

8. To which emotion does Elizabeth's speech most strongly appeal? Explain your answer, citing examples from the speech to support it.
   a. patriotism
   b. fear
   c. anger
   d. friendship

   _____

   _____

   _____

9. According to her speech, why is Elizabeth unafraid to come among her people?

   _____

   _____

   _____

10. Which of these points does Elizabeth most want to convey about herself as a monarch? Select the best answer, then explain why each answer is or is not correct.
a. Although she is a woman, she is a strong leader and a just and beloved monarch.

   _____

b. Because she is a woman, her people love her more than they would a male monarch.

   _____

c. If she, a weak woman, can face the enemy, then her all-male troops can face the enemy too.

   _____

d. Because she is a woman, she cannot fight the Spanish herself and must have a lieutenant general do it for her.

   _____

Extended Response

11. Write a brief description of the kind of monarch that Sir Thomas More seems to admire, based on the passage from *Utopia*, or write a one- or two-paragraph character sketch of Elizabeth I, based on the details in her speech. Include specific details or quotations from the selections to help you make your points.

12. In a sentence or brief paragraph, sum up the argument that More makes in the first ten sentences in the selection from *Utopia*. Then, in another paragraph or two, consider how his argument applies to political leaders today.

13. Imagine that you were one of Queen Elizabeth's subjects listening to her speech on the day she made it. Write a paragraph or two explaining your own reaction to the speech. Discuss your reaction to the queen's message and the feelings that her message inspired in you.

14. In a short essay, examine how Elizabeth's use of language helps make her speech more persuasive. Consider her word choice and also her use of word repetition and parallel grammatical structures to make her statements stronger and more memorable. You might organize your examples on a chart like this one.

Word Choice	Word Repetition	Parallel Structure

15. Based on the passage from More's *Utopia*, what would you guess was his purpose in writing it? Whom do you think was his primary audience? Answer these questions in a brief essay that examines how persuasive you think the passage is.

Oral Response

16. Go back to questions 1, 2, 5, 8, 10, or 13 or one assigned to you by your teacher, and take five to ten minutes to expand your answer and prepare an oral response. Find additional details in the selections that will support your points. If necessary, make notes to guide your response.

Rubric for Evaluating Extended Responses

0	1	2	3	4
Blank paper Foreign language Illegible, incoherent Not enough content to score	Incorrect purpose, mode, audience Brief, vague Unelaborated Rambling Lack of language control Poor organization	Correct purpose, mode, audience Some elaboration Some details Gaps in organization Limited language control	Correct purpose, mode, audience Moderately well elaborated Clear, effective language Organized (perhaps with brief digressions)	Correct purpose, mode, audience Effective elaboration Consistent organization Sense of completeness, fluency

from **The King James Bible**

Open-Book Test

Multiple Choice and Short Answer

Write your answers to all questions in this section on the lines provided.
For multiple-choice questions, circle the letter of the best answer.

1. Whom does Psalm 23 most clearly praise? Use examples to help explain your answer.
    a. the Lord   c. the speaker's beloved
    b. shepherds   d. the speaker's enemies

    _____

    _____

2. What sort of life does Psalm 23 most clearly suggest that a person should lead? Explain
    why each choice seems correct or incorrect.
    a. a quiet, isolated life far from the world's woes

    _____

    b. a life spent in seeking vengeance on one's enemies

    _____

    c. a pious, righteous life

    _____

    d. a simple rural life

    _____

3. In Psalm 23, to whom do "thou" and "thy" refer?
    a. the Lord
    b. the other members of the shepherd's flock
    c. the speaker's friends
    d. the speaker's enemies

    _____

    _____

4. At one point in Psalm 23, the speaker says, "My cup runneth over." What is the meaning
    of this remark?

    _____

    _____

5. Which word best describes the Sermon on the Mount? Explain your answer.
    a. a song   b. a speech   c. a dialogue   d. a parable

    _____

    _____

6. In the passage from the Sermon on the Mount, who are the two "masters" to which the opening sentence refers? Briefly explain your answer.

_____

_____

7. In the passage from the Sermon on the Mount, what does Jesus most likely mean with his examples about the fowls of the air and the lilies of the field? Select the best inference, and then explain your choice.
   a. God has created both beauty and ugliness in the natural world.
   b. People should trust God to take care of their worldly needs.
   c. People should nurture beauty, even if it is hard work.
   d. God provides for animals or plants, but people must provide for themselves.

_____

_____

_____

8. Which word best describes the elder brother in the Parable of the Prodigal Son? Cite details from the parable to support your answer.
   a. lazy
   b. dutiful
   c. generous
   d. greedy

_____

_____

_____

9. State in a single sentence the chief moral or religious lesson that the Parable of the Prodigal Son conveys.

_____

_____

_____

10. Which of these people could best be described as *prodigal?* Choose the best answer. Then explain your answer.
   a. an action hero
   b. a long-time enemy
   c. a wanderer
   d. a spendthrift

_____

_____

_____

Extended Response

11. In a paragraph or two, describe the kind of life Psalm 23 suggests people lead. Include specific examples from the psalm to support your statements.

12. In a brief essay, discuss the use of figurative language in Psalm 23 or in the selection from the Sermon on the Mount. If you choose Psalm 23, explain how the details in the psalm extend the comparison made in the opening metaphor, "The Lord is my shepherd." If you choose the passage from the Sermon on the Mount, explain how the figurative examples support the main idea of the first paragraph. You might use a chart like the one below to organize the examples you plan to use.

Figurative Language	Literal Meaning	How It Supports Opening Idea

13. Compare and contrast the two brothers in the Parable of the Prodigal Son. How do the brothers differ in terms of their experiences and in terms of their attitudes? What, if anything, do the two brothers have in common? Answer these questions in a brief essay that cites examples from the parable to support your ideas.

14. Write a brief character sketch of the father in the Parable of the Prodigal Son. Discuss his personality and behavior, and also consider the motives for his behavior.

15. Write a brief reaction to the advice given in one of these selections. Do you find the advice practical? Do you think it will be easy to follow? Why or why not? Answer these questions in a few paragraphs that use examples and logical reasons to support your ideas.

Oral Response

16. Go back to questions 2, 4, 7, 9, 11, or 13 or one assigned to you by your teacher, and take five to ten minutes to expand your answer and prepare an oral response. Find additional details in the selections that will support your points. If necessary, make notes to guide your response.

Rubric for Evaluating Extended Responses

0	1	2	3	4
Blank paper Foreign language Illegible, incoherent Not enough content to score	Incorrect purpose, mode, audience Brief, vague Unelaborated Rambling Lack of language control Poor organization	Correct purpose, mode, audience Some elaboration Some details Gaps in organization Limited language control	Correct purpose, mode, audience Moderately well elaborated Clear, effective language Organized (perhaps with brief digressions)	Correct purpose, mode, audience Effective elaboration Consistent organization Sense of completeness, fluency

Name _____ Date _____

The Tragedy of Macbeth, **Act I,** by William Shakespeare

Open-Book Test

Multiple Choice and Short Answer

Write your answers to all questions in this section on the lines provided.
For multiple-choice questions, circle the letter of the best answer.

1. What is the general setting of Act I? Cite details from the play to explain your answer.
    a. ancient Rome   c. Elizabethan England
    b. medieval Scotland   d. Stratford-upon-Avon

    _____

    _____

2. Why do the stage directions in Act I make no detailed references to lighting and sets?
    Explain your responses.
    a. In Shakespeare's day, plays did not have artificial lighting or elaborate sets.
    b. In Shakespeare's day, the acting companies could not read.
    c. Shakespeare put all his stage directions at the very end of the play, not in Act I.
    d. Shakespeare wanted to leave the lighting and sets up to future generations of
       directors.

    _____

    _____

    _____

3. How does Macbeth come to be Thane of Cawdor? Cite lines from the play to support your
    response.

    _____

    _____

    _____

4. Using the marginal notes to help you, restate Macbeth's aside in Scene iii, lines 127–129,
    in contemporary English.

    _____

    _____

    _____

5. Which action most clearly is an act of valor?
    a. Macbeth's courage in battle before the opening of the play
    b. Macbeth's willingness to believe the three witches
    c. Macbeth's decision to kill Duncan to become king
    d. Lady Macbeth's influencing her husband to kill Duncan

    _____

    _____

6. Using the marginal notes to help you, explain what Lady Macbeth begins planning after reading her husband's letter in Scene v. Use details to support your answer.

_____

_____

_____

_____

7. Circle the character flaw that most seems to motivate Lady Macbeth to plan Duncan's murder. After each response, explain why it is or is not correct.
a. excessive love of money

_____

b. excessive ambition for her husband

_____

c. fear of losing her husband in battle

_____

d. insecurity about whether her husband really loves her

_____

8. Which line or lines from Scene vi identify the specific setting for the audience?

_____

_____

_____

9. What is the "double trust" (Scene vii, line 12) that Macbeth would be breaking if he kills Duncan?

_____

_____

_____

10. Which statement comparing Lady Macbeth to her husband in Act I seems most accurate? Explain why each choice is accurate or inaccurate.
a. She is kinder and gentler than her husband.

_____

b. She is less ambitious than her husband.

_____

c. She understands the consequences of violent actions far better than her husband.

_____

d. She is more decisive than her husband.

_____

Extended Response

11. In a paragraph of two, explain the significance of the witches' remark, "Fair is foul and foul is fair." How does it help to set the mood for the play?

12. Why do you think Macbeth is so quick to take the witches' predictions seriously? Answer your questions in a brief essay that cites details from the play to support your ideas.

13. Write a paragraph or two comparing and contrasting Macbeth and Banquo. Consider each character's personality, motive, and attitude; also decide which character seems more admirable to you, and why. To organize your thoughts, list each character's qualities on the diagram below, putting common qualities in the shared area.

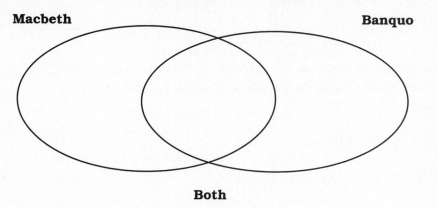

Macbeth   **Banquo**

Both

14. Write a short essay exploring the character of Lady Macbeth and the influence she seems to have on her husband. Focus especially on her remarks in Scenes v and vii and the attitudes and personality traits that those remarks reveal. Also consider what Macbeth says to her in his next-to-last speech in Scene vii.

15. Dramatic irony exists when what appears true to one or more characters is not what the audience or reader knows to be true. Discuss Shakespeare's use of dramatic irony in his portrayal of King Duncan. What does Duncan believe to be true? In contrast, what do we know to be true? How does the dramatic irony surrounding Duncan add to the play's effectiveness? Address these questions in a brief essay that uses details from the play to support your ideas.

Oral Response

16. Go back to questions 7, 10, 11, 12, 14, or 15 or one assigned to you by your teacher, and take five to ten minutes to expand your answer and prepare an oral response. Find additional details in the play that will support your points. If necessary, make notes to guide your response.

Rubric for Evaluating Extended Responses

0	1	2	3	4
Blank paper	Incorrect purpose, mode, audience	Correct purpose, mode, audience	Correct purpose, mode, audience	Correct purpose, mode, audience
Foreign language				
Illegible, incoherent	Brief, vague	Some elaboration	Moderately well elaborated	Effective elaboration
	Unelaborated	Some details		
Not enough content to score	Rambling	Gaps in organization	Clear, effective language	Consistent organization
	Lack of language control	Limited language control	Organized (perhaps with brief digressions)	Sense of completeness, fluency
	Poor organization			

Name _____ Date _____

The Tragedy of Macbeth, **Act II,** by William Shakespeare

Open-Book Test

Multiple Choice and Short Answer

Write your answers to all questions in this section on the lines provided.
For multiple-choice questions, circle the letter of the best answer.

1. By killing Duncan, what does Macbeth most clearly seek to augment? Explain your answer.
   a. riches   b. power   c. his family's safety   d. God's wrath

   _____

   _____

2. Which of these feelings or attitudes does Macbeth most clearly express in his final speech in Scene i, lines 31–64? Explain why each answer is correct or incorrect.
   a. hatred

   _____

   b. loyalty

   _____

   c. glee

   _____

   d. hesitation

   _____

3. Carefully read lines 62–64 in Scene i, paying attention to where the sentences end. Then explain in your own words what Macbeth suggests about the bell he hears.

   _____

   _____

4. What is the general effect of the blank verse that Shakespeare uses? Explain why each answer is correct or incorrect.
   a. Though poetry, it tries to capture the rhythm of spoken English.

   _____

   b. Its extensive use of end rhyme makes it easier for the actors to remember their lines.

   _____

   c. It helps achieve variety by creating lines of varying lengths.

   _____

   d. Its short, abrupt lines startle the audience.

   _____

5. Consider the incident in Scene ii, lines 34–42, where Macbeth hears the words, "Sleep no more! Macbeth does murder sleep." In what sense might Macbeth have murdered sleep?

   _____

   _____

   _____

6. According to Lady Macbeth, why doesn't she kill Duncan herself? Indicate which lines in the play pointed you toward your answer.

_____

_____

7. Carefully read the blank verse in Scene ii, lines 59–62. Which statement below best sums up what the lines say? Explain your answers.
    a. Will all the ocean clean the blood from my hands? No, my hands will bloody the ocean instead.
    b. Will the ocean wash ashore? No, it will turn from green to red instead.
    c. Will the ocean's water turn to blood? No, the ocean is too large and green.
    d. Will Neptune wash the ocean? No, his large body will make it seem green and red.

_____

_____

8. Which of the following objects or details in Act II is *palpable?* Select the best answer, and then explain your answer.
    a. the dagger that Macbeth sees in Scene i, lines 33-39
    b. the bell that Macbeth hears in Scene i, line 62
    c. the knocking that Macbeth hears at the end of Scene ii
    d. the door against which Macduff knocks

_____

_____

_____

9. Which character in Act II does not speak in blank verse? Prove your answer by offering an example of that character's lines.
    a. Macbeth
    b. Lady Macbeth
    c. the porter in Scene iii
    d. the old man in Scene iv

_____

_____

10. Based on Malcolm's and Donalbain's remarks at the end of Act II, Scene iii, what seems to be their reason for leaving Scotland? How do their actions play into the Macbeths' hands? Indicate which remarks led you to your conclusions.

_____

_____

Extended Response

11. Write a brief essay analyzing how Shakespeare uses characters' remarks about the setting to help establish not only the setting but also the atmosphere or mood of Act II. Be sure to support your ideas with several specific examples of dialogue.

12. Act II, Scene iii, is the famous knocking-at-the-gate scene in *Macbeth*. What role, if any, does the scene play in forwarding the plot? How does the scene affect the audience? Address these questions in a brief essay.

13. Write an essay comparing and contrasting the characters of Macbeth and Lady Macbeth as they are presented up until the end of Act II. Consider each character's motives, attitudes, and actual deeds, as well as his or her effect on the other. To organize your thoughts, use the diagram below, putting shared elements in the shared area.

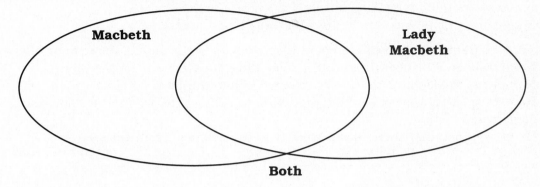

14. Would you say that Macbeth has a good imagination? Answer this question in a paragraph or two, citing details from Act II to support your evaluation.

15. Choose a single character's speech of five or more lines that appears in Act II and is written in blank verse. Then, in a brief essay, consider how the poetic language and rhythm work together to convey the character's thoughts and feelings. Also make clear how you would have an actor or actress say the speech if he or she were delivering it aloud.

Oral Response

16. Go back to questions 4, 5, 11, 12, 13, or 14 or one assigned to you by your teacher, and take five to ten minutes to expand your answer and prepare an oral response. Find additional details in the play that will support your points. If necessary, make notes to guide your response.

Rubric for Evaluating Extended Responses

0	1	2	3	4
Blank paper Foreign language Illegible, incoherent Not enough content to score	Incorrect purpose, mode, audience Brief, vague Unelaborated Rambling Lack of language control Poor organization	Correct purpose, mode, audience Some elaboration Some details Gaps in organization Limited language control	Correct purpose, mode, audience Moderately well elaborated Clear, effective language Organized (perhaps with brief digressions)	Correct purpose, mode, audience Effective elaboration Consistent organization Sense of completeness, fluency

The Tragedy of Macbeth, Act III, by William Shakespeare

Open-Book Test

Multiple Choice and Short Answer

Write your answers to all questions in this section on the lines provided.
For multiple-choice questions, circle the letter of the best answer.

1. What does Banquo reveal in the opening lines 1–10 of the act)? Explain your answer.
   a. He is jealous of Macbeth and wants to be king himself.
   b. He is loyal to Macbeth and wants to serve him faithfully.
   c. He is suspicious that Macbeth had a hand in making the witches' prophesies come true.
   d. He is skeptical that there is any validity to the witches' prophesies.

   _____

   _____

2. Reading between the lines in Scene i, explain how Macbeth has apparently managed to claim the Scottish throne even though Malcolm and Donalbain are closer relatives to the slain King Duncan.

   _____

   _____

   _____

3. Which person is most *dauntless*? Explain your answer.
   a. a fearless soldier
   b. a loyal subject
   c. a hired murderer
   d. an uneasy king

   _____

4. Why does Macbeth order the death of Fleance as well as Banquo?

   _____

5. Reading between the lines, what can you conclude about the Macbeths from Lady Macbeth's speech in Scene ii lines 4–12? Select the best answer. Then, explain why each answer is correct or incorrect.
   a. They are finally happy now that they have become Scotland's king and queen.

   _____

   b. They are not happy because they live in fear of discovery.

   _____

   c. They are happy because they are finally able to spend time together.

   _____

   d. They are not happy because they no longer love each other and are always quarreling.

   _____

6. What is the outcome of Macbeth's conflict with Banquo and Fleance? Indicate where in the play you found the details that reveal this outcome.
    a. Both men escape.
    b. Both men are killed.
    c. Banquo is killed, but Fleance escapes.
    d. Fleance is killed, but Banquo escapes.

    _____

    _____

7. In which incident below would Macbeth seem to be suffering from an infirmity? Explain your answer.
    a. when he hesitates about killing Duncan
    b. when he seems ill at the banquet
    c. when he fights bravely in battle
    d. when he puts on his crown and royal robes

    _____

    _____

8. At the banquet, Macbeth says "Were the graced person of our Banquo present" (Scene iv, line 42) and "I drink to th' general joy o' th' whole table,/And to our dear friend Banquo, whom we miss;/Would he were here!" (Scene iv, lines 90–92). What is ironic or surprising about these remarks?

    _____

    _____

    _____

9. Which struggle points to an internal conflict? Explain your answer.
    a. Macbeth's attempts to have Banquo and Fleance killed
    b. the witches' influence on Macbeth's and Banquo's lives
    c. Lady Macbeth's attempts to convince her husband to behave differently
    d. Macbeth's guilt causing him to see Banquo's ghost

    _____

    _____

10. Which of the following statements seems most true about Act III? Explain why each choice is right or wrong.
    a. It contains no internal conflict.

    _____

    b. It contains no external conflict.

    _____

    c. It is the climax of the play.

    _____

    d. It is part of the rising action building to a climax.

    _____

Extended Response

11. Write a paragraph or two explaining why Macbeth tries to arrange the murder of Banquo and Banquo's son, Fleance. Try to cover all his reasons, and back them up with details from the play.

12. In III, i, Macbeth speaks with only two murderers, but later there are three, and the sudden appearance of this third murderer has been a subject of much debate over the centuries. What is your explanation of the third murderer? Write a one- or two-paragraph explanation in which you support your theory with examples and reasons.

13. Consider the lesson that the play thus far teaches about political power and the attempts to achieve it through violent means. What do the events in Acts I-III suggest is the outcome of such efforts? Address this question in an essay that cites examples from the play to support general statements about it. Before writing, you might organize your ideas on the diagram below.

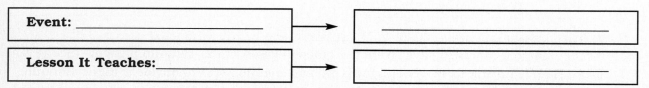

14. Write an essay exploring the role that the supernatural plays in *Macbeth* thus far. How does it affect the play's overall atmosphere, or mood? How is it related to the play's central conflicts? Answer these questions in a brief essay in which you support your ideas by citing details from Acts I-III of *Macbeth*.

15. Despite centuries of tension, England and Scotland united under one monarchy when Scotland's James VI became James I of England not long before Shakespeare wrote *Macbeth*. King James, who became the patron of Shakespeare's acting company, was also known as the author of a book about witchcraft. Keeping all this in mind, write a few paragraphs about how the play seems to reflect Shakespeare's efforts to flatter his new patron. Support general statements with details from the first three acts.

Oral Response

16. Go back to questions 1, 5, 8, 10, 13, or 14 or one assigned to you by your teacher, and take five to ten minutes to expand your answer and prepare an oral response. Find additional details in the play that will support your points. If necessary, make notes to guide your response.

Rubric for Evaluating Extended Responses

0	1	2	3	4
Blank paper	Incorrect purpose, mode, audience	Correct purpose, mode, audience	Correct purpose, mode, audience	Correct purpose, mode, audience
Foreign language	Brief, vague	Some elaboration	Moderately well elaborated	Effective elaboration
Illegible, incoherent	Unelaborated	Some details	Clear, effective language	Consistent organization
Not enough content to score	Rambling	Gaps in organization	Organized (perhaps with brief digressions)	Sense of completeness, fluency
	Lack of language control	Limited language control		
	Poor organization			

Name _____ Date _____

Multiple Choice and Short Answer

Write your answers to all questions in this section on the lines provided.
For multiple-choice questions, circle the letter of the best answer.

1. In the witches' chant in Scene i, lines 1–38, what do all the images have in common?
    Cite examples to show why each choice is correct or incorrect.
    a. They are vivid and beautiful.

    _____
    b. They are vivid and unpleasant.

    _____
    c. They appeal only to the sense of sight.

    _____
    d. They appeal mainly to the sense of smell.

    _____

2. Who or what is the "something wicked" that the second witch hears coming in Scene i,
    line 45? Explain your answer.
    a. Macbeth   c. Hecate
    b. the first witch   d. the first apparition

    _____
    _____

3. Reread Macbeth's speech in Scene i, line 50–61. Identify to which one of the five senses
    these lines most strongly appeal.

    _____

4. Why does Macbeth take comfort in the second and third predictions of the apparitions?

    _____

5. Which phrase best describes the impression we get of Macduff's son before he is
    murdered? Explain your choice, citing details from the play to support your answer.
    a. charming, naive, and affectionate   c. nasty, foolish, and ignorant
    b. cold, calculating, and ambitious   d. sniveling and whining

    _____
    _____

6. What method does Malcolm initially use to test Macduff's loyalty, and why is he so
    suspicious of Macduff? Cite details from the play to support your answer.

    _____
    _____
    _____

7. To which senses do Malcolm's images of Scotland in Scene iii, lines 39–41, most clearly appeal? Explain your answer.
   a. sight, sound, and taste
   b. sight, taste, and smell
   c. touch, smell, and sound
   d. touch, sound, and sight

_____

_____

8. What recurring image is associated with Lady Macduff and her son? Cite examples of this imagery and explain the qualities that it helps to convey.
   a. witches
   b. flowers
   c. birds
   d. eggs

_____

_____

_____

9. Which adjective would Macduff and Malcolm be most likely to use to describe Macbeth's rule on Scotland? Explain why it is right or wrong.
   a. judicious   b. sundry   c. credulous   d. pernicious

_____

_____

10. Reread Ross's description of Scotland in Scene iii, lines 164–173. Then identify the words and images that Ross uses to appeal to the sense of sound.

_____

_____

_____

Extended Response

11. Write a brief essay about the imagery in the witches' chant (IV, i, 1-38) and the mood that the images help create. Examine the senses to which the different images appeal. Then consider how the images, taken as a whole, establish a particular mood or atmosphere. Be sure to cite several examples of images. You can gather them first on the diagram below.

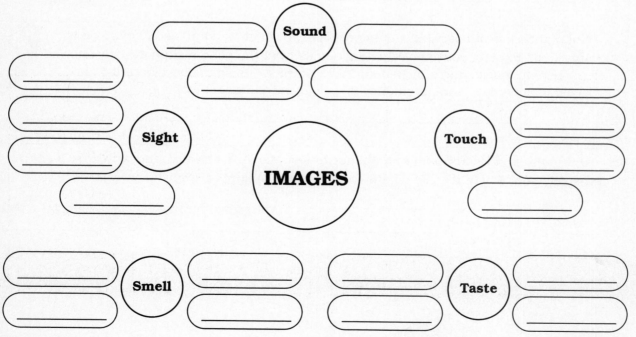

© Prentice-Hall, Inc.

12. In a brief essay, discuss the poetic form of the witches' chant. How is it different from blank verse? Why do you think Shakespeare uses this form instead of blank verse? Answer these questions in a brief essay that cites specific examples to support general statements.

13. Write a few paragraphs tracing the murders thus far. Explain the reasons that Macbeth commits or orders each murder and the mounting horror of his acts. What does his behavior suggest about violence and its outcome?

14. Shakespeare is often praised for his profound understanding of human nature. Evaluate this praise based on the details of Act IV. Setting aside the behavior of the nonhuman characters (the witches, Hecate, and the apparitions), focus on Macbeth, Malcolm, Macduff, Lady Macduff and her son, and Ross. Do their behavior and attitudes seem realistic to you? Would you say that Shakespeare's knowledge of human nature holds up across the centuries? Address these questions in a brief essay that cites specific details to support your opinions.

15. What do you predict about the apparitions' last two predictions? Do you think the seeming impossibility of their happening means that Macbeth is safe, as he believes? Or do you think there will be a way for what seems impossible to happen? Explain your answers in a paragraph or two that speculates about what might occur later. Base your speculations on what has happened so far.

Oral Response

16. Go back to questions 4, 5, 6, 13, 14, or 15 or one assigned to you by your teacher, and take five to ten minutes to expand your answer and prepare an oral response. Find additional details in the play that will support your points. If necessary, make notes to guide your response.

Rubric for Evaluating Extended Responses

0	1	2	3	4
Blank paper Foreign language Illegible, incoherent Not enough content to score	Incorrect purpose, mode, audience Brief, vague Unelaborated Rambling Lack of language control Poor organization	Correct purpose, mode, audience Some elaboration Some details Gaps in organization Limited language control	Correct purpose, mode, audience Moderately well elaborated Clear, effective language Organized (perhaps with brief digressions)	Correct purpose, mode, audience Effective elaboration Consistent organization Sense of completeness, fluency

The Tragedy of Macbeth, **Act V,** by William Shakespeare

Open-Book Test

Multiple Choice and Short Answer

Write your answers to all questions in this section on the lines provided.
For multiple-choice questions, circle the letter of the best answer.

1. Which of the following incidents does Lady Macbeth recall as she sleepwalks?
   Explain your choice, citing lines from the play.
   a. Duncan's murder   c. the murder of Lady Macduff
   b. the appearance of Banquo's ghost   d. all of the above

   _____

   _____

   _____

   _____

2. What earlier remark of Macbeth's does Lady Macbeth clearly echo in lines 51–53 of her
   sleepwalking scene?

   _____

3. Which emotion or attitude does Lady Macbeth display in her sleepwalking scene?
   Explain your answer.
   a. lust for power   c. guilt for her crimes
   b. hatred of Macbeth   d. a desire for revenge against her enemies

   _____

   _____

4. What does the sleepwalking scene suggest about customs and practices of the past?
   Explain why each choice is right or wrong.
   a. Medical knowledge of mental disorders was far more limited than it is today.

   _____

   b. People in the Middle Ages were more prone to sleepwalking than they are today.

   _____

   c. People in Shakespeare's time knew nothing of emotional distress.

   _____

   d. In the past, servants often knew more about medicine than doctors did.

   _____

5. Which word most clearly identifies Macbeth's feelings in his famous soliloquy after
   learning of his wife's death (Scene v, lines 19–28)? Cite details from the soliloquy to
   explain your answer.
   a. anger   c. peace
   b. despair   d. excitement

   _____

   _____

   _____

6. Which of the following incidents is most clearly a *harbinger* of Macbeth's downfall? Explain your response.
   a. the gentlewoman's remark about Lady Macbeth, "She has a light by her continually"
   b. Macbeth's calling his servant a "lily-livered boy"
   c. Macbeth's remark, "Throw physic to the dogs"
   d. the messenger's remark, "I looked toward Birnam, and anon, methought,/The wood began to move"

   _____

   _____

   _____

7. Explain how the two prophesies that Macbeth thought never would come true actually do come true.

   _____

   _____

   _____

8. As the tragedy moves to a climax, how would you describe Macbeth's behavior? Cite examples to help you explain your answer.
   a. courageous   c. wise
   b. cowardly   d. pious

   _____

   _____

9. From the battles in Act V, what can you conclude about warfare in Macbeth's day? Explain why each choice seems correct or incorrect.
   a. Soldiers never faced each other one on one.

   _____

   b. All fighting was done in the open, and the concept of camouflage was unknown.

   _____

   c. The telephone and telegraph were the chief means of sending messages.

   _____

   d. Swords were among the weapons used in close combat.

   _____

10. Think about the definition of tragedy and the events that have unfolded in *Macbeth*. What would you say is Macbeth's tragic flaw, and why?

   _____

Extended Response

11. Choose one recurring image in *Macbeth*—blood, for example, or illness—and discuss how it is used throughout the play. Is the image associated mainly with one or two particular characters? How does the image help to convey ideas and emotions? Address these questions in a brief essay.

12. Write a brief evaluation of Macbeth as a typical tragic hero. Do you think he is an otherwise noble figure with one tragic flaw, or do you find him less noble overall than a tragic hero should be? State your opinions, and be sure to support them with examples and reasons.

13. Some readers of *Macbeth* have observed that Lady Macbeth, by the end of the play, takes on qualities that Macbeth displayed near the beginning, while Macbeth, by the play's end, takes on qualities that Lady Macbeth initially displayed. Write a brief essay exploring this idea. Before you begin, organize details on the chart below.

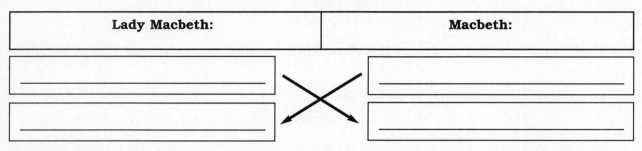

Lady Macbeth:	Macbeth:
_____	_____
_____	_____

14. Choose one of the following sayings, and write a brief essay explaining how it expresses a theme conveyed in *Macbeth*. Cite details from Acts I-V to support your ideas.
    a. Power corrupts, and absolute power corrupts absolutely.
    b. Blood will have blood.
    c. What goes around, comes around.
    d. Look before you leap.
    e. Fair is foul and foul is fair.

15. In a few paragraphs, explain why you think *Macbeth* has endured over the centuries. You may want to discuss the play's relevance today in terms of themes or characters and their experiences, or you may wish to focus on Shakespeare's use of language. Whatever the thrust of your writing, be sure to cite details from the play to support your general statements about it.

Oral Response

16. Go back to questions 5, 8, 10, 12, 14, or 15 or one assigned to you by your teacher, and take five to ten minutes to expand your answer and prepare an oral response. Find additional details in the play that will support your points. If necessary, make notes to guide your response.

Rubric for Evaluating Extended Responses

0	1	2	3	4
Blank paper Foreign language Illegible, incoherent Not enough content to score	Incorrect purpose, mode, audience Brief, vague Unelaborated Rambling Lack of language control Poor organization	Correct purpose, mode, audience Some elaboration Some details Gaps in organization Limited language control	Correct purpose, mode, audience Moderately well elaborated Clear, effective language Organized (perhaps with brief digressions)	Correct purpose, mode, audience Effective elaboration Consistent organization Sense of completeness, fluency

Name _____ Date _____

Open-Book Test

Multiple Choice and Short Answer

Write your answers to all questions in this section on the lines provided.
For multiple-choice questions, circle the letter of the best answer.

1. Which of the following lines from "Holy Sonnet 10" contains a paradox about death? Explain your answer choice by defining paradox.
   a. "Death be not proud, though some have called thee / Mighty and dreadful, for thou art not so. . ."
   b. "And soonest our best men with thee do go, / Rest of their bones. . ."
   c. "Thou art slave to fate, chance, kings, and desperate men, / And dost with poison, war, and sickness dwell. . . "
   d. "One short sleep past, we wake eternally, / And death shall be no more; Death, thou shalt die."

   _____

   _____

2. In "Holy Sonnet 10," what conclusion can you draw about the speaker's opinion about death and the way it affects people? Support your answer with lines from the poem.

   _____

   _____

3. What might you recognize about the speaker's relationship to his beloved in "Song"? Support your answer by citing a line or two from the poem.

   _____

   _____

4. When the speaker in "Song" says, "When thou sigh'st, thou sigh'st not wind, /But sigh'st my soul away . . . ," what inference can you make about the speaker's situation and motivation?

   _____

   _____

5. In "Song," the speaker attempts to comfort his beloved about their temporary separation. Why does the speaker suggest that the beloved view their separation as if they were ". . . but turned aside to sleep" (line 38)? Explain the speaker's suggestion in your answer.

   _____

   _____

6. In "A Valediction: Forbidding Mourning," which word is an antonym for *breach*, based on how this word is used in stanza 6, line 24? Use *breach* in a sentence of your own.
   a. eruption   c. distraction
   b. unification   d. expansion

   _____

7. Identify the metaphysical conceit used in "A Valediction: Forbidding Mourning" by citing the line numbers in which it is found. Explain what this conceit illustrates about the relationship between the speaker and his beloved.

_____

_____

8. In "Meditation 17," what is presented as being analogous to God? Choose the correct answer. Explain why the answer that you chose is correct.
   a. an island   b. a book   c. a bell   d. a child

_____

9. In "Meditation 17," Donne discusses the special connection that the church creates among its members. What does Donne mean when he writes, "The church is catholic, universal, so are all her actions; all that she does belongs to all"? Support your answer with one example from the text.

_____

_____

10. Select the answer that contains an example of a metaphysical conceit that is found in "Meditation 17." Explain why your answer is correct, and why each of the others is incorrect.
    a. "All mankind is of one author and one volume. When one man dies, one chapter is not torn out of the book, but translated into a better language. . ."

    _____

    b. "Any man's death diminishes me because I am involved in mankind. . ."

    _____

    c. "Who casts not up his eye to the sun when it rises?"

    _____

    d. "Another man may be sick too, and sick to death, and this affliction may lie in his bowels as gold in a mine and be of no use to him. . ."

    _____

Extended Response

11. "Holy Sonnet 10" is a poem in which the speaker asserts his acceptance of death. Why is the speaker unafraid of dying? Answer this question in a short essay. Support your ideas with examples from the poem.

12. In "Song," the length of time that will elapse while the speaker and his beloved are separated is described in numerous ways. In a short essay, explain how the passage of time is described in "Song" and why it is portrayed in this way. Support your interpretation citing details from the poem.

13. Using the Venn diagram below, compare and contrast how "Song" and "A Valediction: Forbidding Mourning" portray the parting of the speaker and his beloved, the effect that parting has on the speaker, and the effect that parting has on the beloved. Write an essay comparing and contrasting the two poems using the information compiled in the Venn diagram. Support your interpretation with examples from each poem.

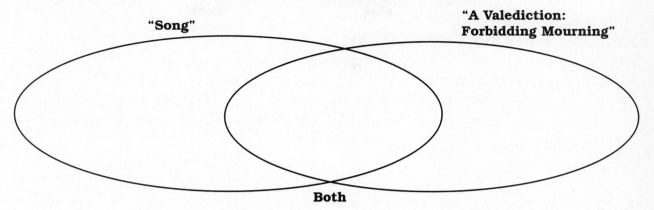

"Song"

"A Valediction: Forbidding Mourning"

Both

14. In "Meditation 17," Donne reveals his views about the value of suffering. In one or two paragraphs, explain what Donne's views about the value of suffering are and why he feels this way. Cite examples from "Meditation 17" to support your interpretation.

15. In "Meditation 17," Donne repeatedly refers to how the events in one person's life, such as birth and death, may affect another person directly, even if the people are not related to each other. Write a short essay in which you discuss why Donne believes this idea to be true. Cite details from "Meditation 17" to support your interpretation.

Oral Response

16. Go back to question 4, 8, 10, 11, 13, or 15 or one assigned by your teacher, and take five to ten minutes to expand your answer and prepare an oral response. Find additional details in the works by Donne that will support your points. If necessary, make notes to guide your response.

Rubric for Evaluating Extended Responses

0	1	2	3	4
Blank paper Foreign language Illegible, incoherent Not enough content to score	Incorrect purpose, mode, audience Brief, vague Unelaborated Rambling Lack of language control Poor organization	Correct purpose, mode, audience Some elaboration Some details Gaps in organization Limited language control	Correct purpose, mode, audience Moderately well elaborated Clear, effective language Organized (perhaps with brief digressions)	Correct purpose, mode, audience Effective elaboration Consistent organization Sense of completeness, fluency

"On My First Son," "Song: To Celia,"
and **"Still to Be Neat"** by Ben Jonson

Open-Book Test

Multiple Choice and Short Answer

Write your answers to all questions in this section on the lines provided.
For multiple-choice questions, circle the letter of the best answer.

1. In "On My First Son," the speaker mourns the loss of his young son. Explain what the speaker means when he says, "Seven years thou wert lent to me, and I thee pay, / Exacted by thy fate, on the just day" (lines 3–4)?

   _____

   _____

2. In "On My First Son," the speaker tries to comfort himself over the loss of his son. Why does he suggest that his son's death is a "state he should envy"? (line 6) Support your answer with one other line from the poem.

   _____

   _____

3. In "On My First Son," the speaker reveals to the reader a lesson he has learned from the loss of his son. What twist in meaning exists in the following line: "What he loves may never like too much"? (line 12)

   _____

   _____

4. Based on your reading of "On My First Son," whom can you hypothesize is the speaker of this poem? Explain why your answer choice is correct.
   a. Ben Jonson   b. a minister   c. a father   d. a son

   _____

5. In "Song: To Celia," what does the act of drinking represent in the poem? Support your answer with evidence from the poem.

   _____

   _____

6. Why does the speaker give his beloved a wreath of flowers in "Song: To Celia"? Explain your answer choice, citing details from the poem.

   a. He gives her the wreath as a token of his love.

   b. He gives her a wreath in order to prevent it from drying out.

   c. He gives her a wreath as a symbol of her beauty.

   d. He gives her a wreath in order to persuade her to return to him.

   _____

7. In "Song: To Celia," what feelings of the speaker about the beloved are reflected in the last two lines of the poem? Explain your answer.

_____

_____

8. In "Still to Be Neat," the speaker is troubled about the lady whom he addresses. Why does the speaker feel that "All is not sweet, all is not sound" (line 6) about the lady he describes in stanza 1?

_____

_____

9. An epigram is a short poem in which brevity, clarity, and permanence are emphasized. In his poetry, Jonson uses statements that appear to go against common sense, giving his work a memorable "twist." In "Still to Be Neat," which of the following lines contains an example of a twist? Explain why the answer that you selected is correct.

   a. "Still to be neat, still to be dressed, / As you were going to a feast..." (lines 1–2)

   b. "Lady, it is to be presumed, / Though art's hid causes are not found..." (lines 4–5)

   c. "Give me a look, give me a face, / That makes simplicity a grace..." (lines 7–8)

   d. "Robes loosely flowing, hair as free; / Such sweet neglect more taketh me than all th' adulteries of art." (lines 9–10)

_____

_____

10. How does the repetitive use of the word *still* in various phrases in stanza 1 of "Still to Be Neat" help you to hypothesize about what the speaker regards as beautiful? Explain your answer, citing details from the poem.

_____

_____

Extended Response

11. In "On My First Son," Jonson writes about the loss of his young son and how he views this loss. In one or two paragraphs, explain how Jonson views the loss of his son and how he comforts himself about it. Cite examples from the poem to support your response.

12. In "Song: To Celia," the speaker describes his feelings for his beloved through a figurative description of actions that both he and the beloved undertake. How does the speaker convey his romantic feelings for his beloved through these descriptions? Respond to this question in a short essay, citing examples from the poem to support your statements.

13. Why is the use of the second-person narrator an effective means of presenting the poems "On My First Son" and "Song: To Celia"? In a short essay, explain how Jonson's choice of this narrator helps to express the speaker's feelings about his subject and the message in the poems. Use examples from both poems to support your response.

14. Using the Venn diagram below, compare and contrast the types of love and how they are portrayed in "On My First Son" and "Song: To Celia." Identify the type of love that is discussed, and how the speaker presents it in the poem. Using the information in the Venn diagram, write an essay comparing and contrasting these two poems. Support your interpretation with examples from both poems.

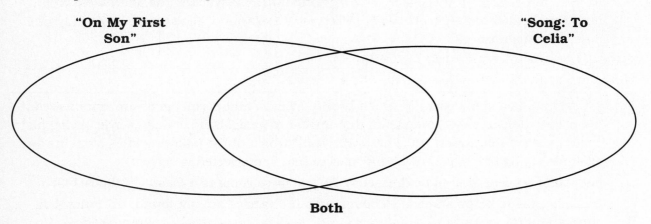

"On My First Son"

"Song: To Celia"

Both

15. The epigrams presented in this unit demonstrate Jonson's ability to craft works that contain messages that hold true for all time. How does Jonson make the ideas presented in "On My First Son," "Song: To Celia," and "Still to Be Neat" memorable ones? Respond to this question in an essay, citing examples from these poems to support your response.

Oral Response

16. Go back to question 4, 10 11, 12, 13, 14, or 15 or one assigned by your teacher, and take five or ten minutes to expand your answer and prepare an oral response. Find additional details in the poems by Jonson that will support your points. If necessary, make notes to guide your response.

Rubric for Evaluating Extended Responses

0	1	2	3	4
Blank paper Foreign language Illegible, incoherent Not enough content to score	Incorrect purpose, mode, audience Brief, vague Unelaborated Rambling Lack of language control Poor organization	Correct purpose, mode, audience Some elaboration Some details Gaps in organization Limited language control	Correct purpose, mode, audience Moderately well elaborated Clear, effective language Organized (perhaps with brief digressions)	Correct purpose, mode, audience Effective elaboration Consistent organization Sense of completeness, fluency

"To His Coy Mistress" by Andrew Marvel
"To the Virgins, to Make Much of Time" by Robert Herrick
"Song" by Sir John Suckling

Open-Book Test

Multiple Choice and Short Answer

Write your answers to all questions in this section on the lines provided.
For multiple-choice questions, circle the letter of the best answer.

1. In "To His Coy Mistress," the speaker describes how, if he had time, he would spend it in love with his beloved. How does the speaker describe time in stanza 1? Support your answer with one example from the poem.

    _____

    _____

2. Throughout the poem "To His Coy Mistress," the speaker describes aspects of his beloved's appearance. What can you infer about the speaker's attitude about his beloved's appearance? Explain why your answer choice is correct.
    a. The speaker thinks that the beloved is old.
    b. The speaker thinks that the beloved is beautiful.
    c. The speaker thinks that the beloved is losing her beauty.
    d. The speaker is uninterested in the beloved's appearance.

    _____

    _____

3. The speaker in "To His Coy Mistress" likens himself and his lover to a pair of "amorous birds of prey" (line 38). Based on how it is used in line 38 of the poem, select the answer that contains the word that means the opposite of *amorous*. Explain why your answer choice is correct.
    a. hateful   b. aggressive   c. loving   d. unemotional

    _____

    _____

4. In Herrick's "To the Virgins, to Make Much of Time," what does the flower image in stanza 1 represent? Explain your answer.

    _____

    _____

5. In "To the Virgins, to Make Much of Time," the speaker discusses how a woman's youth should be spent. Which of the lines from the poem listed below capture the speaker's attitude about this idea? Explain why the answer that you chose is correct.
    a. "That age is best which is the first, / When youth and blood are warmer. . ." (lines 9–10)

    _____

    b. "Then be not coy, but use your time, / And, while ye may, go marry . . ." (lines 12–13)

    _____

    c. "And this same flower that smiles today / Tomorrow will be dying." (lines 3–4)

    _____

    d. "For, having lost but once your prime, / You may forever tarry." (lines 15–16)

    _____

6. "To the Virgins, to Make Much of Time" is a poem that attempts to persuade young women to make the most of their youth. How does the speaker structure his argument persuasively in this poem? Explain your answer, citing one or two lines from the poem.

_____

_____

7. In "Song," the speaker is an outsider who is speaking to a lover about his attempts to win his beloved's affections. Why does the speaker ask various questions of the lover in the first three stanzas? Explain your answer.

_____

_____

8. In "Song," what can you infer about the speaker's attempts to gain his beloved's affections? Explain why your answer choice is correct.
   a. The speaker's attempts are futile.
   b. The speaker's attempts inspire him with hope.
   c. The speaker's attempts are unnecessary because his beloved is willing to become involved with him.
   d. The speaker's attempts reflect his impatience with his beloved.

_____

9. Which lines listed below expresses the *carpe diem* theme presented in "Song"? Explain why your answer choice is correct, and why the other choices are incorrect.
   a. "Will, when looking well can't move her, / Looking ill prevail?" (lines 2–3)

_____

   b. "Why so dull and mute, young sinner?" (line 6)

_____

   c. "Will, when speaking well can't win her, / Saying nothing do't?" (lines 8–9)

_____

   d. "If of herself she will not love, / Nothing can make her, / The devil take her!" (lines 13–14)

_____

10. Which of the following best contrasts the purposes of the speakers in "To His Coy Mistress" and "Song" ? Explain why your answer choice is correct.
   a. The speaker in "To His Coy Mistress" tries to pressure his mistress, while the speaker in "Song" wants to persuade the lover.
   b. The speaker in "To His Coy Mistress" wants to enrage his mistress, while the speaker in "Song" attempts to confuse the lover.
   c. The speaker in "To His Coy Mistress" tries to frighten the mistress, while the speaker in "Song" wants to anger the lover.
   d. The speaker in "To His Coy Mistress" wants to humor the mistress, while the speaker in "Song" wants to criticize the lover.

_____

_____

Extended Response

11. Throughout "To His Coy Mistress," the speaker argues that he and the beloved must make the most of their time together in order to persuade her to enter into a relationship with him. In a short essay, explain how the speaker structures his argument in his efforts to persuade the beloved to seize the moment and engage in a relationship with him. Cite lines from the poem to support your response.

12. In "To the Virgins, to Make Much of Time," the speaker describes the passage of time through various images in the poem. In one or two paragraphs, explain how the images in the poem convey the passage of time.

13. The speaker in "Song" is an outsider who comments on the lover's futile efforts to win his beloved's affections. In one or two paragraphs, explain why and how the use of an outside speaker effectively conveys the *carpe diem* theme in the poem. Cite lines from the poem to support your response.

14. "To His Coy Mistress" and "To the Virgins, to Make Much of Time" both convey the speaker's feelings about love. In the Venn diagram below, compare and contrast the speakers' attitude about love. Cite one or two images in each poem that support your analysis of the speakers' attitudes. Then, in a comparative essay, explain how the images in each poem illustrate your points about these attitudes.

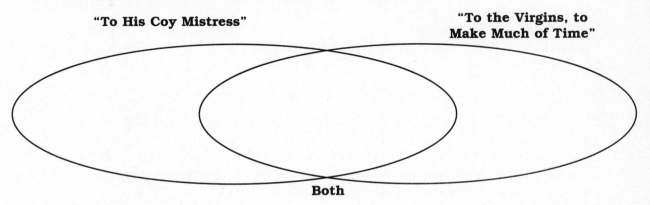

"To His Coy Mistress"

"To the Virgins, to Make Much of Time"

Both

15. Each of the poems in this section—"To His Coy Mistress," "To the Virgins, to Make Much of Time," and "Song"—illustrates the *carpe diem* theme. Based on your reading and analysis of each poem, which poem most effectively portrays this theme? In a short essay, explain how your choice presents this theme most effectively. Cite lines from the poem to support your response.

Oral Response

16. Go back to question 1, 6, 7, 10, 11, or 13 or one assigned to you by your teacher, and take five or ten minutes to expand your answer and prepare an oral response. Find additional details in the poems in the sections that will support your points. If necessary, make notes to guide your response.

Rubric for Evaluating Extended Responses

0	1	2	3	4
Blank paper Foreign language Illegible, incoherent Not enough content to score	Incorrect purpose, mode, audience Brief, vague Unelaborated Rambling Lack of language control Poor organization	Correct purpose, mode, audience Some elaboration Some details Gaps in organization Limited language control	Correct purpose, mode, audience Moderately well elaborated Clear, effective language Organized (perhaps with brief digressions)	Correct purpose, mode, audience Effective elaboration Consistent organization Sense of completeness, fluency

Poetry of John Milton

Open-Book Test

Multiple Choice and Short Answer

Write your answers to all questions in this section on the lines provided.
For multiple-choice questions, circle the letter of the best answer.

1. Explain the problem that troubles the speaker in "Sonnet VII."

   _____

   _____

   _____

2. The speaker in Sonnet VII describes time as a "subtle thief of youth" (line 1). Why does he describe time in this way?

   _____

   _____

   _____

3. In the last six lines of Sonnet VII, the speaker presents a solution to the problem he presented earlier in the poem. Choose the answer below that most accurately reflects his solution. Explain why your answer choice is correct.
   a. Time cannot be stopped; the speaker puts his faith in heaven to help him deal with aging.
   b. The speaker vows to follow time no matter where it leads him.
   c. The speaker hires a Taskmaster to help him deal with his issues about aging.
   d. Time is really the speaker's Taskmaster, and the speaker realizes that he must obey time.

   _____

   _____

   _____

4. In the octet of Sonnet VII, the speaker discusses the contrast between his physical appearance and his inner self. Why is the speaker concerned about this difference? Support your response with lines from the poem.

   _____

   _____

   _____

5. The speaker in Sonnet XIX contemplates the loss of his eyesight (lines 1–6). How is this loss of eyesight represented? Explain your answer, citing details from the sonnet as support.

   _____

   _____

   _____

   _____

6. The last six lines of Sonnet XIX are a response to the speaker's questions about the loss of his eyesight. What is the purpose of the response in these lines? Explain why the answer you chose is correct.
    a. to give the speaker patience
    b. to comfort the speaker
    c. to fool the speaker
    d. to explain to the speaker how he will suffer

    _____

    _____

7. Based on how it is used in lines 22–23 of *Paradise Lost*, what does *illumine* mean? Explain your answer on the lines provided.

    _____

    _____

8. In *Paradise Lost*, how does the account of the devil's fall from heaven reflect the theme of good versus evil? Support your answer with lines or phrases from the poem.

    _____

    _____

    _____

    _____

9. Reread lines 81–83. Break down this complex sentence into shorter sentences, and explain what it means.

    _____

    _____

    _____

    _____

10. In *Paradise Lost*, Satan reflects on his defeat by God. What conflicting feelings does Satan have about this defeat? Support your answer with lines from the poem.

    _____

    _____

    _____

Extended Response

11. In Sonnet VII, Milton expresses his concern over the difference between his physical age and his inner development. In one or two paragraphs, explain the view that Milton has about his ability to control this conflict in his life. Cite lines from the poem to support your response.

12. Milton uses two speakers in Sonnet XIX to present the poem's problem and solution. In one or two paragraphs, explain why two speakers in Sonnet XIX are necessary to resolve Milton's issue with his blindness. Cite lines from the poem to support your response.

13. Examine the rhyme structure of the sestets in Sonnet VII and Sonnet XIX. Which rhyme scheme is more regular? Why? In a short essay, explain how the rhyme scheme of each sestet serves to convey the speaker's feelings about the answer posed in the sestets of each poem. Cite lines from the poem to support your response.

14. In *Paradise Lost*, Milton employs Hebrew allusions in the first twenty-five lines in order to set the stage for his account of the battle between God and the devil. In one or two paragraphs, explain why Milton uses these allusions to prepare the reader for the events in this epic poem. Support your response with lines from *Paradise Lost*.

15. In this excerpt from *Paradise Lost*, the reader learns only about Satan's perspective of the battle. Using the herringbone organizer, list the devil's characteristics on the diagonal lines, and list examples to support the existence of these characteristics on the horizontal lines. You may not need to use all of the lines in the herringbone organizer. Then, in a short essay, use the information compiled in the herringbone organizer to explain how Satan portrays himself in this section. Support your response with lines from the poem.

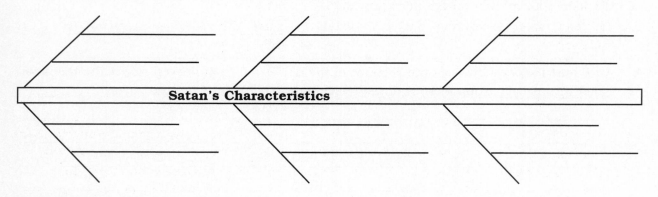

Oral Response

16. Go back to question 4, 10, 11, 12, 13, or 15 or one assigned by your teacher, and take five to ten minutes to expand your answer and prepare an oral response. Find additional details in the poems by Milton that will support your points. If necessary, make notes to guide your response.

Rubric for Evaluating Extended Responses

0	1	2	3	4
Blank paper Foreign language Illegible, incoherent Not enough content to score	Incorrect purpose, mode, audience Brief, vague Unelaborated Rambling Lack of language control Poor organization	Correct purpose, mode, audience Some elaboration Some details Gaps in organization Limited language control	Correct purpose, mode, audience Moderately well elaborated Clear, effective language Organized (perhaps with brief digressions)	Correct purpose, mode, audience Effective elaboration Consistent organization Sense of completeness, fluency

from **"Eve's Apology in Defense of Women"** by Amelia Lanier
"To Lucasta, on Going to the Wars" and **"To Althea, from Prison"**
by Richard Lovelace

Open-Book Test

Multiple Choice and Short Answer

Write your answers to all questions in this section on the lines provided.
For multiple-choice questions, circle the letter of the best answer.

1. How is Eve portrayed as a victim in the last stanza of "Eve's Apology in Defense of Women"? Cite lines from stanza 4 to support your response.

   _____

   _____

   _____

2. Through "Eve's Apology to Women," Lanier calls for equality between men and women by analyzing the story of Adam and Eve. Based on your reading of stanzas 1 and 2, how does Lanier assert that Adam's "breach" (line 12) is the more serious one? Use the herringbone organizer to respond to this question. List the ways in which Lanier asserts this argument on the diagonal lines. List the lines of the poem that support your responses on the horizontal lines. You may not need to use all of the lines in order to respond completely to this question.

   "Eve's Apology in Defense of Women"

3. Why does Lanier base her proposal for equality between the sexes on a reinterpretation of a biblical story? Explain your answer.

   _____

   _____

4. Based on how the word *inconstancy* is used in line 9 of "To Lucasta, on Going to the Wars," what type of *inconstancy* is described in stanza 3? Explain why your answer choice is correct.
   a. The speaker shifts his affections from his beloved to war.
   b. The speaker shifts his affections from his beloved to a new mistress.
   c. The speaker shifts his affections from his beloved to honor.
   d. The speaker shifts his affections from his beloved to his faith.

   _____

   _____

5. Based on your knowledge of the historical context of this period, why is it appropriate that "To Lucasta, on Going to the Wars" deals with a lover going off to fight a war? Cite one example from the historical section of this text to support your response.

_____

_____

6. In "To Althea, from Prison," the speaker is visited by his beloved, Althea. How does the speaker feel when Althea visits him? Cite one or two lines to support your answer.

_____

_____

7. The "Guide for Interpreting" states that Lovelace was a Royalist and was chosen by the Royalists to demand that Parliament restore the king's authority. How are Lovelace's Royalist views presented in "To Althea, from Prison"? Support your response with citations from the poem.

_____

_____

8. Why does Lovelace use the poem "To Althea, from Prison" to argue for the restoration of the king to his throne? Explain your answer, citing details from the poem.

_____

_____

_____

9. Based on your reading of "To Althea, from Prison," what can you infer about how the speaker feels about his imprisonment? Explain why your answer choice is correct.
   a. defiant
   b. free
   c. careless
   d. happy

_____

_____

10. In each stanza of the poem, "To Althea, from Prison," how does the speaker reinforce his feelings that he is free from prison? Support your answer with one or two examples from the poem.

_____

_____

_____

Extended Response

11. England experienced a time of instability during the period that Lanier wrote her works. In one or two paragraphs, explain how Lanier's poem, "Eve's Apology in Defense of Women" is an example of the instability of this period. Support your response with lines from the poem.

12. The speaker in "To Lucasta, on Going to the Wars" informs his beloved that he is going to war. In one or two paragraphs, explain how the speaker feels about going to war. Cite lines from the poem to support your response.

13. In "To Althea, from Prison," the speaker describes his feelings about imprisonment through various images in each of the poem's stanzas. In a short essay, explain how the speaker attempts to defy his physical imprisonment through these images. Support your response with evidence from the poem.

14. In "To Althea, from Prison," the speaker reveals his personality through his account of his imprisonment. In an essay, analyze the speaker's personality, based on how he describes his imprisonment. Use examples from the poem to support your response.

15. In both "To Lucasta, on Going to the Wars" and "To Althea, from Prison," the speakers take an optimistic outlook on potentially bleak circumstances—war and imprisonment, respectively. In an essay, explain how each speaker presents this positive outlook in the poems. Cite examples from the poems to support your response.

Oral Response

16. Go back to question 1, 3, 8, 12, or 14 or one assigned by your teacher, and take five or ten minutes to expand your answer and prepare an oral response. Find additional details in the poems by Lanier and Lovelace that will support your points. If necessary, make notes to guide your response.

Rubric for Evaluating Extended Responses

0	1	2	3	4
Blank paper Foreign language Illegible, incoherent Not enough content to score	Incorrect purpose, mode, audience Brief, vague Unelaborated Rambling Lack of language control Poor organization	Correct purpose, mode, audience Some elaboration Some details Gaps in organization Limited language control	Correct purpose, mode, audience Moderately well elaborated Clear, effective language Organized (perhaps with brief digressions)	Correct purpose, mode, audience Effective elaboration Consistent organization Sense of completeness, fluency

from *The Diary* by Samuel Pepys
from *A Journal of the Plague Year* by Daniel Defoe

Open-Book Test

Multiple Choice and Short Answer

Write your answers to all questions in this section on the lines provided.
For multiple-choice questions, circle the letter of the best answer.

1. In the excerpt from *The Diary*, Pepys describes the plague and the toll it takes on the people of London. Explain why Pepys names and describes the fates of specific people.

   _____

   _____

2. Based on the group of men with whom Pepys meets on September 3, 1665, what can you conclude about Pepys's social position? Explain your answer.

   _____

   _____

3. In his September 14, 1665, entry in *The Diary*, why does Pepys feel some hope about the conditions in London? Explain why your answer choice is correct.
   a. Pepys has learned that his money and valuables are safe and that fewer people have died of the plague.
   b. Pepys has learned that his money and valuables are safe and that his wife and family are happy.
   c. Pepys has learned that the local pub is open and that fewer people have died of the plague.
   d. Pepys has learned that his waiter is alive and fewer people have died of the plague recently.

   _____

   _____

4. Which of the following lines reflects Pepys's growing alarm about the fire? Explain why the answer you chose is correct and why the other answers are incorrect.
   a. ". . . Jane called us up about three in the morning, to tell us of a great fire they saw in the city."

   _____

   b. ". . . there I did see the houses at that end of the bridge all on fire, and an infinite great fire on this and the other side the end of the bridge. . ."

   _____

   c. "We stayed till, it being darkish, we saw the fire as only one entire arch of fire from this to the other side of the bridge, and in a bow up the hill for an arch above a mile long; it made me weep to see it."

   _____

   d. "About four o'clock in the morning, my Lady Batten sent me a cart to carry away all my money and plate, and best things. . ."

   _____

5. Based on your reading of his diary, what can you conclude about what Pepys values the most? Support your response with examples from Pepys's diary.

_____

_____

6. In *A Journal of the Plague Year*, the narrator describes the effect that the plague has on the people he observes. How does the narrator convey the grief-stricken mood of the people?

_____

_____

7. In his account of the numbers of people who die from the plague, the narrator cites specific numbers of people who died. Why does the narrator cite these numbers in the excerpt from *A Journal of the Plague Year?* Explain your answer.

_____

_____

8. Which of the following words is a synonym for *prodigious*, based on how it is used in the last sentence of the excerpt from *A Journal of the Plague Year?* Explain why the answer you chose is correct.
   a. various   b. wealthy   c. enormous   d. insignificant

_____

9. What details does Defoe use to make *A Journal of the Plague Year* seem like an authentic journal? Cite one or two details and explain how they make the journal appear authentic.

_____

_____

_____

_____

10. Based on your reading of *The Diary* and *A Journal of the Plague Year*, what can you conclude about the similarity in the way that Pepys and the narrator of the journal present their accounts? Cite examples from each diary to support your response.

_____

_____

_____

Extended Response

11. Although it does provide insight into the time period about which it was written, Pepys's diary contains only his viewpoint about the major historical events of his age. In a short essay, explain how *The Diary* provides a biased point of view of events such as the plague and the fire of London. Support your response with examples from the diary.

12. A diary or journal may not only offer a daily account of a writer's experiences and reactions, it may also offer insights into important historical events. In one or two paragraphs, explain what you learned about English society during the 1660's from *The Diary*. Cite examples from *The Diary* to support your response.

13. Defoe's *A Journal of the Plague Year* is a fictional journal that describes the effect the bubonic plague had on England's people. Analyze the structure of this journal excerpt by using the story map below. Using the information that you compile in the story map, explain in one or two paragraphs how you can conclude that Defoe intended that the journal become public.

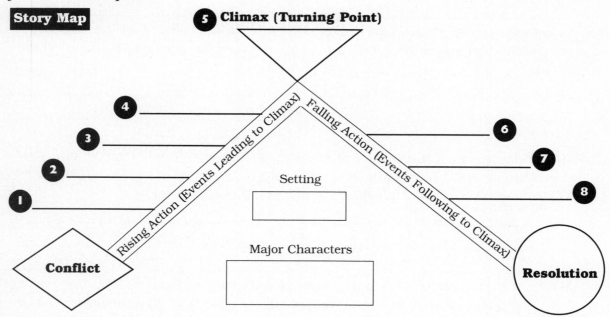

14. Both *The Diary* and *A Journal of the Plague Year* offer two different accounts of the same historical event—the bubonic plague. In a brief essay, explain which excerpt offered a more personalized account of the event. Cite examples from both works to support your response.

15. Both *The Diary* and Defoe's *A Journal of the Plague Year* describe the effects of the plague on English society. In an essay, explain why the diary form is an effective means of presenting the effects of catastrophes such as the bubonic plague on people. Cite examples from both excerpts to support your response.

Oral Response

16. Go back to question 5, 6, 9, 10, or 12 or one assigned by your teacher, and take five or ten minutes to expand your answer and prepare an oral response. Find additional details in *The Diary* and *A Journal of the Plague Year* that will support your points. If necessary, make notes to guide your response.

Rubric for Evaluating Extended Responses

0	1	2	3	4
Blank paper	Incorrect purpose, mode, audience	Correct purpose, mode, audience	Correct purpose, mode, audience	Correct purpose, mode, audience
Foreign language	Brief, vague	Some elaboration	Moderately well elaborated	Effective elaboration
Illegible, incoherent	Unelaborated	Some details	Clear, effective language	Consistent organization
Not enough content to score	Rambling	Gaps in organization	Organized (perhaps with brief digressions)	Sense of completeness, fluency
	Lack of language control	Limited language control		
	Poor organization			

from *Gulliver's Travels* by Jonathan Swift

Open-Book Test

Multiple Choice and Short Answer

Write your answers to all questions in this section on the lines provided.
For multiple-choice questions, circle the letter of the best answer.

1. In *Gulliver's Travels*, Swift satirizes the conflict between the Catholics and the Protestants by recounting a fictional tale about a conflict between the Little-Endians and the Big-Endians. Which sentence below is an example of how Swift makes the actual historical conflict seem silly through the telling of this tale? Explain why the answer you chose is correct.
   a. "It is allowed on all hands, that the primitive way of breaking eggs before we eat them was upon the larger end. . ."
   b. ". . . but his present Majesty's grandfather, while he was a boy, going to eat an egg, and breaking it according to the ancient practice, happened to cut one of his fingers."
   c. "Whereupon the Emperor, his father, published an edict, commanding all his subjects, upon great penalties, to break the smaller end of their eggs."
   d. "These civil commotions were constantly fomented by the monarchs of Blefescu; and when they were quelled, the exiles always fled for refuge to that empire."

   _____

   _____

2. Many of Swift's opinions about the conflict between England and France need to be interpreted from the fictional story that he tells in *Gulliver's Travels.* What can you interpret about Swift's view of the two countries from the following quote: "Besides, our histories of six thousand moons make no mention of any other regions, than the two great empires of Lilliput and Blefescu"?

   _____

   _____

   _____

3. Gulliver is described as a giant in size compared to the inhabitants of Lilliput and Blefescu. How does this difference in size serve to reinforce Swift's opinion about the rift between England and France as presented in *Gulliver's Travels?* Cite one or two examples from the text to support your answer.

   _____

   _____

   _____

   _____

4. After Gulliver captures the entire fleet of the Blefuscudians and brings it to Lilliput, why does he refuse to assist the king of Lilliput in reducing the Blefuscudian empire into a province of Lilliput?

   _____

   _____

5. In the excerpt from a "A Voyage to Brobdingnag," Gulliver finds himself in a kingdom of giants. What can you infer about the King's attitude toward Gulliver's accounts of his homeland from the following quotation from Gulliver:

> "But I confess, that after I had been a little too copious in talking of my own beloved country, of our trade, and wars by sea and land, of our schisms in religion, and parties in the state, the prejudices of his education prevailed so far, that he could not forbear taking me up in his right hand, and stroking me gently with the other, after an hearty fit of laughing, asked me whether I was a Whig or A Tory."

Explain why your answer choice is correct.
a. The King is interested in learning about Gulliver's political connections.
b. The King finds England's politics and society, based on Gulliver's account of them, to be ridiculous.
c. The King thinks that Gulliver told him a joke.
d. The King did not understand what Gulliver said.

_____

_____

6. How does the King's huge size in relation to Gulliver's small size serve to emphasize Swift's satire of English politics and society? Support your answer with one or two examples from the text.

_____

_____

7. Based on the King's reactions to Gulliver's account of events in English society, what can you infer about the state of the King's society? Explain why your answer choice is correct.
a. It is peaceful.   b. It is primitive.   c. It is poor.   d. It is warlike.

_____

8. In "A Voyage to Brobdingnag," Gulliver tells stories about England that reflect his pride in his country's accomplishments and position in the world. The King's reactions to these stories, however, surprise and embarrass Gulliver. What can you interpret about Swift's motives for including the following quotation, "Nothing but an extreme love of truth could have hindered me from concealing this part of my story"?

_____

_____

_____

9. Based on the way that the word *odious* is used in the text, which word is the synonym for *odious*? Explain why your answer choice is correct.
a. beautiful   b. sneaky   c. disgusting   d. small

_____

10. Gulliver describes the composition and uses of gunpowder to the King in a very graphic way, provoking a strong reaction from the King. Based on this scene, what can you interpret about Swift's views on warfare? Support your answer with one or two examples from the text.

_____

_____

_____

Extended Response

11. In the excerpt from "A Voyage to Lilliput," Swift satirizes the religious conflict between Catholics and Protestants in England that has also developed into a larger dispute involving a conflict between Britain and France. In a short essay, identify the satirical elements in the passage that represent these conflicts and explain how Swift uses these elements to explain his position on the conflicts.

12. In "A Voyage to Brobdingnag," Swift satirizes English politics and society through the interaction between Gulliver and the King. In a short essay, describe Gulliver's earnest explanation of the way that his society functions and the King's responses.

13. In "A Voyage to Brobdingnag," the King expresses his opinions of English politics and society based on what Gulliver tells him about them. Despite the fact that the King disagrees with Gulliver's view of England on more than one occasion, Gulliver admires him. In one or two paragraphs, analyze the elements of personality that Swift suggests are admirable, based on how the King is portrayed in this section.

14. In both "A Voyage to Lilliput" and "A Voyage to Brobdingnag," Swift satirizes various aspects of the society in which he lives. In a brief essay, explain which excerpt provides a more optimistic picture of English society. Support your response with examples from the text.

15. Gulliver finds himself in different political positions in each of these stories. In "A Voyage to Lilliput," Gulliver is a giant who assists the Lilliputians in preventing an invasion of their shores by the Blefuscudians. In "A Voyage to Brobdingnag," Gulliver's tiny size reduces him to being the pet of the giant King. In an essay, analyze the experiences that Gulliver has as a result of his size in each of these kingdoms.

Oral Response

16. Go back to question 3, 5, 6, 11, 12, or 14 or one assigned by your teacher, and take five to ten minutes to expand your answer and prepare an oral response. Find additional details in *Gulliver's Travels* that will support your points. If necessary, make notes to guide your response.

Rubric for Evaluating Extended Responses

0	1	2	3	4
Blank paper Foreign language Illegible, incoherent Not enough content to score	Incorrect purpose, mode, audience Brief, vague Unelaborated Rambling Lack of language control Poor organization	Correct purpose, mode, audience Some elaboration Some details Gaps in organization Limited language control	Correct purpose, mode, audience Moderately well elaborated Clear, effective language Organized (perhaps with brief digressions)	Correct purpose, mode, audience Effective elaboration Consistent organization Sense of completeness, fluency

from *An Essay on Man* and from *The Rape of the Lock*
by Alexander Pope

Open-Book Test

Multiple Choice and Short Answer

Write your answers to all questions in this section on the lines provided.
For multiple-choice questions, circle the letter of the best answer.

1. In *An Essay on Man*, Pope states that "The proper study of mankind is man." (line 2)
    What does he mean by this statement? Explain why your answer choice is correct.
    a. Mankind does not know how to study man properly.
    b. In order to understand how and why the human race behaves as it does, one must
       study individuals and analyze the individuals' behaviors.
    c. There is no room for the study of individuals if one is to understand the way that the
       human race behaves.
    d. To properly understand men, mankind must be studied.

    _____

    _____

2. In *An Essay on Man*, Pope asserts that man is "Placed on this isthmus of a middle
    state. . ." (line 3) What does this assertion suggest about Pope's view of a human
    being's place in the universe?

    _____

    _____

    _____

3. In lines 4–18 of *An Essay on Man*, Pope sets up a series of contrasting descriptions about
    a person's behavior and character. What is his purpose in presenting these contrasts to
    the reader? Cite one or two examples to support your answer.

    _____

    _____

4. About man's thought processes, Pope writes,
    > "Whether he thinks too little, or too much: / Chaos of thought and passion,
    > all confused; / Still by himself abused, or disabused. . ." (lines 12–14)

    Based on how it is used within the context of these lines from *An Essay on Man*, choose
    the answer that contains the definition for *disabused*. Explain why your answer choice is
    correct.
    a. no longer abused
    b. abused by other people
    c. freed from false ideas
    d. tricked by a cunning ploy

    _____

    _____

5. In the opening lines of *The Rape of the Lock*, Pope describes the royal court and courtiers. How does Pope mock the courtly talk described in lines 10–16? Explain why your answer choice is correct.
    a. He suggests that the talk is trivial.
    b. He suggests that the talk is patriotic.
    c. He suggests that the talk has deadly consequences.
    d. He suggests that the talk is instructive.

    _____

6. Pope describes the activities that cease as day comes to an end in lines 19–24 of *The Rape of the Lock*. How do the activities described in lines 19–23 contrast with the activity mentioned in line 24 of this part of the poem? Explain your answer.

    _____

    _____

7. In *The Rape of the Lock*, how is the card game of omber presented as a war? (lines 25–44) Support your answer with one or two examples from the poem.

    _____

    _____

8. In *The Rape of the Lock*, the players stop to drink coffee. During this break, the baron manages to cut a lock of Belinda's hair. Explain how the baron managed to cut the lock of Belinda's hair. (lines 120–154)

    _____

    _____

9. In Canto V of *The Rape of the Lock*, Belinda and the baron exchange words about the stolen lock of hair. (lines 51–56) Why did Pope include a conversation between Belinda and the baron in this section? In your answer, cite one or two examples from the poem to support your response.

    _____

10. In the last lines of Canto V of *The Rape of the Lock*, the lock of hair is described as ascending into heaven behind a "sudden star." (line 77) How does Pope mock the conflict that exists between Belinda and the baron through his description of the lock's ascent to the heavens? (lines 75–88) Cite examples from the poem to support your response.

    _____

    _____

    _____

    _____

Extended Response

11. In *An Essay on Man,* Pope describes the human condition through a series of contrasting phrases. In one or two paragraphs, explain what Pope's view of the human condition is, based on his description. Cite examples from the poem to support your response.

12. In *The Rape of the Lock,* Pope adapts the style of the epic poem to present a mockery of social matters that he considers to be petty. In a short essay, identify the elements of the true epic that Pope uses to structure his mock epic, and explain how he incorporates these elements. Cite examples from the poem to support your response.

13. While *The Rape of the Lock* was intended to mock the pretentious behavior of the English upper class, Pope accomplished his intention by adopting a humorous tone in the poem. In a short essay, identify and explain how various lines and passages in the poem contribute to this humorous tone.

14. Much attention is paid to the stolen lock of hair in *The Rape of the Lock;* it is the source of intrigue and conflict throughout the poem. In one or two paragraphs, analyze what this lock of hair represents in the poem. Cite examples from *The Rape of the Lock* to support your response.

15. In both *An Essay on Man* and *The Rape of the Lock,* Pope examines human nature. Based on your reading of these two pieces, write a short essay analyzing which poem contains a more hopeful outlook on human nature. Support your response with examples from the text.

Oral Response

16. Go back to question 2, 3, 9, 11, or 14 or one assigned by your teacher, and take five to ten minutes to expand your answer and prepare an oral response. Find additional details in the works by Pope that will support your points. If necessary, make notes to guide your response.

Rubric for Evaluating Extended Responses

0	1	2	3	4
Blank paper Foreign language Illegible, incoherent Not enough content to score	Incorrect purpose, mode, audience Brief, vague Unelaborated Rambling Lack of language control Poor organization	Correct purpose, mode, audience Some elaboration Some details Gaps in organization Limited language control	Correct purpose, mode, audience Moderately well elaborated Clear, effective language Organized (perhaps with brief digressions)	Correct purpose, mode, audience Effective elaboration Consistent organization Sense of completeness, fluency

from The Preface to a Dictionary of the English Language and
from A Dictionary of the English Language by Samuel Johnson
from The Life of Samuel Johnson by James Boswell

Open-Book Test

Multiple Choice and Short Answer

Write your answers to all questions in this section on the lines provided.
For multiple-choice questions, circle the letter of the best answer.

1. In *The Preface to a Dictionary of the English Language*, Johnson describes the role of the dictionary writer, or lexicographer. Which answer states what Johnson thinks this role was? Explain why your answer choice is correct.
    a. The lexicographer clarifies the meanings of words so that other people may use the words for their own ends.
    b. The lexicographer works for scientists and writers by assisting them to write their works.
    c. The lexicographer clears garbage in order to allow others to walk freely.
    d. The lexicographer is the critic who edits the work of others.

    _____

    _____

2. According to the information presented in *The Preface to a Dictionary of the English Language*, how do people view the lexicographer as opposed to other writers?

    _____

    _____

3. Based on what he writes in *The Preface to a Dictionary of the English Language*, circle the answer that explains what Johnson hopes to accomplish by creating his dictionary. Explain why the answer you chose is correct.
    a. Johnson wanted to be criticized for his efforts.
    b. Johnson wanted to create a standard, universal reference work that cataloged the English language and how it is used.
    c. Johnson needed to find something to take his mind off the immense suffering that he experienced during this period in his life.
    d. Johnson wanted to write something that would make him famous.

    _____

    _____

4. In *The Preface to a Dictionary of the English Language*, after he has described his efforts to create this dictionary, Johnson states, "It may repress the triumph of malignant criticism to observe that if our language is not here fully displayed, I have only failed in an attempt which no human powers have hitherto completed." What does Johnson mean by this statement?

    _____

    _____

    _____

5. Using *The Preface to a Dictionary of the English Language*, complete the first two columns of the K-W-L chart below. Then, after examining the excerpt from *A Dictionary of the English Language*, complete the final column of the chart.

K	W	L
"What did you learn about *A Dictionary of the English Language* from the preface?"	"What do you want to know about *A Dictionary of the English Language?*"	"What have you learned from your examination of *A Dictionary of the English Language?*"

6. In *A Dictionary of the English Language*, how does the definition for *patron* reflect Johnson's view of patrons?

_____

_____

7. How does this section of *The Preface to a Dictionary of the English Language*, which precedes the excerpt of *A Dictionary of the English Language*, help you to understand Johnson's purpose for writing the dictionary?

_____

_____

8. In the excerpt from *The Life of Samuel Johnson*, the section entitled "Boswell Meets Johnson" details the circumstances in which Boswell began his friendship with Johnson. How does this section serve to prepare the reader for Boswell's account of Johnson's character in the section entitled "Johnson's Character"? Explain your answer, citing details from the selection.

_____

_____

9. In this section of *The Life of Samuel Johnson*, Boswell discusses some of Johnson's personality traits and reveals information about the values and concerns of the society in which both men lived. Describe Johnson and the society of his time, citing details from the selections.

> He was a sincere and zealous Christian, of high Church of England and monarchical principles, which he would not tamely suffer to be questioned. . .

_____

_____

10. In the excerpt from *The Life of Samuel Johnson*, Boswell writes that Johnson "was prone to superstition, but not to *credulity*." Define *credulity*, and write a sentence of your own that demonstrates the meaning of the word.

_____

_____

Extended Response

11. In *The Preface to a Dictionary of the English Language*, Johnson asserts that his purpose for writing the dictionary was to provide an organized and systematic means to locate words, their meanings, and their uses. In one or two paragraphs, explain how Johnson attempts to persuade the reader that his efforts in creating this dictionary deserve to be respected.

12. In *A Dictionary of the English Language*, Johnson cites excerpts from famous writers and works to support or explain his definition. In one or two paragraphs, explain how and why these excerpts reveal Johnson's opinions about the ideas, people, and things that the words represent. Cite examples from the text to support your response.

13. It is important to read *The Preface to a Dictionary of the English Language* in order to understand the format of *A Dictionary of the English Language*. In one or two paragraphs, explain how *A Dictionary of the English Language* reflects the purpose that Johnson set forth in his preface.

14. By definition, a good biography portrays its subject accurately and within the context of the times that he or she lived. In a short essay, explain how Boswell's *The Life of Samuel Johnson* gives a biased portrayal of Johnson's character. Cite examples from the work to support your response.

15. Though Boswell focuses his efforts on describing Samuel Johnson in *The Life of Samuel Johnson*, we learn about Boswell's personality through this work. In one or two paragraphs, explain what we learn about Boswell's personality based on his assessment of Johnson's personality. Cite examples from the text to support your response.

Oral Response

16. Go back to question 4, 8, 12, 14, or 15 or one assigned by your teacher, and take five to ten minutes to expand your answer and prepare an oral response. Find additional details in the works by Johnson and Boswell that will support your points. If necessary, make some notes to guide your response.

Rubric for Evaluating Extended Responses

0	1	2	3	4
Blank paper Foreign language Illegible, incoherent Not enough content to score	Incorrect purpose, mode, audience Brief, vague Unelaborated Rambling Lack of language control Poor organization	Correct purpose, mode, audience Some elaboration Some details Gaps in organization Limited language control	Correct purpose, mode, audience Moderately well elaborated Clear, effective language Organized (perhaps with brief digressions)	Correct purpose, mode, audience Effective elaboration Consistent organization Sense of completeness, fluency

"Elegy Written in a Country Churchyard" by Thomas Gray
"A Nocturnal Reverie" by Ann Finch, Countess of Winchilsea

Open-Book Test

Multiple Choice and Short Answer

Write your answers to all questions in this section on the lines provided.
For multiple-choice questions, circle the letter of the best answer.

1. In "Elegy Written in a Country Churchyard," the speaker introduces an atmosphere of
    solitude and mystery in his description of the transition from day to night. Which answer
    best represents this solitary, mysterious mood? Explain why your answer is correct.
    a. "The lowing herd winds slowly o'er the lea, / The plowman homeward plods his weary
       way. . ." (lines 2–3)
    b. "Now fades the glimmering landscape on the sight, / And all the air a solemn stillness
       holds. . ." (lines 5–6)
    c. "Save where the beetle wheels his droning flight, / And drowsy tinklings lull the
       distant folds. . ." (lines 7–8)
    d. "Save that from yonder ivy-mantled tower, / The moping owl does to the moon
       complain. . ." (lines 9–10)

    _____

    _____

2. The sentence structure in "Elegy Written in a Country Churchyard" is sometimes complex
    and difficult to understand, since Gray frequently manipulates the construction of the
    sentences in order to keep the rhythm and rhyme of the entire poem consistent. Examine
    lines 17–20 of the poem, and express their meaning in your own words.

    _____

    _____

    _____

3. "Elegy Written in a Country Churchyard" is a reflection on death—that is, the speaker
    speculates about the former lives of those people who are buried in the churchyard and
    wonders if anyone thinks of them now that they are gone. How does the speaker envision
    the lives of these dead? Support your response with one or two examples from the text.

    _____

    _____

    _____

4. The speaker of the poem "Elegy Written in a Country Churchyard" is a young man who is
    walking through the churchyard. At one point in the poem, he speculates what a "hoary-
    headed swain" (line 97) might say about his walks through the courtyard. Why does the
    speaker speculate about what this old man might say about him? Support your response
    with one or two examples from the poem.

    _____

    _____

    _____

5. The end of "Elegy Written in a Country Churchyard" is entitled "The Epitaph." To whom is this epitaph dedicated? Support your response with at least one example from the poem.

_____

_____

6. The dreamlike mood in "A Nocturnal Reverie" is conjured up by the speaker's description of the oncoming night. Which answer contains a line from the poem that reflects this dreamlike atmosphere? Explain why your answer is correct.
   a. "When scattered glow-worms, but in twilight fine, / Show trivial beauties watch their hour to shine. . ." (lines 17–18)
   b. "When through the gloom more venerable shows / Some ancient fabric, awful in repose. . ." (lines 25–26)
   c. "When nibbling sheep at large pursue their food, / And unmolested kine rechew the cud. . ." (lines 33–34)
   d. "Our cares, our toils, our clamors are renewed, / Or pleasures, seldom reached, again pursued." (lines 49–50)

_____

7. Examine lines 43–50 of "A Nocturnal Reverie," and express the ideas in these lines in your own words.

_____

_____

8. In "A Nocturnal Reverie," the speaker describes the movements and actions of a horse in the following lines: "When the loosed horse now, as his pasture leads, / Comes slowly grazing through the adjoining meads, / Whose stealing pace, and lengthened shade we fear, / Till torn up forage in his teeth we hear. . ." (lines 29–32). Using clues in this quotation, select the answer that gives the best meaning for the word *forage*. Explain why your answer is correct.
   a. animal feed   b. horse's whinny   c. paper   d. a bridle

_____

9. The speaker in "A Nocturnal Reverie" explains that the night produces a different emotional reaction in her than the morning does. Explain the contrasting emotions that the speaker feels during these different times. Support your response with one or two examples from the poem.

_____

_____

_____

10. Throughout "A Nocturnal Reverie," the speaker sets the mood of the poem and describes the nightfall through her observations of the plants and animals. Why do these descriptions make the poem a pre-romantic one? Support your answer with one or two examples from the poem.

_____

_____

Extended Response

11. The speaker contemplates the lives and deaths of people buried in the churchyard in "Elegy Written in a Country Churchyard." In a short essay, explain the speaker's attitudes toward death. Cite examples from the poem to support your response.

12. In "Elegy Written in a Country Churchyard" the speaker walks through the churchyard, examining the graves of the villagers. In an essay, explain how the speaker feels about the people buried in the churchyard. Support your response with examples from the poem.

13. The speaker in "A Nocturnal Reverie" feels at ease during the nighttime. In one or two paragraphs, explain how the speaker's description of her environment reflects her sense of ease. Support your response with examples from the poem.

14. "A Nocturnal Reverie" is essentially one long sentence punctuated by brief pauses. In an essay, explain how the structure of this poem contributes to its dreamlike quality.

15. In both "Elegy Written in a Country Churchyard" and "A Nocturnal Reverie," night serves as an inspiration for reflection. In the Venn diagram below, compare and contrast the way in which night serves to inspire the speakers. Using the information that you have gathered, write an essay analyzing how and why night serves as an inspiration for the speakers. Support your response with examples from each poem.

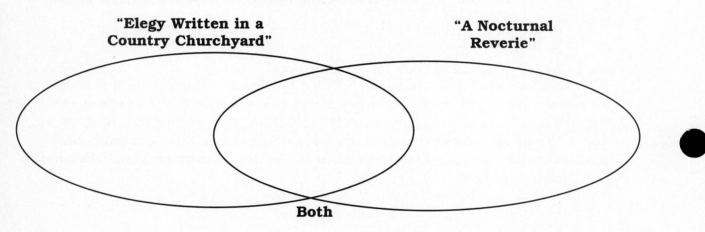

"Elegy Written in a Country Churchyard"   "A Nocturnal Reverie"

Both

Oral Response

16. Go back to question 4, 9, 10, 11, or 13 or one assigned by your teacher, and take a five to ten minutes to expand your answer and prepare an oral response. Find additional details in "Elegy Written in a Country Churchyard" and "A Nocturnal Reverie" that will support your points. If necessary, make notes to guide your response.

Rubric for Evaluating Extended Responses

0	1	2	3	4
Blank paper Foreign language Illegible, incoherent Not enough content to score	Incorrect purpose, mode, audience Brief, vague Unelaborated Rambling Lack of language control Poor organization	Correct purpose, mode, audience Some elaboration Some details Gaps in organization Limited language control	Correct purpose, mode, audience Moderately well elaborated Clear, effective language Organized (perhaps with brief digressions)	Correct purpose, mode, audience Effective elaboration Consistent organization Sense of completeness, fluency

Name _____ Date _____

Open-Book Test

Multiple Choice and Short Answer

Write your answers to all questions in this section on the lines provided.
For multiple-choice questions, circle the letter of the best answer.

1. In "On Spring," Johnson recounts the story of a man who looks forward to spring, even if the coming of spring does not alleviate any of his problems. Why does Johnson relate this story in his essay?

   _____

   _____

2. What does Johnson mean when he says in "On Spring" that "when a man cannot bear his own company there is something wrong"? Explain your answer, citing details from the text.
   a. People should be able to appreciate solitude.
   b. People should respect their employers.
   c. People should always seek the company of others.
   d. Employers should respect their employees.

   _____

   _____

3. In "On Spring," Johnson discusses the value of taking a walk. How does Johnson's discussion of the value of taking a walk relate to his thoughts on the value of observing the natural world during springtime?

   _____

   _____

4. Johnson makes several points to support his hypothesis about the value of natural observation. Cite one quotation from the selection that contains one such point.

   _____

   _____

5. What can you infer from the last paragraph of "On Spring" about why Johnson considers spring to be such an important season? Support your answer with one example from the text.

   _____

   _____

6. In "The Aims of the Spectator," Addison states, "And to the end that their virtue and discretion may not be short, transient, intermitting starts of thought, I have resolved to refresh their memories from day to day, till I have recovered them out of that desperate state of vice and folly into which the age is fallen." What can you infer about Addison's attitude about his magazine and his readership from this statement?

   _____

   _____

7. Why does Addison compare himself to Socrates when he states, "It was said of Socrates that he brought philosophy down from heaven; and I shall be ambitious to have it said of me that I have brought philosophy out of closets and libraries, schools and colleges, to dwell in clubs and assemblies, at tea tables and in coffeehouses"?

    _____

    _____

8. Based on his remarks in "The Aims of the Spectator," how can you infer that Addison's attitude about men who do not work for a living is a humorous one? Support your response with one or two examples from the text.

    _____

    _____

9. In "The Aims of the Spectator," Addison asserts in a humorous manner that reading his paper is a necessary activity for all people to undertake. How does Addison explain that reading this paper will be good for women?

    _____

    _____

    _____

10. Write an antonym of the word *trifles* used in "The Aims of the Spectator."

    _____

Extended Response

11. "On Spring" presents the reader with Johnson's views on spring and how he thinks other people should view it as well. In a short essay, explain how Johnson advances his hypothesis about spring. Support your response with examples from the essay.

12. Johnson discusses the benefits of contemplating nature during spring that go beyond emotional or spiritual renewal. In one or two paragraphs, identify these benefits and explain how Johnson feels that observing and contemplating nature in the springtime will lead to them. Support your points with examples from the essay.

13. While discussing the goals of his paper in "The Aims of the Spectator," Addison adopts a humorous, conversational tone. Identify how Addison employs humor, citing examples to support your statements. On the diagonal lines of the herringbone diagram, list characteristics of Addison's humor. On the horizontal lines, qive quotations that provide examples. You may not need to use the entire diagram. Write a short essay explaining how and why Addison employs such a tone in this piece.

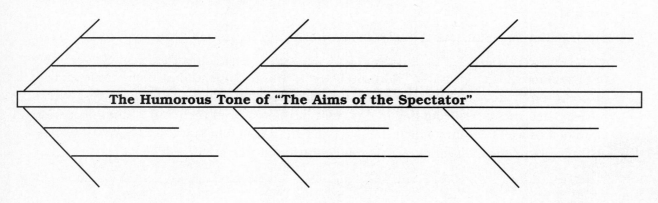

The Humorous Tone of "The Aims of the Spectator"

14. In "The Aims of the Spectator," Addison puts forth his goals for his paper in a humorous way. In one or two paragraphs, explain how Addison views his journalistic goals based on your analysis of this essay.

15. Both Johnson and Addison put forth hypotheses and test them in their respective essays "On Spring" and "The Aims of the Spectator." However, the two writers advance their arguments in different ways. In a short essay, analyze the different ways in which Johnson and Addison structure their arguments in their works. Support your response with examples from each essay.

Oral Response

16. Go back to question 1, 3, 8, 9, or 12 or one assigned by your teacher, and take five to ten minutes to expand your answer and prepare an oral response. Find additional details in "On Spring" and "The Aims of the Spectator" that will support your points. If necessary, make notes to guide your response.

Rubric for Evaluating Extended Responses

0	1	2	3	4
Blank paper Foreign language Illegible, incoherent Not enough content to score	Incorrect purpose, mode, audience Brief, vague Unelaborated Rambling Lack of language control Poor organization	Correct purpose, mode, audience Some elaboration Some details Gaps in organization Limited language control	Correct purpose, mode, audience Moderately well elaborated Clear, effective language Organized (perhaps with brief digressions)	Correct purpose, mode, audience Effective elaboration Consistent organization Sense of completeness, fluency

"To a Mouse" and **"To a Louse"** by Robert Burns
"Woo'd and Married and A'" by Joanna Baillie

Open-Book Test

Multiple Choice and Short Answer

Write your answers to all questions in this section on the lines provided.
For multiple-choice questions, circle the letter of the best answer.

1. What happens to the mouse's home in "To a Mouse"?

    _____

    _____

2. Which word best describes the attitude of the speaker toward the mouse in Burns's "To a
    Mouse?" Explain why the answer you selected is correct and the others are not.
    a. pity   c. respect
    b. disgust   d. scorn

    _____

    _____

3. Interpret the following lines (33–36) from "To a Mouse":
    "Now thou's turned out, for a' thy trouble, / But house or hald, / To thole the
    winter's sleety dribble, / An cranreuch cauld!"

    _____

    _____

4. In "To a Mouse," how does the poet compare humankind with the mouse in lines 43–48?

    _____

    _____

5. Which of the following lines from "To a Louse" contain dialect? Identify and define the
    dialect words.
    a. "dare unsettle / Your thick plantations."
    b. "and seek your dinner / On some poor body."
    c. "How dare ye set your fit upon her . . ."
    d. "a blunder free us / And foolish notion. . . ."

    _____

    _____

6. Which words best describe the object of the poet's scorn in "To a Louse"? Explain why
    the answer you selected is correct.
    a. pomp and circumstance   c. gossip and slander
    b. fashion and finery   d. vanity and conceit

    _____

    _____

7. What does the louse symbolize in "To a Louse"?

    _____

8. Which word is an antonym for *winsome?* Write a sentence of your own using *winsome.*
   a. gruff   b. unlucky   c. poor   d. cute

   _____

   _____

9. Judging from the dialect in "Woo'd and Married and A,'" what can you conclude about the social standing of the characters?

   _____

   _____

10. Paraphrase this line from "Woo'd and Married and A'."
    "Is na' she very weel aff..."

    _____

Extended Response

11. In the poems "To a Mouse" and "To a Louse," Robert Burns expresses an idea by having a speaker address an animal. However, the ideas he expresses in the two poems are very different. In an essay, summarize, and then compare, the themes of the poems, analyzing how Burns uses the animals in his poems. What does each animal symbolize?

12. The poetry of Robert Burns was extremely popular in Scotland; when he died, thousands attended his funeral, and he was consequently named the national poet. Write an essay explaining how "To a Mouse" and "To a Louse" would help Burns achieve such a reputation with the masses of Scotland. How do you think the use of dialect contributed to his popularity?

13. Dialect—the language of a particular social class, region, or group—features prominently in the poems of Robert Burns and Joanna Baillie. Write an essay that analyzes the use of dialect in relation to the subject matter of the poems "To a Louse" and "Woo'd and Married and A'."

14. Write an essay comparing and contrasting the use of dialect in "To a Mouse," "To a Louse," and "Woo'd and Married and A'" to the use of slang, or colloquial speech, in contemporary poetry, fiction, drama, or music.

15. Use the following graphic organizer to identify the conflict and resolution in Baillie's poem "Woo'd and Married and A'." In the beginning the bride is unhappy on the day of the marriage, but by the end of the poem her outlook has changed. In the first box, identify the conflict—why the bride is unhappy. In the middle three boxes, summarize what the different speakers have to say about the bride's state. In the last box, identify the resolution—how the bride's outlook has changed—and circle the box of the speaker you think is responsible for changing the bride's outlook. Then, in a brief essay, summarize the information from the graphic organizer.

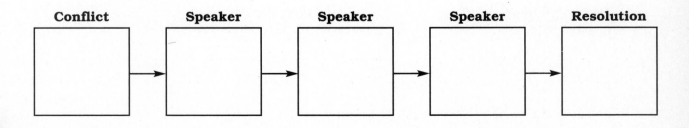

Conflict	Speaker	Speaker	Speaker	Resolution

Oral Response

16. Choose question 6, 11, 12, 13, 14, or 15 or one your teacher assigns you. Take a few minutes to look through the poems to prepare an oral response to give in class. If necessary, make notes to be clear about the order in which you want to present your answer.

Rubric for Evaluating Extended Responses

0	1	2	3	4
Blank paper	Incorrect purpose, mode, audience	Correct purpose, mode, audience	Correct purpose, mode, audience	Correct purpose, mode, audience
Foreign language	Brief, vague	Some elaboration	Moderately well elaborated	Effective elaboration
Illegible, incoherent	Unelaborated	Some details	Clear, effective language	Consistent organization
Not enough content to score	Rambling	Gaps in organization	Organized (perhaps with brief digressions)	Sense of completeness, fluency
	Lack of language control	Limited language control		
	Poor organization			

"The Lamb," "The Tyger," "Infant Sorrow," and **"The Chimney Sweeper"**
by William Blake

Open-Book Test

Multiple Choice and Short Answer

Write your answers to all questions in this section on the lines provided.
For multiple-choice questions, circle the letter of the best answer.

1. What idea does the lamb symbolize in Blake's poem "The Lamb"? Explain your answer, citing a detail from the poem.
   a. knowledge
   b. innocence
   c. reason
   d. courage

   _____

   _____

   _____

2. In the following lines from "The Lamb," to whom does Blake refer as "He"?
   "He is called by thy name, / For he calls himself a Lamb..."

   _____

3. Which word describes the mood of the illustration accompanying the poem "The Lamb"? Explain why the answer you selected is correct.
   a. jubilant
   b. serene
   c. chaotic
   d. ecstatic

   _____

   _____

4. How does Blake's illustration of the tiger compare with how it is represented in the poem "The Tyger"?

   _____

   _____

   _____

5. Which word is a synonym for *aspire*? Write a sentence of your own using *aspire* in a way that demonstrates the word's meaning.
   a. inspire
   b. achieve
   c. strive
   d. descend

   _____

6. Paraphrase the following lines from "The Tyger."
   "What immortal hand or eye, / Could frame thy fearful symmetry?"

   _____

   _____

   _____

7. What do the "swaddling bands" symbolize in the second stanza of "Infant Sorrow"?

   _____

   _____

8. Describe the tone of the second stanza of "Infant Sorrow."

   _____

   _____

9. What do the "bags" symbolize in the following lines from "The Chimney Sweeper"?
   "Then naked & white, all their bags left behind, / They rise upon the clouds, and
   sport in the wind."

   _____

   _____

10. What is the message of the following lines from "The Chimney Sweeper"?
    "Hush Tom never mind it, for when your head's bare, / You know that the soot
    cannot spoil your white hair."

    _____

    _____

    _____

Extended Response

11. Use the Venn diagram to record the similarities and differences between Blake's poems
    "The Lamb" and "The Tyger." Then, using the notes in the diagram, write an essay in
    which you compare and contrast the ways that Blake uses the animals to convey
    different meanings in the two poems.

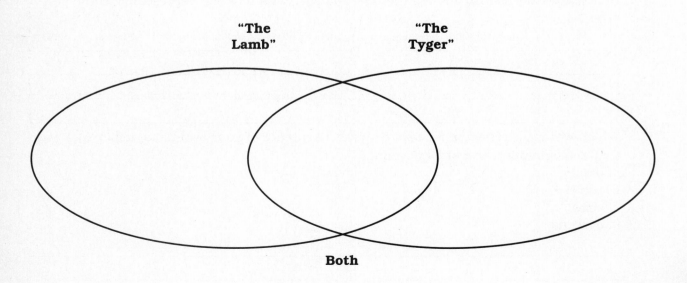

"The Lamb"   "The Tyger"

Both

12. In an essay, compare the different speakers in Blake's poems "The Lamb," "The Tyger," "Infant Sorrow," and "The Chimney Sweeper." Who are they? Whom are they addressing? What are their concerns? Discuss their similarities and their differences, citing specific details from the poems to support your interpretation.

13. In an essay, discuss Blake's social commentary in poem "The Chimney Sweeper." Identify the social issue Blake is addressing, and then analyze how Blake uses the poem to touch upon the issue. What message does the poem contain? Cite details from the poem to support your interpretation.

14. Write an essay, analyzing how Blake uses symbols in his poetry. Choose two symbols from any of the four poems—"The Lamb," "The Tyger," "Infant Sorrow," and "The Chimney Sweeper"— and interpret them. How does Blake use the symbols to create meaning? Cite details from the poem you select to support your interpretation.

15. In each of Blake's poems, "The Chimney Sweeper" and "Infant Sorrow," the speaker is a child. Write an essay, exploring other similarities between these poems. Do they have similar messages about the way Blake perceives the meaning of life? Cite details from the poems to support your interpretation.

Oral Response

16. Choose question 4, 11, 12, 13, 14, or 15 or one your teacher assigns you. Take a few minutes to look through the poems to prepare an oral response to give in class. If necessary, make notes to be clear about the order in which you want to present you answer.

Rubric for Evaluating Extended Responses

0	1	2	3	4
Blank paper Foreign language Illegible, incoherent Not enough content to score	Incorrect purpose, mode, audience Brief, vague Unelaborated Rambling Lack of language control Poor organization	Correct purpose, mode, audience Some elaboration Some details Gaps in organization Limited language control	Correct purpose, mode, audience Moderately well elaborated Clear, effective language Organized (perhaps with brief digressions)	Correct purpose, mode, audience Effective elaboration Consistent organization Sense of completeness, fluency

Introduction to *Frankenstein* by Mary Wollstonecraft Shelley

Open-Book Test

Multiple Choice and Short Answer

Write your answers to all questions in this section on the lines provided.
For multiple-choice questions, circle the letter of the best answer.

1. Which statement best summarizes why Mary Shelley felt she had to write the introduction to *Frankenstein*? Explain why the answer you selected is correct.
    a. Because some people thought she was too young to expand upon an idea.
    b. Because some people thought she wasn't intelligent enough to come up with the idea for the book.
    c. Because some people thought it was a hideous idea to write the book.
    d. Because some people thought it was shocking for a young girl to conceive of and expand upon such a hideous tale.

    _____

    _____

    _____

2. In which sentence is the word *platitude* used correctly? Explain why the answer you selected is correct.
    a. The scholar's work is full of remarkably original platitudes.
    b. The story is so full of platitudes that the ending is predictable.
    c. *Frankenstein* can be understood at many different platitudes.
    d. I thought the platitudes in the prose made the story unpredictable.

    _____

    _____

    _____

3. How does Mary Shelley politely state that her husband, Percy, isn't suited for writing a good ghost story?

    _____

    _____

    _____

4. Which quotation from "The Introduction to *Frankenstein*" describes the frustration Mary Shelley encounters when she tries to think of a good ghost story? Explain why the answer you selected is correct.
    a. "I felt that blank incapability of invention which is the greatest misery of authorship, when dull Nothing replies to our anxious invocations."
    b. "I busied myself to *think of a story*— a story to rival those which had excited us to this task."
    c. "If I did not accomplish these things, my ghost story would be unworthy of its name."
    d. "But it proved a wet, ungenial summer, and incessant rain often confined us for days to the house."

    _____

    _____

5.   What are Shelley's criteria for a good ghost story?

_____

6.   Briefly explain the connection between Dr. Darwin's experiment and Mary Shelley's novel,
     Frankenstein.

_____

_____

_____

7.   The "Introduction to *Frankenstein*" contains basic story elements—setting, characters,
     situations (conflicts), and resolution. List the elements in the following chart.

Story Element	"Introduction to *Frankenstein*" Elements
Setting	
Characters	
Situation or conflict	
Resolution	

8.   List the literary elements of "The History of the Inconsistent Lover" that categorize it as
     an example of Gothic literature.

_____

_____

9.   Identify and explain the characteristic of the Gothic novel that connects it with the
     Romantic Tradition.

_____

_____

10. Based on Shelley's description of her dream, what would you say is her attitude towards
     science?

_____

_____

_____

Extended Response

11. Mary Shelley's novel, *Frankenstein*, is considered a classic example of the Gothic novel.
     With what you have learned from reading the "Introduction to *Frankenstein*," write an
     essay explaining what characteristics of Shelley's novel classify it as Gothic literature.
     Cite specific examples.

12. Write an essay that compares and contrasts the ghost story "The Inconsistent Lover" with Mary Shelley's *Frankenstein.* How are they alike? How are they different?

13. Write an essay that describes how and why Mary Shelley's *Frankenstein* is a product of the Romantic period. In your essay, define the characteristics of the Romantic period, and provide specific examples from the "Introduction to Frankenstein" that support your thesis.

14. One theme of *Frankenstein* is that technology and science can be used for the wrong purposes. Write an essay comparing *Frankenstein* with a more contemporary work—a novel, short story or even a horror movie—that addresses the same issues as Mary Shelley's novel.

15. Think about some of the ethical controversies that have arisen in the last few years due to advances in technology. Write an essay that compares and contrasts the ethical issues of Mary Shelley's *Frankenstein* with a present-day ethical issue.

Oral Response

16. Choose questions 8, 9, 11, 12, or 13 or one your teacher assigns you. Take a few minutes to look through the essay to prepare an oral response to give in class. If necessary, make notes to be clear about the order in which you want to present your answer.

Rubric for Evaluating Extended Responses

0	1	2	3	4
Blank paper Foreign language Illegible, incoherent Not enough content to score	Incorrect purpose, mode, audience Brief, vague Unelaborated Rambling Lack of language control Poor organization	Correct purpose, mode, audience Some elaboration Some details Gaps in organization Limited language control	Correct purpose, mode, audience Moderately well elaborated Clear, effective language Organized (perhaps with brief digressions)	Correct purpose, mode, audience Effective elaboration Consistent organization Sense of completeness, fluency

"Lines Composed a Few Miles Above Tintern Abbey," from *The Prelude*, "The World is Too Much with Us," and "London, 1802"
by William Wordsworth

Open-Book Test

Multiple Choice and Short Answer

Write your answers to all questions in this section on the lines provided.
For multiple-choice questions, circle the letter of the best answer.

1. Why is Wordsworth's "Lines Composed a Few Miles Above Tintern Abbey" identified as Romantic poetry?

   _____

   _____

   _____

2. In "Lines Composed a Few Miles Above Tintern Abbey," Wordsworth remembers when he was young and visited the abbey for the first time. How does he characterize his youth? Support your interpretation, citing details from the poem.
   a. ignorant
   b. romantic
   c. thoughtless
   d. sublime

   _____

   _____

3. Summarize the following lines from "Lines Composed a Few Miles Above Tintern Abbey."
   "To [these beauteous forms] I may have owed another gift, / Of aspect more sublime; / that blessed mood, / In which the burthen of the mystery, / In which the heavy and the weary weight / Of all this unintelligible world / Is lightened . . ."

   _____

   _____

   _____

4. Explain why the lines quoted in question 3 exemplify Romantic thought.

   _____

   _____

   _____

5. The following excerpt from Wordsworth's poem, "The Prelude," was written within the context of which historical event? Explain your answer choice, citing details from the poem.
   "But now, become oppressors in their turn, / Frenchmen had changed a war of self-defense / for one of conquest, losing sight of all / Which they had struggled for . . . "

   a. the War of 1812   c. the French-Indian Wars
   b. the Industrial Revolution   d. the French Revolution

   _____

   _____

6. In which of the following sentences is the word *confounded* correctly used? Explain your answer.
   a. Together we confounded the construction site.
   b. The complexity of the issue confounded me.
   c. The confounded ship sunk off the coast.
   d. The simple addition problems confounded the mathematicians.

   _____

7. How do the following lines from the excerpt from *The Prelude* relate to Romanticism? "So I fared, / Dragging all precepts, judgements, maxims, creeds, / Like culprits to the bar . . ."

   _____

   _____

   _____

8. Which phrase best describes what Wordsworth mourns in "The World is Too Much with Us"? Explain your answer.
   a. the declining interest in Greek mythology
   b. the loss of wonder for nature in the Age of Reason
   c. the loss of the time he spent thinking by the sea
   d. the frenzied quest for wealth

9. In "The World is Too Much with Us," why does Wordsworth write, "Great God! I'd rather be / A Pagan suckled in a creed outworn . . ."?

   _____

   _____

10. What is the state of England in "London, 1802"?

    _____

    _____

Extended Response

11. William Wordsworth is considered one of the founders of the Romantic movement. Write an essay describing the characteristics of Romanticism and Romantic poetry. Explain how Wordsworth's work is exemplary of the period, citing examples from at least two of these poems: "Lines Composed a Few Miles Above Tintern Abbey," *The Prelude*, "The World is Too Much with Us," or "London, 1802."

12. In "London, 1802," Wordsworth remembers the seventeenth-century English poet John Milton as someone who possessed "manners, virtue, freedom, power"—attributes that Wordsworth feels are lacking in his 1802 countrymen. Identify a heroic figure from the past who exhibited virtues many people take for granted today. Write a short essay describing this person. Cite examples of how he or she is a good role model for the contemporary world.

13. Write an essay describing the attitudes of the Romantic poets regarding emotions. How important are feelings and passions to the life of the artist? Support your opinion by citing specific passages from Wordsworth's poems.

14. Wordsworth revisits the area where he grew up in "Lines Composed a Few Miles Above Tintern Abbey." He describes his attitude toward the French Revolution in the excerpt from *The Prelude.* Although each poem focuses on a different subject matter, both describe a change that has occurred over time. Write an essay summarizing the changes examined in these two poems. What are some of the attitudes Wordsworth expresses about these changes?

15. Sometimes, when an author is distinctive and influential, adjectives are constructed from their names. A certain brand of humor, for instance, can be called "Chaucerian"; the clothing of a certain period is known as "Shakespearean dress." Think of some attributes of Wordsworth's work which could be given the term "Wordsworthian." Using the following chart, make a list of these attributes, illustrating your points with specific lines from "Lines Composed a Few Miles Above Tintern Abbey," from *The Prelude,* "The World is Too Much with Us," and "London, 1802." Finally, write a paragraph summarizing the features that would make something Wordsworthian.

Wordsworthian attributes	lines from poems

Oral Response

16. Choose question 11, 12, 13, 14, or 15 or the question your teacher assigns you. Take a few minutes to look through the poems to prepare an oral response to give in class. If necessary, make notes to be clear about the order in which you want to present your answer.

Rubric for Evaluating Extended Responses

0	1	2	3	4
Blank paper Foreign language Illegible, incoherent Not enough content to score	Incorrect purpose, mode, audience Brief, vague Unelaborated Rambling Lack of language control Poor organization	Correct purpose, mode, audience Some elaboration Some details Gaps in organization Limited language control	Correct purpose, mode, audience Moderately well elaborated Clear, effective language Organized (perhaps with brief digressions)	Correct purpose, mode, audience Effective elaboration Consistent organization Sense of completeness, fluency

"The Rime of the Ancient Mariner" and "Kubla Khan"
by Samuel Taylor Coleridge

Open-Book Test

Multiple Choice and Short Answer

Write your answers to all questions in this section on the lines provided.
For multiple-choice questions, circle the letter of the best answer.

1. Which line from "The Rime of the Ancient Mariner" contains alliteration? Explain why your choice illustrates this poetic sound device.
   a. "Rested the broad bright Sun"
   b. "As green as emerald"
   c. "To Mary Queen the praise be given!"
   d. "For all averred, I had killed the bird"

   _____

   _____

2. Identify some of the qualities the albatross symbolizes. Cite details from the poem to support your interpretation.

   _____

   _____

   _____

3. Identify the central theme of "The Rime of the Ancient Mariner." Briefly explain why you chose your answer.
   a. pleasure in all imaginative voyages.
   b. love of storytelling.
   c. sanctity of all wild creatures.
   d. importance of fantasy over reality.

   _____

   _____

   _____

4. Locate the passage in "The Rime of the Ancient Mariner" where the spell of the albatross is broken. What occurrence illustrates the breaking of the spell? Why do you think this happens?

   _____

   _____

5. Which choice best describes the tone used by the mariner throughout his narration?
   a. nostalgia and profound sorrow.
   b. weariness and apathy.
   c. dread, horror, and awe.
   d. coyness and teasing amusement.

   _____

   _____

6. Which of the following pairs of poetic sound devices does Coleridge employ in the line, "The western wave was all aflame"? Briefly explain your answer choice, defining the literary terms.
   a. internal rhyme and alliteration
   b. alliteration and assonance
   c. assonance and consonance
   d. consonance and internal rhyme

_____

7. The closing lines of "Kubla Khan" add another dimension to the poem's meaning because they
   a. take the reader to yet another exotic location.
   b. shift the focus to the poet as the inspired creator.
   c. hint at historical references from Coleridge's day and age.
   d. discuss the dangers and pitfalls of imagination.
   Explain your answer.

_____

_____

8. Which of the following instruments' music probably sounds most similar to the dulcimer played by the damsel in "Kubla Khan"? Briefly explain your answer.
   a. harp
   b. snare drum
   c. flute
   d. trumpet

_____

9. Rearrange the order of the inverted words in the following passage—"In Xanadu did Kubla Khan / A stately pleasure dome decree"—to mirror a more contemporary-sounding English. What are two purposes served by Coleridge in inverting the words of these and other lines?

_____

_____

10. Which pair of adjectives best describes a feature of Romantic subject matter so evident in "Kubla Khan"? Explain your answer, citing details from the poem.
   a. simple and mundane
   b. political and pedantic
   c. nostalgic and forlorn
   d. faraway and fantastic

_____

_____

Extended Response

11. The actual geographical journey taken by the Mariner in "The Rime of the Ancient Mariner" is obvious. It might be noted, however, that Coleridge is more interested in another "journey" his narrator takes. Write an essay examining the emotional and spiritual journey of the Mariner. Cite passages from the poem that illustrate this journey.

12. What can you infer about Coleridge's feelings for the sinister and supernatural from reading "The Rime of the Ancient Mariner"? How do the presence of characters such as Death and Life-in-Death affect the overall atmosphere of the poem? Cite passages from the poem to support your interpretation.

13. Use the chart to examine three lines from Coleridge's "The Rime of the Ancient Mariner" that employ sound devices. Identify and list specific lines in column one. In the second column, identify the sound devices used in the line. In the third column, describe Coleridge's purpose in using the sound devices and the ultimate effect generated.

Line	Sound Device	Purpose

14. Compare and contrast Coleridge's use of water imagery in both "The Rime of the Ancient Mariner" and "Kubla Khan." What descriptive words or sound devices does he use in the poems, and what are their effects? Cite specific passages from both poems to support your points.

15. How does Romanticism's fascination with exotic and faraway places suffuse Coleridge's "Kubla Khan"? What feelings about Xanadu—and all other exotic places—does Coleridge seem to be stating in the final stanza? Support your interpretation with specific examples from the poem.

Oral Response

16. Choose question 7, 12, 13, 14, or 15 or the question the teacher assigns you. Take a few minutes to look through the poems to prepare an oral response to give in class. If necessary, make notes to be clear about the order in which you want to present your answer.

Rubric for Evaluating Extended Responses

0	1	2	3	4
Blank paper Foreign language Illegible, incoherent Not enough content to score	Incorrect purpose, mode, audience Brief, vague Unelaborated Rambling Lack of language control Poor organization	Correct purpose, mode, audience Some elaboration Some details Gaps in organization Limited language control	Correct purpose, mode, audience Moderately well elaborated Clear, effective language Organized (perhaps with brief digressions)	Correct purpose, mode, audience Effective elaboration Consistent organization Sense of completeness, fluency

Name _____   Date _____

"She Walks in Beauty," from *Childe Harold's Pilgrimage,* and from *Don Juan*
by George Gordon, Lord Byron

Open-Book Test

Multiple Choice and Short Answer

Write your answers to all questions in this section on the lines provided.
For multiple-choice questions, circle the letter of the best answer.

1. Which pair of adjectives best describes the woman in "She Walks in Beauty" as the
    speaker presents her? Explain your answer choice.
    a. virtuous and intriguing
    b. lonely and mournful
    c. odd and untouchable
    d. cheerful and childlike

    _____

    _____

2. In "She Walks in Beauty," what is meant by the line, "A mind at peace with all below"?
    Explain what the line tells you about the speaker's attitude toward the subject.

    _____

    _____

3. What type of figurative language does Byron employ in the lines,
        "Where thoughts serenely sweet express / How pure, how dear their dwelling place?"

    _____

    _____

4. Which of the following sentences best explains the speaker's attitude toward the ocean in
    the selection from *Childe Harold's Pilgrimage?* Explain your answer.
    a. He wishes it were not so limitless and terrifying.
    b. He longs for the feelings it generated in him as a young boy.
    c. He curses it for destroying ships and empires.
    d. He celebrates it for its permanence and sublime power.

    _____

    _____

5. What is meant by the speaker's recollection that "from a boy / I wantoned with thy
    breakers"? Explain.
    a. During his childhood, the speaker was too afraid to swim in the ocean.
    b. Although the ocean was merciless, the speaker delighted in playing in its waters.
    c. The ocean nearly drowned the speaker.
    d. The speaker often played on board the ships that sailed the oceans.

    _____

    _____

6. Define "*leviathans*," citing context clues from *Childe Harold's Pilgrimage* to support your definition.

_____

_____

7. In *Childe Harold's Pilgrimage*, what are the narrator's feelings toward the "empires" described in stanza five? Support your interpretation, citing details from the poem.

_____

_____

_____

8. To which question do these lines from *Don Juan* best provide an answer?
   "No more—no more—Oh! never more on me / The freshness of the heart can fall like dew"
   a. Does the speaker believe he is invincible?
   b. Why is the speaker's attitude toward childhood?
   c. Have the speaker's ideals and illusions changed since he has grown?
   d. How does the speaker feel about the loves of his past?
   Explain your answer choice.

_____

_____

9. Which of the following lines from *Don Juan* contains a metaphor? Briefly defend your answer.
   a. "Ambition was my idol, which was broken"
   b. "And flesh (which Death mows down to hay) is grass"
   c. "For God's sake, reader! take them not for mine!"
   d. "The freshness of the heart can fall like dew"

_____

_____

10. "I / Have spent my life, both interest and principal . . ." What comparison is the speaker making in these lines? Explain your answer, and note why you think the comparison is, or is not, effective.

_____

_____

_____

Extended Response

11. Write four paragraphs in which you compare and contrast the tone used by the speakers in Byron's excerpt from *Childe Harold's Pilgrimage* and the excerpt from *Don Juan*. Cite specific passages or lines in which you can almost hear the tone of voice used by the speaker, and use these lines to illustrate your points.

12. Throughout the excerpt from *Childe Harold's Pilgrimage*, Byron uses figurative language to heightened effect. Organize what you have learned about similes, metaphors, and personification, using the grid organizer. List three separate lines that employ figurative language. Examine what Byron is describing, and explain in an essay how he makes an abstract idea or image concrete by using figurative language.

Line	Type of Figurative Language

13. During Byron's time, his adoring public imagined him to be a mirror image of his characters: a dark and brooding figure who passionately defended the causes of his day. Write an essay, examining the narrators of "She Walks in Beauty" and "Apostrophe to the Ocean" from *Childe Harold's Pilgrimage*. Why do you think Byron's audience wanted to associate their literary hero with the heroes he describes in his works? Cite examples from the poems to support your interpretation.

14. Write an essay focusing on the humor used in Byron's *Don Juan*. What are some specific lines that strike you as especially humorous, mocking, or clever? Identify and describe some of the methods Byron employs to convey his humorous message.

15. In an essay, examine how the speakers of "She Walks in Beauty" and *Childe Harold's Pilgrimage* express love and admiration for their subjects. How do the poems use figurative language to convey their messages?

Oral Response

16. Choose question 2, 7, 11, 13, 14, or 15 or one the teacher assigns you. Take a few minutes to look through the poems to prepare an oral response to give in class. If necessary, make notes to be clear about the order in which you want to present your answer.

Rubric for Evaluating Extended Responses

0	1	2	3	4
Blank paper Foreign language Illegible, incoherent Not enough content to score	Incorrect purpose, mode, audience Brief, vague Unelaborated Rambling Lack of language control Poor organization	Correct purpose, mode, audience Some elaboration Some details Gaps in organization Limited language control	Correct purpose, mode, audience Moderately well elaborated Clear, effective language Organized (perhaps with brief digressions)	Correct purpose, mode, audience Effective elaboration Consistent organization Sense of completeness, fluency

"Ozymandias," "Ode to the West Wind," and **"To a Skylark"**
by Percy Bysshe Shelley

Open-Book Test

Multiple Choice and Short Answer

Write your answers to all questions in this section on the lines provided.
For multiple-choice questions, circle the letter of the best answer.

1. Which of the following ideas can you infer from the closing image of Shelley's "Ozymandias"? Explain why you chose your answer.
   a. Kings from ancient times were less intelligent than men and women of today.
   b. The spiritual world carries more importance than the physical world.
   c. Exotic lands are more important to the imagination than familiar settings.
   d. All forms of wealth and power are ultimately impermanent and meaningless.

   _____

   _____

2. Think for a moment of the description of what the traveler saw in "Ozymandias." Now provide your own brief description of other images, sights, sounds, and smells—things beyond "the decay / Of that colossal wreck"—which might have been part of that physical setting.

   _____

   _____

   _____

3. Which passage from "Ode to the West Wind" is written in the subjunctive mood? Explain your answer.
   a. "If I were a dead leaf thou mightest bear"
   b. "Make me thy lyre, even as the forest is"
   c. "As thus with thee in prayer in my sore need"
   d. "Thine azure sister of the Spring shall blow"

   _____

   _____

4. Which choice best approximates the theme of the final section of "Ode to the West Wind"? Support your interpretation, citing details from the poem.
   a. The poet wants to have a singing voice as musical and lovely as the sound of the West Wind.
   b. The poet wishes his verse could empower and enliven all people with the potency carried by the West Wind.
   c. The poet wants to be resurrected after his death.
   d. The poet wants to fly across the earth on the driving power of the West Wind.

5. Which pair of adjectives best categorizes the images Shelley uses to describe the West Wind in the first two stanzas of "Ode to the West Wind"? Briefly explain your answer.
   a. radiant and colorful
   b. dark and destructive
   c. lazy and peaceful
   d. animating and fantastic

   _____

   _____

6. Which passage from "Ode to the West Wind" best illustrates the ultimate request the speaker has for the wind? Explain.
   a. "Be through my lips to unawakened earth / The trumpet of a prophecy!"
   b. "Oh, lift me as a wave, a leaf, a cloud!"
   c. "I would ne'er have striven / As thus with thee in prayer in my sore need."
   d. "If I were a dead leaf thou mightest bear"

   _____

   _____

7. Explain how the depiction of the wind in "Ode to the West Wind" is similar to the depiction of the skylark in "To a Skylark." Shelley describes two distinctly different things, but in what ways are they also similar?

   _____

   _____

8. In "To a Skylark," Shelley speaks of "love's sad satiety." Briefly define *satiety*. Then use the word in a sentence that demonstrated the word's meaning.

   _____

   _____

9. Which adjective is an antonym of the word *blithe*? Explain your answer choice, and write a sentence of your own using *blithe*.
   a. busy   b. ill   c. woebegone   d. carefree

   _____

   _____

10. Which quality of the skylark is most admired by the speaker throughout "To a Skylark"? Support your interpretation, citing details from the poem.
    a. The skylark is essentially the muse of all poets.
    b. The skylark has the power to shift shape and become other beings.
    c. The skylark is often invisible, yet its joyous music is heard everywhere.
    d. The skylark is the most colorful and beautiful bird in the world.

    _____

    _____

Extended Response

11. Like the other Romantic poets, Shelley celebrated the beauty and power of nature. In an essay examine Shelley's feelings about nature in "Ozymandias," "Ode to the West Wind," and "To a Skylark." How does he depict the natural world, and how does he compare it to humans? Cite specific lines and images from the poems to support your interpretation.

12. Both "Ode to the West Wind" and "To a Skylark" contain references to music. Examine these specific passages in a short essay. How does Shelley use his musical references to add meaning and depth to the subjects addressed? Are there instances of musical language in Shelley's poems? Illustrate your points with specific examples from the text.

13. Coleridge had a fascination with exotic and mysterious worlds like Xanadu in "Kubla Khan," a fascination common to many of the Romantic poets. Is Shelley as interested in places that exist in the imagination? Would you argue that his subjects and settings are more mundane, or does he achieve a certain mystery and exoticism in his works through different means? Answer these questions in a short essay.

14. In "To a Skylark," Shelley compares his subject to many different things—humans, animals, flowers, and so on. Use the graphic organizer to list three of these comparisons. After each item, explain why the comparison is effective in describing the Skylark.

Skylark Comparison	How Comparison Works

15. In "Ode to the West Wind," as important to the attributes and changes in the West Wind are the attributes and changes in the speaker himself. In an essay, discuss the method and purpose by which the speaker addresses the Wind. Examine the problems and questions arising from the relationship between the Wind and the speaker, as well as the effect the West Wind ultimately has on him. Cite examples from the poem to support your ideas.

Oral Response

16. Choose question 2, 7, 12, 13, or 15 or the question the teacher assigns you. Take a few minutes to look through the poems to prepare an oral response to give in class. If necessary, make notes to be clear about the order in which you want to present your answer.

Rubric for Evaluating Extended Responses

0	1	2	3	4
Blank paper Foreign language Illegible, incoherent Not enough content to score	Incorrect purpose, mode, audience Brief, vague Unelaborated Rambling Lack of language control Poor organization	Correct purpose, mode, audience Some elaboration Some details Gaps in organization Limited language control	Correct purpose, mode, audience Moderately well elaborated Clear, effective language Organized (perhaps with brief digressions)	Correct purpose, mode, audience Effective elaboration Consistent organization Sense of completeness, fluency

Poetry of John Keats

Open-Book Test

Multiple Choice and Short Answer

Write your answers to all questions in this section on the lines provided.
For multiple-choice questions, circle the letter of the best answer.

1. What assumption can you make about the speaker in the first four lines of "On First Looking into Chapman's Homer"? Support your interpretation, citing details from the poem.
    a. The speaker has travelled across the globe.
    b. The speaker has become immortal, and has experienced different worlds throughout time.
    c. The speaker has read many books about different lands and historical figures.
    d. The speaker has been wealthy throughout his life.

    _____

    _____

2. Paraphrase these lines from "On First Looking into Chapman's Homer:"
    "Then felt I like some watcher of the skies / When a new planet swims into his ken"

    _____

3. What mood is evoked in the last two lines of "When I Have Fears That I May Cease to Be"? List some adjectives you could use to describe the character of the poet in this closing.

    _____

    _____

4. What is Keats symbolizing when he speaks of the "full ripened grain" in "When I Have Fears That I May Cease to Be"? Explain your answer choice.
    a. the words on the pages of the books he loves.
    b. the poems and other works which he, as the artist, will create.
    c. the future romances he may have.
    d. the memories he will gather at the close of his life.

    _____

5. What word makes Keats return to reality in "Ode to a Nightingale"? Why is this word so important to the poem? Explain your answer.

    _____

6. What type of ode is "Ode on a Grecian Urn"? Define the literary term that identifies this type of ode.

    _____

    _____

7. What type of ode is "Ode to a Nightingale"? Define the literary term that identifies this type of ode.

_____

_____

8. What can you surmise about Keats's theories of art by reading "Ode on a Grecian Urn"?

_____

_____

9. Which of the following statements best describes the urn as Keats depicts it in the final stanza of "Ode on a Grecian Urn"? Support your answer choice, citing details from the poem.
   a. The urn is made of marble and elaborately shaped.
   b. The urn is elegant and simply shaped with a pattern of Greek human figures.
   c. The urn is stately, with a shape that reminds Keats of a human figure.
   d. The urn is graceful and simple with a gray, veined surface like marble.

_____

_____

10. Which of the following attributes does Keats admire and celebrate most in "Ode on a Grecian Urn? Support your answer choice, citing details from the poem.
    a. The quality of the artist's craftmanship.
    b. The simplicity and grace of the shape of the urn.
    c. The fact that the scene seems to tell a fascinating story.
    d. The timelessness of the scene and the eternal youth represented by the figures.

_____

_____

Extended Response

11. Compare and contrast "Ode to a Nightingale" with "Ode on a Grecian Urn." What does Keats does Keats admire, envy, or question about the two subjects? Cite examples from the poems to support your interpretation.

12. Perhaps more than any other Romantic poet, John Keats often focused on feelings of sorrow and melancholy in his poems. In an essay, focus on at least two of the Keats poems in your textbook, examining the significance of melancholy in his work. Cite specific images and passages to support your interpretation. Examine how Keats's style and language convey sorrowful feelings or emotions.

13. "Ode to a Nightingale" is a poem that appeals to every sense. Complete the graphic organizer, listing specific lines and images from Keats's poem that appeal to each sense. Finally, in a short essay, discuss how Keats's generous usage of sensory detail affects the theme of the poem.

	Sight	Taste	Touch	Sound	Smell
Images					

14. The final two lines of Keats's "Ode on a Grecian Urn" are among the most famous in all of poetry. Why do you think this is so? What do the lines say about poetry and about art, in general? Answer these questions in an essay. Find other references in the poem to support your points.

15. How does Keats feel about the unknown? What are his attitudes about places he has never visited, things he has not seen, or the mysteries of the world? Write an essay that cites examples from all four of the poems. Judging by the way Keats presents the unknown and mysterious in his works, draw conclusions about how he might have felt anticipating his own untimely death.

Oral Response

16. Choose question 5, 8, 11, 12, 14, or 15 or the question the teacher assigns you. Take a few minutes to look through the poems to prepare an oral response to give in class. If necessary, make notes to be clear about the order in which you want to present your answer.

Rubric for Evaluating Extended Responses

0	1	2	3	4
Blank paper Foreign language Illegible, incoherent Not enough content to score	Incorrect purpose, mode, audience Brief, vague Unelaborated Rambling Lack of language control Poor organization	Correct purpose, mode, audience Some elaboration Some details Gaps in organization Limited language control	Correct purpose, mode, audience Moderately well elaborated Clear, effective language Organized (perhaps with brief digressions)	Correct purpose, mode, audience Effective elaboration Consistent organization Sense of completeness, fluency

"Speech to Parliament: In Defense of the Lower Classes"
by George Gordon, Lord Byron
"A Song: 'Men of England'" by Percy Bysshe Shelley
"On the Passing of the Reform Bill" by Thomas Babington Macaulay

Open-Book Test

Multiple Choice and Short Answer

Write your answers to all questions in this section on the lines provided.
For multiple-choice questions, circle the letter of the best answer.

1. Examine the first three paragraphs of Byron's "In Defense of the Lower Classes." What comparison is he making in this first section? What was Byron's purpose in making this comparison?

    _____

    _____

2. Which of the following words is an antonym of *"emancipate"*? Briefly explain your choice.
    a. confuse
    b. murder
    c. imprison
    d. attempt

    _____

3. In which sentence is Byron using exaggeration to effectively convey his message? Explain your answer choice.
    a. "Will you erect a gibbet in every field, and hang up men like scarecrows?"
    b. "These men were willing to dig, but the spade was in other hands . . ."
    c. "If you proceed by the forms of law, where is your evidence?"
    d. "I have traversed the seat of war in the Peninsula . . ."

    _____

    _____

4. Which pair of adjectives best describes Byron's tone in this sentence?
    "When death is a relief, and the only relief it appears that you will afford him, will he be dragooned into tranquillity?"
    a. curious and pleading
    b. teasing and comic
    c. angry and sarcastic
    d. tired and surrendering

    Explain your answer choice.

    _____

    _____

5. To what type of bee does Shelley compare the rich and powerful "tyrants" in "A Song: Men of England"? Why is this comparison effective?

    _____

    _____

6. Which of the following would not be an appropriate and effective purpose for reading Shelley's "A Song: 'Men of England'"? Explain your answer choice.
   a. to compare Shelley's examination of working conditions in nineteenth-century England with your own feelings on a contemporary situation.
   b. to examine the poetic devices and figurative language Shelley uses in the poem.
   c. to compare Shelley's political stance in the poem with Byron's political stance in "In Defense of the Lower Classes."
   d. to compare the lives of the rich and the poor in nineteenth-century England.

7. Which of the following choices could not be accurately associated with the word *balm*? Explain your answer choice.
   a. a healing sunburn
   b. a baseball team's first aid kit
   c. a crowded city street
   d. a gentle and pleasing piece of music

8. Which line from "On the Passing of the Reform Bill" contains correlative conjunctions? Explain your answer choice.
   a. "It is clear that the Reform Bill must pass, either in this or in another Parliament."
   b. "And no sooner were the outer doors opened than another shout answered that within the house."
   c. "I have little news for you, except what you will learn from the papers as well as from me."
   d. "For we did not yet know what the hostile force might be."

9. What is the purpose of a political commentary?

10. In "On the Passing of the Reform Bill," Thomas Babington Macaulay asserts that even a "majority of one" in Parliamentary voting promises a good outcome. Why is this so? Explain your answer.

Extended Response

11. In an essay, compare and contrast the audiences for whom Byron, Shelley, and Macaulay were writing. How do their backgrounds differ, for instance, and what are their respective audiences? What might the audiences of the day have expected from each of the writers?

12. Use the Venn diagram to record the similarities and differences between Byron's "In Defense of the Lower Classes" and Macaulay's "On the Passing of the Reform Bill." Using the notes in the diagram, write an essay in which you compare and contrast their specific purposes.

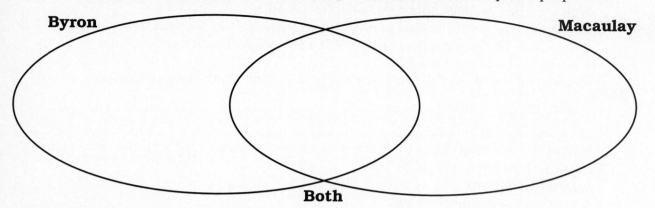

Byron

Macaulay

Both

13. Write an essay comparing and contrasting Shelley's style and poetic language in "A Song: 'Men of England'" with the style and language of his other poems. Do you think Shelley's political poem works as well as the others? Would you classify it as great literature like the other poems, or does it function primarily as a rallying tool for his cause? Support your ideas citing passages from Shelley's poems.

14. Which of "In Defense of the Lower Classes," "A Song: 'Men of England'," or "On the Passing of the Reform Bill" is most effective in its politics? Write an essay, supporting your selection. What does one of the pieces achieve that the other two do not? If you were to write a piece about a political cause of your choice, whose method—Byron's, Shelley's, or Macaulay's—would you follow, and why? Cite examples from the three works to support your interpretation.

15. In an essay, discuss the relationship between politics and art in the works of Byron and Shelley. Describe the politics in their writing. Is it possible to create art without political content? Should politics be kept separate from art, or are there cases where art or poetry might be the best medium for conveying the message? Support your position, citing examples from the poets' works.

Oral Response

16. Choose question 5, 8, 11, 12, 14, or 15 or a question your teacher assigns you. Take a few minutes to look through the selections to prepare an oral response to give in class. If necessary, make notes to be clear about the order in which you want to present your answer.

Rubric for Evaluating Extended Responses

0	1	2	3	4
Blank paper	Incorrect purpose, mode, audience	Correct purpose, mode, audience	Correct purpose, mode, audience	Correct purpose, mode, audience
Foreign language	Brief, vague	Some elaboration	Moderately well elaborated	Effective elaboration
Illegible, incoherent	Unelaborated	Some details	Clear, effective language	Consistent organization
Not enough content to score	Rambling	Gaps in organization	Organized (perhaps with brief digressions)	Sense of completeness, fluency
	Lack of language control	Limited language control		
	Poor organization			

"On Making an Agreeable Marriage" by Jane Austen
from *A Vindication of the Rights of Woman* by Mary Wollstonecraft

Open-Book Test

Multiple Choice and Short Answer

Write your answers to all questions in this section on the lines provided.
For multiple-choice questions, circle the letter of the best answer.

1. What might be Jane Austen's purpose for writing "On Making an Agreeable Marriage"?

   _____

   _____

2. Briefly summarize Jane Austen's feelings for "Mr. J. P." in "On Making an Agreeable
   Marriage."

   _____

   _____

3. Which of the following does Jane Austen not reveal about Fanny's suitor in "On Making
   an Agreeable Marriage"? Explain your answer choice.
   a. He was the first man who courted Fanny.
   b. He excelled in his university studies.
   c. He has become increasingly indifferent to Fanny.
   d. He refuses to boast of his many qualities.

   _____

   _____

4. What societal institutions might be affected by the arguments in Mary Wollstonecraft's *A
   Vindication of the Rights of Woman?* Support your answer, citing details from the selection.
   a. the voting booth
   b. the university
   c. the English social circle
   d. the church

   _____

   _____

5. What was the focus of education for women during the time of Jane Austen and Mary
   Wollstonecraft? Explain your answer.

   _____

   _____

   _____

6. A person behaving *solicitously* might be acting _____
   a. cautiously.
   b. recklessly.
   c. courageously.
   d. frivolously.
   Explain your answer choice.

   _____

   _____

7. A major point of *A Vindication of the Rights of Woman* is that
   a. women should be admired for their beauty.
   b. women should be given more respect and opportunity.
   c. women naturally have more intellect than men.
   d. women should marry into wealth.
   Explain your answer choice, citing details from the selection.

   _____

   _____

8. What does the word *vindication* mean in the context of Wollstonecraft's title? Explain how the word's meaning reflects her purpose for writing the essay.

   _____

   _____

   _____

9. Which choice is best to describe the opposite of *fastidious*? Explain why you chose your answer.
   a. easily satisfied
   b. careless and sloppy
   c. weak
   d. angry

   _____

   _____

10. To what does Mary Wollstonecraft compare women's minds? Support your answer, citing details from the selection.

   _____

   _____

Extended Response

11. In a short essay, examine the letter as a literary device. Are the arguments made by Jane Austen in "On Making an Agreeable Marriage" strengthened or hindered by the letter form? How might the arguments differ if Austen—like Wollstonecraft—had written an essay? Support your points with specific passages from Austen's letter.

12. Do you agree with Austen's judgments of character and human nature in "On Making an Agreeable Marriage"? If you were Fanny Knight, how seriously would you consider Jane Austen's advice? Support your opinions with specific examples from Austen's letter.

13. Write an essay in which you examine the effectiveness of both Austen's letter and Wollstonecraft's essay. Which of the authors' points do you find effective? Which do you not find effective? Compare and contrast the two citing specific examples from the texts.

14. Using the graphic organizer, list examples from Jane Austen's "On Making an Agreeable Marriage" and Mary Wollstonecraft's *A Vindication of the Rights of Woman* to show how women were treated and regarded in England during that period. Then list examples of how women are treated today. Write an essay examining how women's rights have changed. How has the treatment of women changed or stayed the same?

	In Austin	In Wollstonecraft	Today
Treatment of Women			

15. Wollstonecraft's style in *A Vindication of the Rights of Woman* is direct and blunt. How might this have affected the contemporary audience who read the essay? Do you think the men and women of Wollstonecraft's time were accustomed to this sort of opinion from women? In an essay, examine the style used by Wollstonecraft. Compare and contrast how audiences of today would react to the same type of directness. Support your points, citing examples from the text.

Oral Response

16. Choose question 5, 8, 11, 12, 13, or 15 or a one your teacher assigns you. Take a few minutes to look through the selections to prepare an oral response to give in class. If necessary, make notes to be clear about the order in which you want to present your answer.

Rubric for Evaluating Extended Responses

0	1	2	3	4
Blank paper Foreign language Illegible, incoherent Not enough content to score	Incorrect purpose, mode, audience Brief, vague Unelaborated Rambling Lack of language control Poor organization	Correct purpose, mode, audience Some elaboration Some details Gaps in organization Limited language control	Correct purpose, mode, audience Moderately well elaborated Clear, effective language Organized (perhaps with brief digressions)	Correct purpose, mode, audience Effective elaboration Consistent organization Sense of completeness, fluency

**from "In Memoriam, A.H.H.," "The Lady of Shalott," "Ulysses," and
from *The Princess:* "Tears, Idle Tears"** by Alfred, Lord Tennyson

Open-Book Test

Multiple Choice and Short Answer

Write your answers to all questions in this section on the lines provided. For multiple-choice questions, circle the letter of the best answer.

1. In "In Memoriam, A.H.H.," Tennyson expresses his grief over the death of a friend. Which line or lines from the poem best describe how he has come to terms with the loss? Explain your choice.

   _____

   _____

2. Reread lines 9–16 of "In Memoriam, A.H.H." Analyze the poets message and compare it to your own observations and experiences. What is your judgement of the poet's message?

   _____

   _____

3. Circle the letter of the sentence that best states the theme of "In Memoriam, A.H.H." Explain your answer.
   a. Memories of loved ones who have died remain with the living.
   b. One must forget in order to let go of loved ones who have died.
   c. The loss of a loved one is a tragic end to friendship.
   d. A poem is a good way to remember a loved one who has died.

   _____

4. In "The Lady of Shallot," there is a part of the poem where the speaker changes. Identify the line where the change occurs, and explain the effect that this change has on the poem.

   _____

   _____

5. Reread lines 58–63 from "The Lady of Shallot." How does the Lady of Shallot view knights, and how does her view relate to the traditional concept of the behavior of a knight?

   _____

   _____

6. As the thunderclouds rolled in, the light was waning. Circle the letter of the meaning of *waning,* and explain your answer.
   a. suddenly becoming brighter   b. suddenly becoming dimmer
   c. gradually becoming brighter   d. gradually becoming dimmer

   _____

   _____

   _____

7. Who is the speaker of "Ulysses"? List quotations from the poem that indicate who the speaker is and what the speaker's conflict is.

_____

_____

_____

8. "I am a part of all that I have met;/Yet all experience is an arch wherethrough/Gleams that untraveled world, whose margin fades/Forever and forever when I move." (lines 18–21) What does this quotation tell readers about what Ulysses is thinking?

_____

_____

_____

9. The speaker of "Tears, Idle Tears" wonders about the source of sadness and despair. Circle the letter of the phrase that best describes when these thoughts occur. Then cite a line from the poem that supports your answer.
   a. When a loved one has died   b. When remembering the past
   c. During autumn   c. At dawn

_____

_____

10. In "Tears, Idle Tears," Tennyson expresses some ideas about how the world is perceived as people go through the different stages of life. What do you think is his message? How would you judge that message?

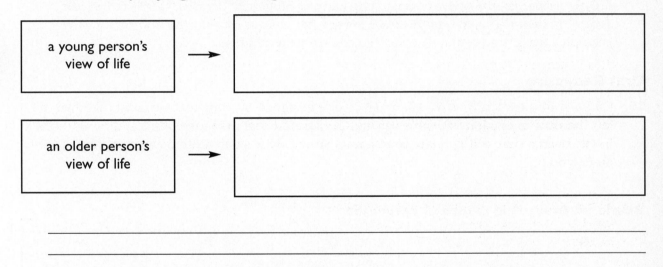

```
┌──────────────────────┐      ┌──────────────────────────────────────┐
│  a young person's    │  →   │                                      │
│  view of life        │      │                                      │
└──────────────────────┘      └──────────────────────────────────────┘

┌──────────────────────┐      ┌──────────────────────────────────────┐
│  an older person's   │  →   │                                      │
│  view of life        │      │                                      │
└──────────────────────┘      └──────────────────────────────────────┘
```

_____

_____

_____

Extended Response

11. Tennyson is the speaker in the poem "In Memoriam, A.H.H." In an essay, describe the conflict the poet faces. Use examples from the poem to explain the conflict.

12. What happens to the Lady at the end of "The Lady of Shalott"? In an essay, answer this question, and explain how the Lady meets her fate. Include quotations or details from the poem that provide information about what happens to her.

13. In the poem "Ulysses," Tennyson details an old man's thoughts on his youth and past adventures. In an essay, discuss Ulysses' attitude toward his earlier life and the way in which it reflects where he is now.

14. Use a chart to analyze the speakers and subjects of each of Tennyson's poems. Compare the speakers' attitude towards the poem's subject.

Poem	Poem's speaker	Poem's subject	Speaker's attitude toward poem's subject
"In Memoriam, A.H.H."			
"The Lady of Shalott"			
"Ulysses"			
"Tear's, Idle Tears"			

15. Tennyson is the identified speaker in only one of the poems you read, "In Memoriam, A.H.H." However, the other poems, "The Lady of Shalott," "Ulysses," and "Tears, Idle Tears," indicate his personal attitude toward his characters and the subjects. Using examples from the poems, discuss Tennyson's general ideas.

Oral Response

16. Go back to question 3, 4, 7, 10, or 14 or one assigned by your teacher, and take five to ten minutes to expand your answer and prepare an oral response. Find additional details in the poems that will support your points. You may wish to write down some notes to guide you.

Rubric for Evaluating Extended Responses

0	1	2	3	4
Blank paper Foreign language Illegible, incoherent Not enough content to score	Incorrect purpose, mode, audience Brief, vague Unelaborated Rambling Lack of language control Poor organization	Correct purpose, mode, audience Some elaboration Some details Gaps in organization Limited language control	Correct purpose, mode, audience Moderately well elaborated Clear, effective language Organized (perhaps with brief digressions)	Correct purpose, mode, audience Effective elaboration Consistent organization Sense of completeness, fluency

Name _____ Date _____

"My Last Duchess," "Life in a Love," "Love Among the Ruins"
by Robert Browning
Sonnet 43 by Elizabeth Barrett Browning

Open-Book Test

Multiple Choice and Short Answer

Write your answers to all questions in this section on the lines provided. For multiple-choice questions, circle the letter of the best answer.

1. To whom the Duke is speaking in "My Last Duchess"? Explain your answer.
    a. the woman in the portrait, who is his late wife and last duchess
    b. the agent who represents the father of the woman he hopes to marry
    c. the woman he hopes to marry so that she will become his next duchess
    d. the father of the woman he hopes to marry and make his next duchess

    _____

    _____

2. When the Duke refers to a gift he offered to his last duchess (line 33–34), why does he want his next duchess to appreciate it more fully than the first, and why does he feel his "gift" is valuable?

    _____

    _____

3. Summarize, in a few sentences, how Browning has the Duke reveal his inner feelings towards his late wife. Use a quotation from "My Last Duchess" to support your answer.

    _____

    _____

4. Reread lines 12–15 of "Life in a Love" and decide who or what strains the nerves, causes a fall and takes up one's life. Explain your answer, using examples.

    _____

    _____

    _____

5. Use an example from "Life in a Love" to show how it works as a dramatic monologue, revealing the most intimate feelings of a single speaker.

    _____

    _____

    _____

6. In "Love Among the Ruins," Browning describes the ruins of a great civilization. Use the chart below to organize details of Browning's description of the city. Summarize your thoughts in a sentence.

"Love Among the Ruins"

Types of People	Activities	Structures

7. Which sentence best describes the speaker's attitude toward comparing love to the ruined civilization in "Love Among the Ruins"? Cite one quotation from the poem that supports your answer.
   a. The advancement of civilization propels feelings of love.
   b. Successful civilizations provide a basis for people to live and love.
   c. The greatness of the city overshadows the simplicity of love.
   d. Love is better than the sublime achievements that the ruins represent.

   _____

   _____

8. If every <u>vestige</u> of the city has disappeared, it means that _____ is left. Explain your answer choice.
   a. everything   b. nothing   c. something   d. one thing

9. Which description indicates the meaning of the last lines of Sonnet 43, ". . . —and, if God choose, I shall but love thee better after death"? Explain your answer.
   a. The speaker's love has died, but the feelings continue.
   b. The speaker is expressing feelings for a loved one who has died.
   c. The speaker's love will continue even after death.
   d. The speaker feels that love is worth more than life.

10. "How do I love thee? Let me count the ways." Why does the speaker feel compelled to count the ways of romantically loving someone?

   _____

   _____

Extended Response

11. Briefly describe the type of person the Duke perceives his last duchess to have been. Use examples from "The Last Duchess" to support your description. Do you think the Duke is justified in thinking that his 900-year-old name deserves more respect?

12. Reread Sonnet 43 and discuss which of the "ways" of loving someone have more impact and why. Cite examples from the poem.

13. Use a Venn diagram to compare and contrast the views of love that are presented in "Love Among the Ruins" and Sonnet 43. Then write an essay discussing how the poems' portrayal of love supports an understanding of the poets' ideas.

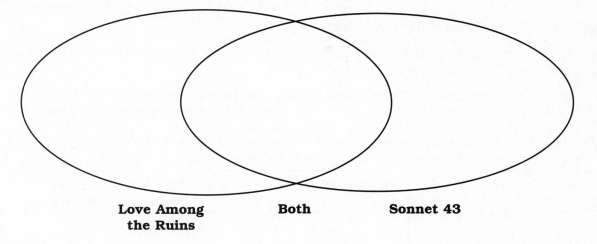

Love Among the Ruins　　　　**Both**　　　　**Sonnet 43**

14. Each of these poems by Robert and Elizabeth Barrett Browning: "My Last Duchess," "Life in a Love," "Love Among the Ruins," and Sonnet 43 illustrates a relationship with another person. Select two of the poems to discuss the various messages about relationships. Cite similarities and differences.

15. In the 1800s, the Brownings often wrote about love, as do poets and songwriters of modern times. Write an essay on why you think the Brownings and other modern writers choose love as a topic.

Oral Response

16. Go back to question 3, 5, 6, 12, or 15 or one assigned by your teacher, and take five to ten minutes to expand your answer and prepare an oral response. Find additional details in the poems that will support your points. You may wish to write down some notes to guide you.

Rubric for Evaluating Extended Responses

0	1	2	3	4
Blank paper Foreign language Illegible, incoherent Not enough content to score	Incorrect purpose, mode, audience Brief, vague Unelaborated Rambling Lack of language control Poor organization	Correct purpose, mode, audience Some elaboration Some details Gaps in organization Limited language control	Correct purpose, mode, audience Moderately well elaborated Clear, effective language Organized (perhaps with brief digressions)	Correct purpose, mode, audience Effective elaboration Consistent organization Sense of completeness, fluency

from *Hard Times* by Charles Dickens
from *Jane Eyre* by Charlotte Brontë

Open-Book Test

Multiple Choice and Short Answer

Write your answers to all questions in this section on the lines provided. For multiple-choice questions, circle the letter of the best answer.

1. What is the social issue addressed and criticized in the excerpt from *Hard Times*?
   a. education   b. economics   c. being a student   d. being a teacher

2. Use a diagram to list the details of *Hard Times* that are clues to Dickens's purpose for writing the novel. Write a short statement summarizing Dickens's purpose.

Subject of Excerpt	Characters' Names	Dickens's Attitudes towards Characters

3. Describe Thomas Gradgrind's teaching style, as seen in the excerpt from *Hard Times*.
   _____
   _____

4. Explain the significance of the "Facts" in the excerpt from *Hard Times*. Give details.
   _____
   _____

5. In the excerpt from *Hard Times*, Dickens refers to an "adversary." What is the meaning of this word? In the context of the final paragraph of Hard Times, who or what is the adversary being discussed?
   a. partner   b. opponent   c. favorite fan   d. least favorite fan
   _____

6. Why does Jane talk to Helen Burns in the excerpt from *Jane Eyre*? Explain.
   a. Jane wants to discover Helen's feelings about school.
   b. Jane wants to criticize Helen's performance in class.
   c. Jane wants know what book Helen is reading.
   d. Jane wants to complain about school.
   _____

7. Explain the main differences between Jane's and Helen's ideas about what makes a good student, as described in the excerpt from *Jane Eyre*.
   _____
   _____

8. Using the context of *Jane Eyre,* explain the meaning of the word "obscure." How does Miss Scatcherd make it impossible for Burns to remain obscure?

    _____

    _____

9. Use your own words to explain why Helen's thoughts do not wander when Miss Temple is teaching her.

    _____

    _____

10. Why is *Jane Eyre* considered a novel of social criticism? Explain your answer choice.
    a. It analyzes the growing friendship between two girls.
    b. It condemns the educational practices of a boarding school.
    c. It condemns the characters' dissatisfaction with their schooling.
    d. It analyzes the teachers' personal teaching philosophies.

Extended Response

11. Make some Compare-and-Contrast notes to analyze the novel excerpts from *Hard Times* and *Jane Eyre.* Then summarize the similarities and differences of the two selections.

12. Select the characters of Sissy Jupe and Bitzer from *Hard Times,* or Helen Burns and Jane from *Jane Eyre.* How do the characters demonstrate the author's purpose for writing.

13. Write an essay in which you describe the teaching styles of Miss Scatcherd and Miss Temple from *Jane Eyre.* Why does Helen think that Miss Scatcherd's style is better for her? What is your opinion?

14. Write why you would prefer to be a student of Thomas Gradgrind *(Hard Times)* or of Miss Scatcherd *(Jane Eyre).* Include examples of both teachers' style.

15. In a three-paragraph essay, summarize the educational situation presented in *Hard Times* and in *Jane Eyre.* Then compare and contrast both situations to what you consider a modern-day educational situation.

Oral Response

16. Go back to question 2, 7, 11, 14, or 15 or one assigned by your teacher, and take five to ten minutes to expand your answer and prepare an oral response. Find additional details in the novel excerpts that will support your points. You may wish to write down some notes to guide you.

Rubric for Evaluating Extended Responses

0	1	2	3	4
Blank paper Foreign language Illegible, incoherent Not enough content to score	Incorrect purpose, mode, audience Brief, vague Unelaborated Rambling Lack of language control Poor organization	Correct purpose, mode, audience Some elaboration Some details Gaps in organization Limited language control	Correct purpose, mode, audience Moderately well elaborated Clear, effective language Organized (perhaps with brief digressions)	Correct purpose, mode, audience Effective elaboration Consistent organization Sense of completeness, fluency

"Dover Beach" by Matthew Arnold **"Recessional"** and
"The Widow at Windsor" by Rudyard Kipling

Open-Book Test

Multiple Choice and Short Answer

Write your answers to all questions in this section on the lines provided. For multiple-choice questions, circle the letter of the best answer.

1. From Arnold's description of the sea in the first stanza of "Dover Beach," you can tell the mood of the night is _____. Explain your answer using words from the poem.
   a. melancholy and sad
   b. calm and peaceful
   c. cloudy and rainy
   d. dark and stormy

   _____

   _____

2. Reread the first three stanzas of "Dover Beach" (lines 8–20). How does the speaker perceive the sea, and how does his perception relate to the history of humankind?

   _____

   _____

3. What sad conclusion does the speaker reach in the last stanza of "Dover Beach"?

   _____

   _____

4. In "Recessional," Kipling directs his words towards a particular listener, but his message is designed for a larger goal. Whom does he specifically address, and who represents the broader audience?

   _____

   _____

5. Which word best describes the mood of "Recessional"? Explain how that mood relates to the poem's central theme.
   a. boastful   b. trusting   c. forewarning   d. fearful

   _____

   _____

   _____

6. As reflected in "Recessional," how does Kipling feel about the British Empire? Use quotes or examples from the poem to explain your answer.

   _____

   _____

   _____

7. If you are <u>contrite</u> about your negative behavior, you are _____. Explain your answer, using a context clue from the poem.

    a. willing to boast or exult
    b. willing to question your actions
    c. willing to defend your actions
    d. willing to repent or atone

    _____

    _____

8. Who is the "Widow at Windsor" referred to by the title of Kipling's poem? Explain how you know who she is.

    a. Queen Elizabeth
    b. Queen Victoria
    c. the wife of a beggar who has died
    d. the wife of a trooper who has died

    _____

9. Use a graphic organizer to gather details about the mood of "The Widow at Windsor." Then analyze the mood to determine the theme of the poem and write a statement of the theme in the space provided in the organizer.

Mood Detail:

Mood Detail:

Mood Detail:

Theme:

10. "The Widow at Windsor" is written so that the reader understands the speaker's cockney accent. Give two examples of this dialect and explain why Kipling might have chosen to write the poem in this dialect.

    _____

    _____

    _____

Extended Response

11. Write an essay in which you explore the mood of Matthew Arnold's "Dover Beach." Include examples from the poem and conclude by stating the theme of the poem.

12. Describe the sea that the speaker of "Dover Beach" is observing and the "Sea of Faith" to which the literal sea is compared. As you write, draw conclusions about the connections between the details of the descriptions of each "sea."

13. Using the chart below, list some of the elements in "Recessional" and "The Widow at Windsor." Using these elements and details from each poem, write a short essay that discusses the primary message of both works.

Poem	Style of Language	References to Those in Power	Audience
"Recessional"			
"The Widow at Windsor"			

14. "Recessional" was written toward the end of Queen Victoria's reign. Kipling's impression of the impact of her reign is evident in "Recessional" and also in "The Widow at Windsor." In an essay, discuss Kipling's poems in relation to the overall historical background of the Victorian Age. As you write your essay, you may wish to refer to "The Story of the Times" in your textbook.

15. In an essay, compare and contrast Arnold's and Kipling's attitudes toward the British Empire as indicated by their poems, "Dover Beach, "Recessional," and "The Widow at Windsor."

Oral Response

16. Go back to question 3, 6, 9, 12, or 15 or one assigned by your teacher, and take five to ten minutes to expand your answer and prepare an oral response. Find additional details in the poems that will support your points. You may wish to write down some notes to guide you.

Rubric for Evaluating Extended Responses

0	1	2	3	4
Blank paper Foreign language Illegible, incoherent Not enough content to score	Incorrect purpose, mode, audience Brief, vague Unelaborated Rambling Lack of language control Poor organization	Correct purpose, mode, audience Some elaboration Some details Gaps in organization Limited language control	Correct purpose, mode, audience Moderately well elaborated Clear, effective language Organized (perhaps with brief digressions)	Correct purpose, mode, audience Effective elaboration Consistent organization Sense of completeness, fluency

"Condition of Ireland," *The Illustrated London News*
"Progress in Personal Conflict" by Sydney Smith

Open-Book Test

Multiple Choice and Short Answer

Write your answers to all questions in this section on the lines provided. For multiple-choice questions, circle the letter of the best answer.

1. Why is the work, "Condition of Ireland: Illustrations of the New Poor-Law," considered a journalistic essay? Explain your answer.
   a. The article builds a unique story about the conditions of a poor Irish family.
   b. The article uses a historical perspective to describe the conditions of Ireland's poor.
   c. The article explains the history of the Great Famine.
   d. The article describes the conditions of Ireland's poor in 1849.

   _____

   _____

2. The "Condition of Ireland" implies that certain people are primarily responsible for the plight of the Irish. Who are those people? Support your answer with a quote from the text.

   _____

   _____

   _____

3. "The country abounds in limestone: coal, iron, and lead have been found. It has an area of 827,994 acres, 372,237 of which are uncultivated, or occupied by woods or water." This quotation from the *London News* article is an example of _____ language. Explain your answer.
   a. denotative   b. connotative   c. figurative   d. archaic

   _____

   _____

4. What is the current event about which the *London News* article is written? Give examples from the essay that support your answer.

   _____

   _____

5. What is the best description of the probable accomplishments of a person whose behavior is an example of <u>indolence</u>? Explain your answer.
   a. memorable   b. productive   c. numerous   d. limited

   _____

   _____

6. Describe the solution to the problems in Ireland, as offered in *The Illustrated London News* article.

_____

_____

_____

7. Sydney Smith describes several changes that he has seen during the course of his lifetime. List a few examples. What seems to be the purpose of Smith's essay, and how might the use of these examples assist his purpose?

_____

8. Smith considers the most important aspects of the eighteen changes that he describes in "Progress in Personal Comfort" to be that they are _____. Explain your answer.
   a. time-savers   b. comforts   c. miseries   d. necessities

_____

_____

9. Reread the third and fourth paragraphs, which describe travel. Identify two examples of denotative language and two examples of connotative language in the paragraph, and explain how to distinguish between the examples.

_____

_____

_____

10. Describe the type of writing found in "Progress in Personal Comfort." Explain your answer.

_____

_____

_____

Extended Response

11. Select either "Condition of Ireland" or "Progress in Personal Comfort." In two or three paragraphs, summarize the essayist's main points and ideas, explaining why the piece of writing is considered a journalistic essay.

12. Use a Venn diagram to compare and contrast the style and tone of "Condition of Ireland" and "Progress in Personal Comfort." Then write an essay in which you support the essay's subject.

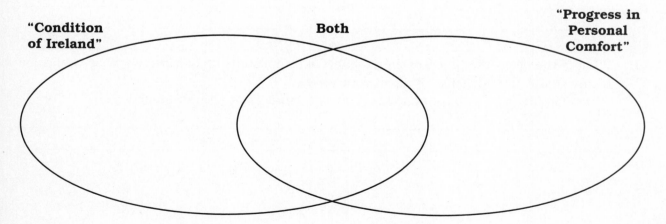

"Condition of Ireland"   **Both**   **"Progress in Personal Comfort"**

13. In an essay, consider the connotative and denotative language in "Condition of Ireland" and "Progress in Personal Comfort." Cite examples of each and explain how their choices fit their purposes.

14. In "Progress in Personal Comfort," Smith describes how progress has affected his life. Choose three examples that appear to be the most significant. Explain your choices in a short essay.

15. The two essays, "Condition of Ireland" and "Progress in Personal Comfort," present the essayists' views on progress. In an essay, compare and contrast their views of progress and explain whether you agree with their presentations of what are or are not considered to be progressive changes.

Oral Response

16. Go back to question 2, 7, 11, 13, or 14 or one assigned by your teacher, and take five to ten minutes to expand your answer and prepare an oral response. Find additional details in the essays that will support your points. You may wish to write down some notes to guide you.

Rubric for Evaluating Extended Responses

0	1	2	3	4
Blank paper	Incorrect purpose, mode, audience	Correct purpose, mode, audience	Correct purpose, mode, audience	Correct purpose, mode, audience
Foreign language	Brief, vague	Some elaboration	Moderately well elaborated	Effective elaboration
Illegible, incoherent	Unelaborated	Some details	Clear, effective language	Consistent organization
Not enough content to score	Rambling	Gaps in organization	Organized (perhaps with brief digressions)	Sense of completeness, fluency
	Lack of language control	Limited language control		
	Poor organization			

"Remembrance" by Emily Brontë
"The Darkling Thrush" and **"Ah, Are You Digging on My Grave?"**
by Thomas Hardy

Open-Book Test

Multiple Choice and Short Answer

Write your answers to all questions in this section on the lines provided. For multiple-choice questions, circle the letter of the best answer.

1. Which phrase best describes the empty world the speaker refers to in the last line of "Remembrance"? Explain your answer.
   a. life without tears
   b. life without thoughts
   c. life without hope
   d. life without love

   _____

   _____

2. In "Remembrance," how long has it been since the speaker has lost "My Only Love"? Cite the stanza that supports your answer.

   _____

   _____

3. Describe at least two patterns that occur in the stanza structure of "Remembrance." Explain the effect of the patterns you describe.

   _____

   _____

   _____

4. Which of the following descriptions best describes the whereabouts of the people mentioned in "The Darkling Thrush"? Support your answer with a line from the stanza.
   a. They are out looking for food.
   b. They are home, staying warm.
   c. They are in the woods, birdwatching
   d. They are home, feeling gloomy.

   _____

5. What is the speaker's perception of Winter in "The Darkling Thrush"? Use examples of words or phrases from the poem to support your answer.

   _____

   _____

   _____

6. Identify the rhyming pattern in "The Darkling Thrush." How does this pattern contribute to the effect of the poem?

   _____

   _____

7. An example of a <u>terrestrial</u> thing in "The Darkling Thrush" is _____. Explain
your answer.
   a. evensong   b. carolings   c. bleak twigs   d. soul

    _____

8. The "digger" in "Ah, Are You Digging on My Grave?" is _____. Explain why the
digger is at the grave.
   a. the speaker's lover   b. the speaker's dog
   c. the speaker's gardener   d. the speaker's cat

    _____

9. Use a graphic organizer to analyze the structure and irony of "Ah, Are You Digging on My
Grave?" In the boxes on the left, write short phrases that summarize the meaning of each
of the poem's stanzas. Then in the box on the right, identify the irony that is created by
the shift between the first five stanzas and the last stanza.

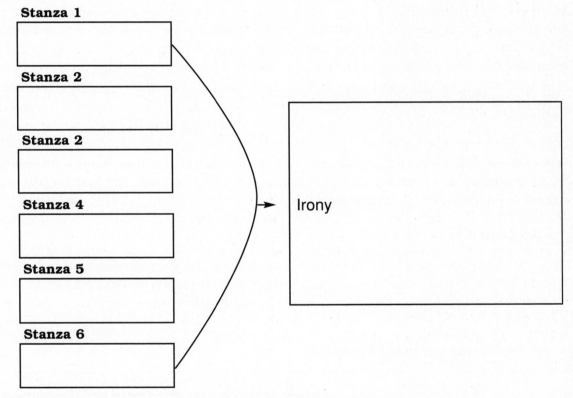

10. Why does the speaker question who is digging on her grave?

    _____

    _____

    _____

Extended Response

11. Use a Cube organizer to analyze "The Darkling Thrush." Then in one or two paragraphs, describe the speaker's outlook and the effect you think Hardy intended his poem to have on readers.

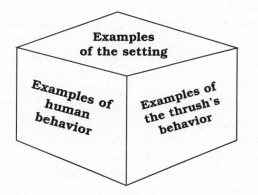

12. In an essay, analyze the poem, "Remembrance." Summarize two or three of the stanzas as individual units of meaning. Then explain how the stanzas support the deeper meaning of the entire poem.

13. Select one of the poems: "Remembrance," "The Darkling Thrush," or "Ah, Are You Digging on My Grave?" In an essay, discuss how the poet creates irony in his or her writing. Use examples from the poem you choose to support the ideas of your essay.

14. Consider the impressions you have from reading each of the poems by Hardy and Brontë. In an essay, analyze the effect of one of the poems, suggesting what the poet wanted the readers to gain from the poem. Use examples of the stanza structure and outcomes of the poem to support your points.

15. Write an essay in which you explain the significance of Hardy's and Brontë's title choices for their poems: "Remembrance," "The Darkling Thrush," and "Ah, Are You Digging on My Grave?" in relation to the meanings of the poems.

Oral Response

16. Go back to question 6, 9, 12, 13, or 15 or one assigned by your teacher, and take five to ten minutes to expand your answer and prepare an oral response. Find additional details in the poems that will support your points. You may wish to write down some notes to guide you.

Rubric for Evaluating Extended Responses

0	1	2	3	4
Blank paper Foreign language Illegible, incoherent Not enough content to score	Incorrect purpose, mode, audience Brief, vague Unelaborated Rambling Lack of language control Poor organization	Correct purpose, mode, audience Some elaboration Some details Gaps in organization Limited language control	Correct purpose, mode, audience Moderately well elaborated Clear, effective language Organized (perhaps with brief digressions)	Correct purpose, mode, audience Effective elaboration Consistent organization Sense of completeness, fluency

"God's Grandeur" and **"Spring and Fall: To a Young Child"**
by Gerard Manley Hopkins

"To an Athlete Dying Young" and **"When I Was One-and-Twenty"**
by A. E. Housman

Open-Book Test

Multiple Choice and Short Answer

Write your answers to all questions in this section on the lines provided. For multiple-choice questions, circle the letter of the best answer.

1. How is Hopkins's religious background evident in "God's Grandeur"? Explain your answer.
   a. The poem has a serious and reverent tone.
   b. There is a reference to the Holy Ghost.
   c. The poem is about the wonder and beauty of nature.
   d. The title of the poem refers to magnificence and splendor.

   _____

   _____

2. Line 12 of "God's Grandeur": "Oh, morning, at the brown brink eastward, springs—" describes an instance of _____. On the lines provided, explain why this instance reflects the work of God.
   a. clarity or precision   b. rarity or scarcity
   c. insignificance or triviality   d. splendor or grandeur

   _____

   _____

3. In "God's Grandeur," Hopkins displays his philosophy of *inscape*—the individuality of all things. Provide an example of *inscape* from the poem and explain how it demonstrates this concept.

   _____

   _____

   _____

4. Why are some syllables of "Spring and Fall: To a Young Child" marked with accents? What is the term used to identify the type of metrical verse found in this poem?

   _____

   _____

5. How does the contrast of "spring and fall" in the title "Spring and Fall: To a Young Child" relate to the poem's meaning?

   _____

   _____

   _____

6. Which sentence best summarizes "To an Athlete Dying Young"? Explain your answer, using examples from the poem.
   a. By dying young, the athlete won't ever lose his glory.
   b. By dying young, the athlete has lost his chance for fame.
   c. By dying young, the athlete will be forgotten.
   d. By dying young, the athlete's records cannot be broken.

   _____

   _____

7. Identify the term that indicates the number of feet per line in "To An Athlete Dying Young," and locate the lines in the poem that are trochaic.
   a. dimeter   b. trimeter   c. tetrameter   d. pentameter

8. Use the diagram to illustrate the possibilities for athletes who die young or those who go on to live out their adult lives. For those who die young, use examples from Housman's poem. Then, using information about the poet, write a few sentences that relate the theme of the poem to Housman's life.

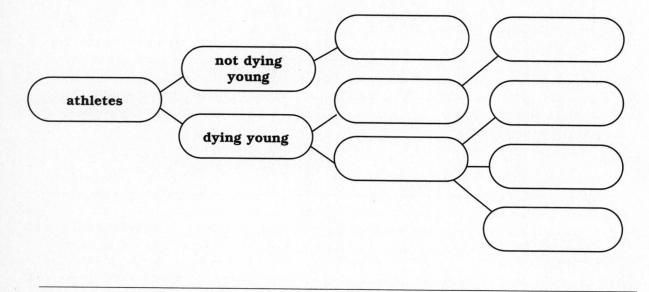

   _____

   _____

9. Reread line 13 of "When I Was One-and-Twenty." What adjustment must the reader make to follow Housman's iambic trimeter and keep the rhythm of the meter?

   _____

   _____

10. What advice does the speaker receive in "When I Was One-and-Twenty"? What conclusion does he read about this advice?

   _____

   _____

   _____

Extended Response

11. Use a chart to organize Hopkins's ideas about nature found in "God's Grandeur" and "Spring and Fall: To a Young Child." Then write one or two paragraphs in which you explain Hopkins's ideas and relate them to his love of the world.

Poem	Ideas about nature	Hopkins's love of the world
"God's Grandeur"		
"Spring and Fall: To a Young Child"		

12. In an essay, discuss the effect of the rhythms of Hopkins's poems "God's Grandeur" and "Spring and Fall: To a Young Child." Consider how the movement of the words affects the impact that the poems have on readers.

13. In each of the four poems you read, "God's Grandeur," "Spring and Fall: To a Young Child," "To an Athlete Dying Young," and "When I Was One-and-Twenty," the speakers are offering philosophical information to an audience. Write an essay about the potential usefulness of this information.

14. Housman once said, "Poetry is not the thing said, but a way of saying it." Discuss how this statement relates to "To an Athlete Dying Young" or "When I Was One-and-Twenty." Use examples from the poem about which you are writing.

15. In an essay, discuss what you think Housman's purpose was for writing "To an Athlete Dying Young." Is it a tribute? Is it a simple statement? Is it a reflection of the poet's attitude toward life? Use examples from the poem to support your main points.

Oral Response

16. Go back to question 3, 8, 10, 12, or 13 or one assigned by your teacher, and take five to ten minutes to expand your answer and prepare an oral response. Find additional details in the poems that will support your points. You may wish to write down some notes to guide you.

Rubric for Evaluating Extended Responses

0	1	2	3	4
Blank paper Foreign language Illegible, incoherent Not enough content to score	Incorrect purpose, mode, audience Brief, vague Unelaborated Rambling Lack of language control Poor organization	Correct purpose, mode, audience Some elaboration Some details Gaps in organization Limited language control	Correct purpose, mode, audience Moderately well elaborated Clear, effective language Organized (perhaps with brief digressions)	Correct purpose, mode, audience Effective elaboration Consistent organization Sense of completeness, fluency

Poetry of William Butler Yeats

Open-Book Test

Multiple Choice and Short Answer

Write your answers to all questions in this section on the lines provided.
For multiple-choice questions, circle the letter of the best answer.

1. In the first stanza of "When You Are Old," the speaker advises the woman to "take down this book" and read it. What does the book symbolize in the poem? Explain your answer, citing details from the poem.
    a. The book represents a reference on sleep disorders.
    b. The book represents memories of youth.
    c. The book represents love.
    d. The book represents the mountains and stars.

    _____

    _____

2. In stanza 2 of "When You Are Old," the speaker describes one man who loved the woman. How does this man differ from the woman's other admirers? Support your answer with one or two examples from the text.

    _____

    _____

3. In the last stanza of "When You Are Old," the speaker explains what happened to the love in the woman's life. What does the speaker mean when he says, ". . . Love fled/And paced upon the mountains overhead/And hid his face amid a crowd of stars" (lines 10–12)? Explain why your answer choice is correct.
    a. The woman lost her opportunity to have love in her life.
    b. Love ran away from her.
    c. The woman chased her love away to the mountains.
    d. Love has aged her.

    _____

    _____

4. In "The Lake Isle of Innisfree," the speaker describes Innisfree in a series of vivid, natural images. On the diagonal lines of the herringbone organizer below, write what the images suggest to you about the qualities of this place. List examples that support your answers on the horizontal lines.

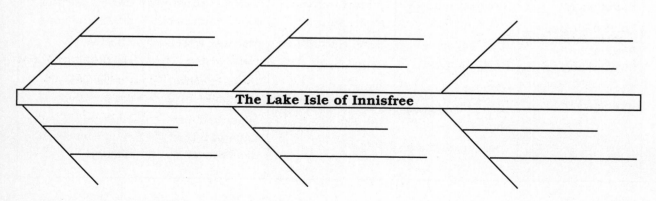

The Lake Isle of Innisfree

5. What does the place in "The Lake Isle of Innisfree" represent to the speaker? Support your response with one or two examples from the poem.

    _____

    _____

6. What does the speaker feel while observing the swans in "The Wild Swans at Coole"? Explain why your answer choice is correct, citing details from the poem.
    a. sadness   b. excitement   c. admiration   d. jealousy

    _____

    _____

7. Reread line 12 of "The Wild Swans at Coole." Which of the following is a synonym for *clamorous*? Explain why your answer choice is correct, citing details from the poem.
    a. white   b. large   c. graceful   d. noisy

    _____

    _____

8. What is the speaker's view of society in "The Second Coming"? Support your answer, citing details from the poem.

    _____

    _____

9. Yeats believed that history occurs in two thousand-year cycles of birth, growth, and decay. Explain how lines 21–22 from "The Second Coming" reflect this philosophy:
    > And what rough beast, its hour come round at last,
    > Slouches toward Bethlehem to be born?

    _____

    _____

10. Which lines from "Sailing to Byzantium" support Yeats's idea that Byzantium symbolizes the world of art? Explain why your answer choice is correct.
    a. "Whatever is begotten, born, and dies./Caught in that sensual music all neglect/Monuments of unaging intellect" (lines 6–8).
    b. "An aged man is but a paltry thing,/A tattered coat upon a stick, unless/Should clap its hands and sing, and louder sing/For every tatter in its mortal dress . . ." (lines 9–12).
    c. "Consume my heart away; sick with desire/And fastened to a dying animal/It knows not what it is . . ." (lines 21–23).
    d. "Once out of nature I shall never take/My bodily form from any natural thing,/But such a form as Grecian goldsmiths make/Of hammered gold and gold enameling . . ." (lines 25–28).

    _____

    _____

Extended Response

11. Yeats's poem "When You Are Old" is about an old woman who is urged to reflect on a lost love. In one or two paragraphs, explain how and why Yeats's relationship with Maude Gonne may have served as an inspiration for this poem. Refer to the biographical information in the Guide for Interpreting. Support your response, citing examples from the poem.

12. Both "The Lake Isle of Innisfree" and "Sailing to Byzantium" express a speaker's intention to leave his familiar world and journey to another, presumably better, place. In a short essay, analyze what each of the places in these poems represents to its respective speaker, and why the speaker desires to go there. Support your response, citing examples from each poem.

13. The speaker in "The Wild Swans at Coole" reflects on the swans that he has observed for the past nineteen years. He states, "All's changed since I, hearing at twilight,/The first time on this shore, the bell-beat of their wings above my head,/Trod with a lighter tread" (lines 15–18). In a short essay, speculate about what the swans might represent to the speaker. Support your response, citing examples from the poem.

14. In "The Second Coming," the speaker ponders the end of a twenty century cycle and what it will bring to humanity. In an essay, explain how the speaker expresses his emotions about this ending through his description of the events that have taken place and may yet take place. Support your response, citing examples from the poem.

15. In "Sailing to Byzantium," the speaker describes the country he left and the world of Byzantium. The descriptions of these two worlds reflect the speaker's attitudes about mortality and immortality. In an essay, explain how the speaker views his former country and Byzantium, and how these views reflect his attitudes about mortality and immortality, respectively. Support your response, citing examples from the poem.

Oral Response

16. Choose question 4, 5, 9, 11, or 12 or one your teacher assigns you. Take a few minutes to look through the poems to prepare an oral response to give in class. If necessary, make notes to be clear about the order in which you want to present your answer.

Rubric for Evaluating Extended Responses

0	1	2	3	4
Blank paper Foreign language Illegible, incoherent Not enough content to score	Incorrect purpose, mode, audience Brief, vague Unelaborated Rambling Lack of language control Poor organization	Correct purpose, mode, audience Some elaboration Some details Gaps in organization Limited language control	Correct purpose, mode, audience Moderately well elaborated Clear, effective language Organized (perhaps with brief digressions)	Correct purpose, mode, audience Effective elaboration Consistent organization Sense of completeness, fluency

"Preludes," "Journey of the Magi," and "The Hollow Men"
by T. S. Eliot

Open-Book Test

Multiple Choice and Short Answer

Write your answers to all questions in this section on the lines provided.
For multiple-choice questions, circle the letter of the best answer.

1. Based on Eliot's descriptions in stanzas one and two of "Preludes," what can you conclude about the quality of modern city life? Support your answer, citing details from the poem.

   _____

   _____

   _____

2. Which line from "Preludes" expresses the speaker's feelings about the person in stanza three? Explain why your answer choice is correct.
   a. "You tossed a blanket from your bed,/You lay upon your back, and waited . . . " (lines 24–25).
   b. "You dozed, and watched the night revealing/The thousand sordid images/Of which your soul was constituted . . . " (lines 26–28).
   c. You had such a vision of the street/As the street hardly understands . . . " (lines 33–34).
   d. "You curled the papers from your hair,/Or clasped the yellow soles of your feet/In the palms of both soiled hands" (lines 36–38).

   _____

   _____

   _____

3. What is the speaker's view of the world described in lines 52–54 of "Preludes"? Support your answer, citing details from the poem.

   _____

   _____

   _____

4. Which statement best describes the trip to Bethlehem in "Journey of the Magi"? Explain why your answer choice is correct, citing details from the poem.
   a. The journey was difficult, but worth it.   c. The journey was cold and agonizing.
   b. The journey was long and foolish.   d. The journey was deadly and long.

   _____

   _____

   _____

5. What does "Journey of the Magi" suggest about Eliot's view of humanity? Support your answer, citing one or two examples from the poem.

   _____

   _____

6. The speaker in "Journey of the Magi" questions whether he has seen a birth or a death. He states, "there was a birth, certainly,/We had evidence and no doubt. I had seen birth and death,/But I had thought they were different; this Birth was/Hard and bitter agony for us, like Death, our death" (lines 36–39). Why is the speaker confused about what he has witnessed? Support your response with one or two lines from the poem.

_____

_____

_____

7. Which lines from Part I of "The Hollow Men" imply that what people say is insignificant ? Explain why your answer choice is correct.
   a. "We are the stuffed men/Leaning together/Headpiece filled with straw." (lines 2–4)
   b. "Our dried voices, when/We whisper together/Are quiet and meaningless/as wind in dry grass/Or rats; feet over broken glass . . . " (lines 5–9).
   c. "Shape without form, shade without color . . . " (line 11).
   d. "Those who have crossed/With direct eyes, to death's other Kingdom/Remember us . . . " (lines 13–15).

_____

_____

_____

8. What do the eyes represent in the "The Hollow Men"? Support your answer, citing one or two examples from the poem.

_____

_____

_____

9. What can you conclude about what the Shadow is in Part V of "The Hollow Men"? Cite one or two lines from the poem to support your response.

_____

_____

10. Reread line 60 of "The Hollow Men" and select the synonym for *tumid*. Explain why your answer choice is correct.
    a. swollen   b. stagnant   c. humid   d. wide

_____

Extended Response

11. In a short essay, explain how the images in "Preludes" convey Eliot's attitude about modern society. Support your response, citing details from the poem.

12. In "Journey of the Magi," Eliot recounts the journey of the Magi to honor the baby Jesus. The account of one of these wise men is presented in modern, everyday language. In a short essay, analyze how effective this language is in presenting the spiritual and actual experiences of the speaker. Support your response, citing details from the poem.

13. In a short essay, explain who the hollow men are, based on how they are presented in the poem. Support your response, citing lines from the poem.

14. Both "Preludes" and "Journey of the Magi" present Eliot's views of modern life. In one or two paragraphs, contrast the visions of life that each poem presents. Support your response, citing examples from each poem.

15. "Preludes" and "The Hollow Men" criticize the effect of modern life on humanity. Using the Venn diagram below, compare and contrast aspects of modern life, and the images that Eliot uses in each poem to illustrate his criticism. Using the information that you have compiled in the Venn diagram, analyze how and why Eliot criticizes modern life in each poem, citing examples from both poems to support your response.

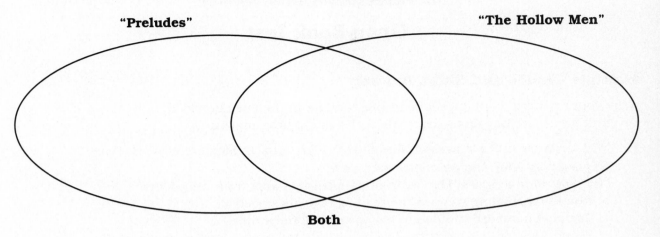

"Preludes"   **"The Hollow Men"**

Both

Oral Response

16. Choose question 1, 5, 8, 12, or 14 or one your teacher assigns you. Take a few minutes to look through the poems to prepare an oral response to give in class. If necessary, make notes to be clear about the order in which you want to present your answer.

Rubric for Evaluating Extended Responses

0	1	2	3	4
Blank paper Foreign language Illegible, incoherent Not enough content to score	Incorrect purpose, mode, audience Brief, vague Unelaborated Rambling Lack of language control Poor organization	Correct purpose, mode, audience Some elaboration Some details Gaps in organization Limited language control	Correct purpose, mode, audience Moderately well elaborated Clear, effective language Organized (perhaps with brief digressions)	Correct purpose, mode, audience Effective elaboration Consistent organization Sense of completeness, fluency

"In Memory of W. B. Yeats" and **"Musée des Beaux Arts"**
by W. H. Auden
"Carrick Revisited" by Louis MacNeice
"Not Palaces" by Stephen Spender

Open-Book Test

Multiple Choice and Short Answer

Write your answers to all questions in this section on the lines provided.
For multiple-choice questions, circle the letter of the best answer.

1. Which statement best paraphrases lines 10–11 from "In Memory of W. B. Yeats"?
   Explain why your answer choice is correct.
   "By mourning tongues/The death of the poet was kept from his poems"
   a. People's mourning stopped the reading of Yeats's poetry.
   b. The poet mourned the loss of his poems before he died.
   c. People kept Yeats's memory alive by reciting his poems even after his death.
   d. Yeats's voice was silenced; thus he could not write any more poetry.

   _____

   _____

2. Yeats is described in "In Memory of W. B. Yeats" as being "scattered among a hundred
   cities" after he has died (line 18). Explain what the speaker means by this phrase.

   _____

   _____

3. Why is the analogy of agriculture appropriate in describing the process involved in
   creating poetry? (lines 70–73)

   _____

   _____

4. Which lines from "Musée des Beaux Arts" describe how people are indifferent to the
   suffering of others? Explain why your answer choice is correct.
   a. ". . .The Old Masters: how well they understood/Its human position; how it takes
   place/While someone else is eating or opening a window or just walking dully
   along . . . " (lines 2–4).
   b. " . . . How, when the aged are reverently, passionately waiting/For the miraculous
   birth, there must always be/Children who did not specially want it to happen . . . "
   (lines 5–7).
   c. "In Brueghel's Icarus, for instance: how everything turns away/Quite leisurely from the
   disaster . . . " (lines 14–15).
   d. "But for him it was not an important failure; the sun shone/As it had to on green legs
   disappearing into the green/Water . . . " (lines 17–19)

   _____

   _____

5. Explain why the fall of Icarus in "Musée des Beaux Arts" "was not an important failure"
   for the ploughman, even though he may have heard Icarus fall (line 17).

   _____

   _____

6. In "Carrick Revisited," the speaker returns to a place where he spent his childhood. What does the speaker mean when he states that "Time and place—our bridgeheads into reality/But also its concealment" (lines 16–17)?

_____

_____

7. In "Carrick Revisited," what theme about controlling the development of one's identity is implied through the author's reminiscences about Carrick and his childhood in general? Support your answer, citing one or two examples from the poem.

_____

_____

8. Reread line 2 of "Not Palaces" and select the synonym for *intrigues*. Explain why your answer choice is correct.
   a. ideas   b. schemes   c. purposes   d. memories

_____

_____

9. Which lines from "Not Palaces" describes the speaker's rejection of the current style of modern poetry? Explain why your answer choice is correct.
   a. "Not palaces, an era's crown/Where the mind dwells, intrigues, rests . . . " (lines 1–2).
   b. It is too late for rare accumulation,/For family pride, for beauty's filtered dusts;/I say, stamping the words for emphasis . . . " (lines 6–8).
   c. "Drink from here energy and only energy/To will this time's change" (lines 9–10).
   d. "Leave your gardens, your singing feasts,/Your dreams of suns circling before our sun,/Of heaven after our world" (lines 16–18).

_____

_____

10. What central idea about poetry's function does Spender present to the reader in "Not Palaces"? Support your answer with one or two examples from the poem.

_____

_____

Extended Response

11. "In Memory of W. B. Yeats" is Auden's homage to Yeats at the time of Yeats's death. In one or two paragraphs, explain what Auden believes about the way that Yeats's poetry has affected the world. Support your response with examples from the poem.

12. In a short essay, analyze how Auden conveys his view of human indifference to suffering in "Musée des Beaux Arts" through the images that he uses. Support your response with examples from the poem.

13. In a short essay, analyze how the speaker's reflections about Carrick are used to explain the formation of his identity in "Carrick Revisited." Support your response with examples from the poem.

14. "Not Palaces" examines the role of poetry as an agent for social change. In one or two paragraphs, explain how Spender attempts to persuade the reader that poetry can act as an agent for social change. Support your response with examples from the poem.

15. Using the Venn diagram below, compare and contrast how the passage of time is presented in each "In Memory of W. B. Yeats" and "Carrick Revisited." Then, using the information that you have compiled in the Venn diagram, write an essay in which you examine how time is portrayed in each poem, and why it is portrayed in this way. Support your response with examples from each poem.

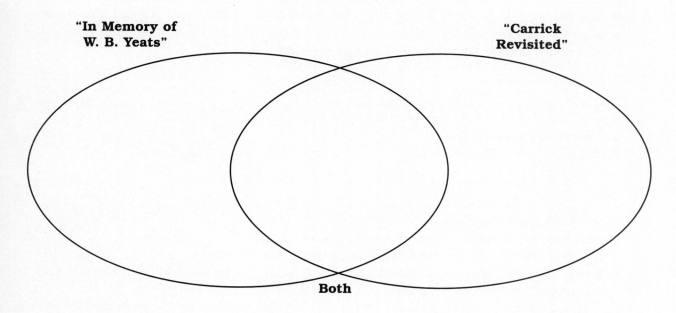

"In Memory of W. B. Yeats"

"Carrick Revisited"

Both

Oral Response

16. Choose question 7, 10, 11, 13, or 15 or one your teacher assigns you. Take a few minutes to look through the poems to prepare an oral response to give in class. If necessary, make notes to be clear about the order in which you want to present your answer.

Rubric for Evaluating Extended Responses

0	1	2	3	4
Blank paper Foreign language Illegible, incoherent Not enough content to score	Incorrect purpose, mode, audience Brief, vague Unelaborated Rambling Lack of language control Poor organization	Correct purpose, mode, audience Some elaboration Some details Gaps in organization Limited language control	Correct purpose, mode, audience Moderately well elaborated Clear, effective language Organized (perhaps with brief digressions)	Correct purpose, mode, audience Effective elaboration Consistent organization Sense of completeness, fluency

Name _____   Date _____

"Shooting an Elephant" by George Orwell

Open-Book Test

Multiple Choice and Short Answer

Write your answers to all questions in this section on the lines provided.
For multiple-choice questions, circle the letter of the best answer.

1. In "Shooting an Elephant," Orwell recounts an incident that occurred in Burma when he
    was a police officer there. What does Orwell mean when he says, "In Moulmein, in lower
    Burma, I was hated by large numbers of people—the only time in my life that I have been
    important enough for this to happen to me"? Explain your answer on the lines provided.

    _____

    _____

2. In "Shooting an Elephant," Orwell explains his attitude about his job as a police officer.
    Which answer best describes how Orwell feels about his job? Explain why the answer you
    chose is correct.
    a. guilty   b. ashamed   c. proud   d. depressed

    _____

    _____

3. Explain the verbal irony present in the following quotation from "Shooting an Elephant":
    "Feelings like this are the normal by-products of imperialism; ask any Anglo-Indian
    official, if you can catch him off guard."

    _____

    _____

4. "It was a very poor quarter, a labyrinth of squalid bamboo huts, thatched with palm leaf,
    winding all over a steep hillside." Based on how *squalid* is used in the above sentence
    from "Shooting an Elephant," choose the answer that contains a synonym for it. Explain
    why your answer choice is correct.
    a. crowded   b. wretched   c. identical   d. dirty

    _____

    _____

5. Before he sees the elephant, Orwell prepares to shoot it only "to defend myself if
    necessary." However, Orwell shoots the elephant so that the Burmese people do not laugh
    at him. Explain why Orwell's decision to shoot the elephant in "Shooting an Elephant" is
    an example of irony of situation.

    _____

    _____

6. Throughout his account of "Shooting an Elephant," Orwell describes the behavior of the
    Burmese people. What is Orwell's attitude about the Burmese, based on how he
    describes them? Support your response with one or two examples from the text.

    _____

    _____

7. Which of the following lines from "Shooting an Elephant" contains an example of verbal irony? Explain why your answer choice is correct.
   a. "The thick blood welled out of him like red velvet, but still he did not die"
   b. "His body did not even jerk when the shots hit him, the tortured breathing continued without a pause."
   c. "He was dying, very slowly and with great agony, but in some world remote from me where not even a bullet could damage him further."
   d. "It seemed dreadful to see the great beast lying there, powerless to move and powerless to die, and not even to be able to finish him."

_____

8. In "Shooting an Elephant," Orwell describes the behavior of the Burmese whom he polices. For example, after Orwell shot the elephant, he states that the Burmese raced to the body of the elephant and "had stripped his body almost to the bones by the afternoon." What can you conclude about the Burmese way of life under British rule, based on this description of them?

_____

_____

9. Why is Orwell glad that the elephant killed the Indian man? Choose the answer that explains why Orwell feels this way. Explain why your answer choice is correct.
   a. This death of the Indian man made Orwell look heroic in the eyes of his fellow officers after he shot the elephant.
   b. The death of the Indian man made Orwell look heroic in the eyes of the Burmese after he shot the elephant.
   c. The death of the Indian man only reinforced Orwell's opinion that he should be killed.
   d. The death of the Indian man gave Orwell a justifiable reason for shooting the elephant.

_____

10. Based on what Orwell writes in the last paragraph of "Shooting an Elephant," choose the answer that explains why he repeatedly mentions how he and his fellow officers feel that he was correct in shooting the elephant. Explain why your answer choice is correct.
    a. Orwell repeats this idea to remind the reader about how heroically he behaves.
    b. Orwell repeats this ideas to reinforce the fact that he took a dangerous risk by shooting the elephant.
    c. Orwell repeats this idea in order to alleviate his own guilt about shooting the elephant.
    d. Orwell repeats this idea to show how other people approved of his actions.

_____

Extended Response

11. In "Shooting an Elephant," Orwell asserts that he "was all for the Burmese and all against their oppressors, the British." However, Orwell's description of the Burmese in this narrative reveals that Orwell had his own biases against them. In one or two paragraphs, explain why Orwell has this ironic attitude toward the Burmese. Support your response with one or two examples from the essay.

12. In "Shooting an Elephant," Orwell reveals his own personality through his description of the incident with the elephant. On the diagonal lines of the herringbone organizer below, list the qualities of Orwell's personality that come to light. Cite evidence from the story to support your findings on the horizontal lines. Then, in a short essay, use the information that you have gathered in the herringbone organizer to explain the conclusions you can draw about Orwell's personality.

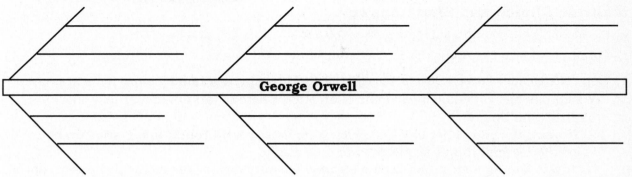

George Orwell

13. "Shooting an Elephant" gives Orwell's insights into the workings of an imperial regime. In a short essay, analyze how the British regime in Burma affected both the British and the Burmese. Support your response with examples from the story.

14. Based on how Orwell describes the actions of the elephant in "Shooting an Elephant," why does Orwell have such conflicting feelings about shooting it? In an essay, respond to this question, supporting your response with examples from the story.

15. There are many examples of Orwell's use of situational and verbal irony throughout "Shooting an Elephant." In an essay, explain how Orwell's use of irony established the critical tone of the piece.

Oral Response

16. Choose question 2, 5, 9, 11, or 13 or one your teacher assigns you. Take a few minutes to look through the essay to prepare an oral response to give in class. If necessary, make notes to be clear about the order in which you want to present your answer.

Rubric for Evaluating Extended Responses

0	1	2	3	4
Blank paper Foreign language Illegible, incoherent Not enough content to score	Incorrect purpose, mode, audience Brief, vague Unelaborated Rambling Lack of language control Poor organization	Correct purpose, mode, audience Some elaboration Some details Gaps in organization Limited language control	Correct purpose, mode, audience Moderately well elaborated Clear, effective language Organized (perhaps with brief digressions)	Correct purpose, mode, audience Effective elaboration Consistent organization Sense of completeness, fluency

"The Demon Lover" by Elizabeth Bowen

Open-Book Test

Multiple Choice and Short Answer

Write your answers to all questions in this section on the lines provided.
For multiple-choice questions, circle the letter of the best answer.

1. In "The Demon Lover," Bowen sets the mood for a story containing supernatural events. Which passage contains an example of an atmosphere of "an unfamiliar queerness"? Explain your answer.
    a. "Toward the end of her day in London Mrs. Drover went round to her shut-up house to look for several things she wanted to take away."
    b. "It was late August; it had been a steamy, showery day; at the moment the trees down the pavement glittered in an escape of humid yellow afternoon sun."
    c. Against the next batch of clouds, already piling up ink-dark, broken chimneys and parapets stood out."
    d. "Dead air came to meet her as she went in."

    _____

    _____

2. When Mrs. Drover enters her house, she notices how empty and deserted it looks. How does Bowen create an image of this emptiness in "The Demon Lover"? Support your answer, citing an example from the story.

    _____

    _____

3. In "The Demon Lover," after she reads the letter, Mrs. Drover examines her reflection in the mirror. What do we learn about Mrs. Drover, based on what she sees in the mirror? Support your answer with an example from the story.

    _____

    _____

4. How does Mrs. Drover perceive the fiancé in "The Demon Lover"? Explain your answer, citing details from the story.
    a. Mrs. Drover has difficulty remembering his name; this makes the reader wonder if he ever existed.
    b. Mrs. Drover envisions that he would be killed, which makes their farewell meeting a haunting one.
    c. Mrs. Drover cannot remember his face and only remembers her fiancé by his touch and from a cut on her hand.
    d. Mrs. Drover has never been kissed by her fiancé, so she has doubts about his existence.

    _____

    _____

5. Based on the last meeting between Mrs. Drover and her fiancé in "The Demon Lover," what type of person is the fiancé? Support your answer with an example from the story.

_____

_____

6. Why does Mrs. Drover feel "so apart, lost, and forsworn" after her fiancé leaves her in "The Demon Lover"? Support your answer choice, citing details from the story.
   a. The departure of her fiancé causes Mrs. Drover to feel this way.
   b. The support from her mother and sister causes Mrs. Drover to feel this way.
   c. The news that the fiancé was missing causes Mrs. Drover to feel this way.
   d. The promise that she makes to her fiancé causes Mrs. Drover to feel this way.

_____

_____

_____

7. Read the following quotation from "The Demon Lover" and select the antonym for *dislocation*. Explain why your answer choice is correct.
   > But her trouble, behind just a little grief, was a complete dislocation from everything.
   a. connection   b. disconnection   c. relocation   d. area

_____

8. In "The Demon Lover," the narrator makes this statement:
   > Unable, for some minutes to go on kneeling with her back exposed to an empty room, Mrs. Drover rose from the chest to sit on an upright chair whose back was firmly against the wall.

   What is your response to this statement? Do you think the author intended for you to feel that way? Why or why not?

_____

_____

_____

9. The effect that the threatening letter has on Mrs. Drover causes her to view her house differently in "The Demon Lover." Explain how the description of the house and its atmosphere reflects Mrs. Drover's alarm about the letter. Support your answer with an example from the story.

_____

_____

10. At the end of "The Demon Lover," Mrs. Drover hails the taxi and gets inside. How does the narrator's description of the actions of the taxi driver at this point add to the supernatural atmosphere of the story? Support your answer with an example from the story.

_____

_____

_____

Extended Response

11. In a short essay, analyze how Bowen develops supernatural effects to make "The Demon Lover" a ghost story. Support your response with examples from the story.

12. On the diagonal lines of the herringbone organizer below, list qualities of Mrs. Drover's personality. List examples from the story that support your assessment of her personality on the horizontal lines. Then, using the information from the organizer, write a short essay citing details about her personality that make her fearful of the letter that she receives.

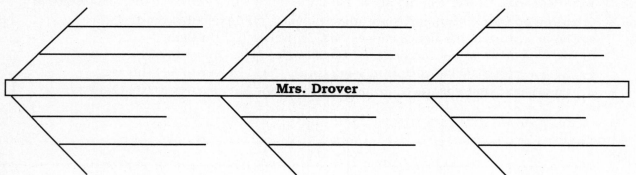

Mrs. Drover

13. Based on Mrs. Drover's recollections of her last meeting with her fiancé in "The Demon Lover," the reader develops an idea about the type of relationship they had. In one or two paragraphs, describe this relationship. Support your response with examples from the story.

14. Events cause the reader to question Mrs. Drover's recollection of her past and the atmosphere in her house. In a short essay, explain why "The Demon Lover" is an appropriate title for this story.

15. In an essay, explain how Bowen builds suspense in "The Demon Lover." Support your response with examples from the text.

Oral Response

16. Choose question 3, 4, 11, 12, or 14 or one your teacher assigns you. Take a few minutes to look through the story to prepare an oral response to give in class. If necessary, make notes to be clear about the order in which you want to present your answer.

Rubric for Evaluating Extended Responses

0	1	2	3	4
Blank paper Foreign language Illegible, incoherent Not enough content to score	Incorrect purpose, mode, audience Brief, vague Unelaborated Rambling Lack of language control Poor organization	Correct purpose, mode, audience Some elaboration Some details Gaps in organization Limited language control	Correct purpose, mode, audience Moderately well elaborated Clear, effective language Organized (perhaps with brief digressions)	Correct purpose, mode, audience Effective elaboration Consistent organization Sense of completeness, fluency

"The Soldier" by Rupert Brooke
"Wirers" by Siegfried Sassoon
"Anthem for Doomed Youth" by Wilfred Owen
"Birds on the Western Front" by Saki (H. H. Munro)

Open-Book Test

Multiple Choice and Short Answer

Write your answers to all questions in this section on the lines provided.
For multiple-choice questions, circle the letter of the best answer.

1. In "The Soldier," the speaker suggests how he should be remembered if he dies on foreign soil. Based on what the speaker describes in the first stanza, which answer states what can be inferred about the speaker's feelings for his country? Explain why your answer is correct.
   a. The speaker mourns for England.
   b. The speaker feels patriotic about England.
   c. The speaker feels pessimistic about England.
   d. The speaker feels curious about England.

   _____

   _____

2. In "The Soldier," the speaker contemplates that after he is buried, his heart will lose any evil that exists within it and be a "pulse in the eternal mind, no less" (line 10). Explain what the speaker means by this remark.

   _____

   _____

3. The speaker in "Wirers" describes the process in which the wire on the the front line is repaired. Based on how this process is described in the first stanza, what can you infer about when and how these wires are repaired?

   _____

   _____

4. After the Boche sends up a flare, the acts of the soldiers illuminated by the flare are described by the speaker in "Wirers." Why are the soldiers described as "ghosts" (line 6)? Support your answer with one or two lines from the poem.

   _____

   _____

5. In the last stanza of "Wirers," the speaker states that one of the soldiers was mortally wounded during the mending of the wire. Even so, he states, "But we can say the front-line wire's been safely mended" (line 13). Based on your interpretation of this line in the poem, what is the tone of the speaker regarding the repair of the wire? Explain how you arrived at your answer.

   _____

   _____

6. Which of the following lines from "Anthem for Doomed Youth" best reflects the poem's embittered tone? Explain why the answer you chose is correct.
   a. "What passing bell for these who die as cattle?" (line 1)
   b. "Not in the hands of boys, but in their eyes/Shall shine the holy glimmers of good-byes" (lines 10–11)
   c. "Their flowers the tenderness of patient minds . . . " (line 13).
   d. "And each slow dusk a drawing down of blinds" (line 14).

_____

7. Based on how *mockeries* is used in the following line from "Anthem for Doomed Youth," select the answer that contains a synonym for it. Explain why the answer you chose is correct.
   "No mockeries for them from prayers or bells . . . " (line 5).
   a. signals   b. praise   c. eulogies   d. ridicule

_____

8. In "Anthem for Doomed Youth," Owen incorporates vivid images of war in the first stanza. How does he describe the weapons of war in stanza one to convey the violence and chaos of battle? Support your answer with one or two examples from the poem.

_____

9. In "Birds on the Western Front," Saki analyzes the effect of war by examining it from the perspective of the wildlife that is affected by it. Based on his examination of how war has affected the owls, select the answer that describes the tone of this piece. Explain why your answer is correct.
   a. sarcastic   b. concerned   c. impressed   d. serious

_____

10. In "Birds on the Western Front," Saki observes, "I once saw a pair of crows engaged in hot combat with a pair of sparrow-hawks, while considerably higher in the sky, but almost directly above them, two Allied battle-planes were engaging an equal number of enemy aircraft." Explain what this quotation illustrates about the nature of the air war during World War I.

_____

Extended Response

11. The speaker in "The Soldier" contemplates how he will be remembered if he dies during the war. In one or two paragraphs, explain how his thoughts in this poem reflect his attitude about death. Cite examples from the poem to support your response.

12. The speaker in "Wirers" describes and questions the great risks that soldiers took while repairing the front-line wire. In one or two paragraphs, analyze how the language that the speaker uses to describe the repair of the front-line wire reflects the danger of the situation. Support your response with examples from the poem.

13. In "Anthem for Doomed Youth," the speaker expresses his bitter feelings about the toll that war has taken on humanity. The two stanzas, however, contain different images to convey this bitterness. In a short essay, analyze the types of images presented in each stanza, and explain why the images in each stanza are different. Support your response with examples from the poem.

14. Saki discusses the war's impact on the natural habitats of birds in "Birds on the Western Front." In a short essay explain what Saki's opinion about this effect on the birds is and and how Saki presents it in the story.

15. The discussion of how birds are affected by war is actually the means by which Saki expresses his opinion about how war affects human beings in "Birds on the Western Front." In the left column of the chart below, list the types of birds in the poem and what each type represents about war. Cite examples to support your explanation in the right column. Then, using the information that you have compiled, write a short essay in which you explain how Saki uses various species of birds to illustrate the effects of war on human beings.

Types of Birds, and What Each Represents	Examples

Oral Response

16. Choose question 5, 8, 13, 14, or 15 or one your teacher assigns you. Take a few minutes to look through the poems and story to prepare an oral response to give in class. If necessary, make notes to be clear about the order in which you want to present your answer.

Rubric for Evaluating Extended Responses

0	1	2	3	4
Blank paper Foreign language Illegible, incoherent Not enough content to score	Incorrect purpose, mode, audience Brief, vague Unelaborated Rambling Lack of language control Poor organization	Correct purpose, mode, audience Some elaboration Some details Gaps in organization Limited language control	Correct purpose, mode, audience Moderately well elaborated Clear, effective language Organized (perhaps with brief digressions)	Correct purpose, mode, audience Effective elaboration Consistent organization Sense of completeness, fluency

"Wartime Speech" by Winston Churchill
"Defending Nonviolent Resistance" by Mohandas K. Gandhi

Open-Book Test

Multiple Choice and Short Answer

Write your answers to all questions in this section on the lines provided.
For multiple-choice questions, circle the letter of the best answer.

1. In "Wartime Speech," Churchill describes the political situation caused by Germany's invasion of France. Explain how Churchill conveys the idea that the situation is serious.

   _____

   _____

2. Churchill discusses various ideas about the war and how the English people should deal with it in "Wartime Speech." What is the main idea of paragraph three of the speech ? Support your response with one or two examples from the text.

   _____

   _____

3. Churchill also informs the English people of the progress that the British and French armed forces are making against the German army. How does Churchill present this information in his speech? Support your answer with one or two examples from the text.

   _____

   _____

4. In "Wartime Speech," Churchill attempts to prepare the English for the hardships and sacrifices of war. Select the answer that contains an example of Churchill's efforts to persuade the English that they must endure the struggles of the approaching war. Explain why the answer you chose is correct.
   a. "We must expect that as soon as stability is reached on the Western Front, the bulk of that hideous apparatus of aggression which gashed Holland into ruin and slavery in a few days, will be turned upon us."
   b. "If the battle is to be won, we must provide our men with ever-increasing quantities of the weapons and ammunition they need."
   c. "There is imperious need for these vital munitions."
   d. "I am sure I speak for all when I say we are ready to face it; to endure it; and to retaliate against it—to any extent that the unwritten laws of war permit."

   _____

   _____

5. Why does Churchill discuss Trinity Sunday and the significance of the day?

   _____

6. Based on how it is used in the speech "Defending Nonviolent Resistance," choose the answer which contains the definition for *disaffection*. Explain why your answer choice is correct.
   a. rejection   b. boredom   c. disillusionment   d. interest

   _____

7. In "Defending Nonviolent Resistance," Gandhi agrees that he is guilty of the crime with which he is charged. He states, "I should have known the consequences of every one of my acts. I know that I was playing with fire. I ran the risk, and if I was set free, I would still do the same." How does Gandhi's admission of guilt serve to underscore his belief in nonviolent resistance?

_____

_____

8. During his speech, Gandhi describes various acts and reforms that the British government enforced in India, as well as the results of those acts and reforms. Choose the answer which explains Gandhi's main purpose for discussing these acts and reforms. Explain why your answer is correct.
   a. to underscore how British rule has oppressed the Indian people
   b. to praise the British for trying to make reforms to help the Indian people
   c. to remind the British that they need to initiate more reforms
   d. to persuade the British that he can help them with ruling India

_____

_____

9. Select the answer which contains a supporting point for Gandhi's assertion that "the British connection had made India more helpless than she ever was before, politically and economically." Explain why the answer you chose is correct.
   a. "A disarmed India has no power of resistance against any aggressor if she wanted to engage in an armed conflict with him."
   b. "This cottage industry, so vital for India's existence, has been ruined by incredibly heartless and inhuman processes as described by English witnesses."
   c. "I have no doubt whatsoever that both England and the town dwellers of India will have to answer, if there is a God above, for this crime against humanity which is perhaps unequaled in history."
   d. "In my opinion, the administration of the law is thus prostituted consciously or unconsciously for the benefit of the exploiter."

_____

_____

10. At the end of his speech, Gandhi tells the judge that he must either resign his post or give Gandhi the most stringent penalty under British law. Why would Gandhi's demand make his speech a memorable one to his audience?

_____

_____

Extended Response

11. In "Wartime Speech," Churchill presents his listeners with an account of the war in Europe and prepares them for their inevitable participation in it. One of the ways that Churchill presents this state of war is by infusing his own opinions about it throughout the speech. In one or two paragraphs, analyze the types of personal comments that Churchill makes and explain what effect these comments are intended to have on his listeners. Support your response with examples from the text.

12. Churchill describes the efforts of the French army in repelling the German advance in "Wartime Speech." Write a short essay in which you analyze how Churchill explains the French army's progress. Support your response with examples from the text.

13. The reader learns about Gandhi's personality from his speech "Defending Nonviolent Resistance." On the herringbone organizer below, use the diagonal lines to list the qualities of Gandhi which are evident from his speech. List examples from the speech which support the traits you have found on the horizontal lines. In a short essay, use the information from the herringbone organizer to explain what you can conclude about Gandhi's personality from this speech.

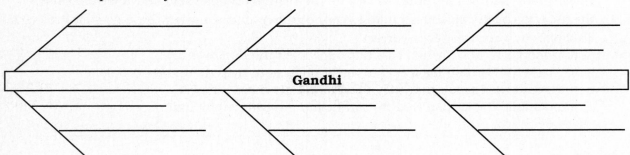

14. Gandhi's speech was delivered just before he was sentenced to six years in prison for his role in stirring up rebellion against British rule in India. However, at many points in his speech, Gandhi seems to be addressing the people of India, rather than only the sentencing judge. In a short essay, explain which segments of Gandhi's speech appear to be addressed to the Indian people, and why Gandhi would want to address them at this moment. Support your response with examples from the text.

15. Both Churchill and Gandhi advocate resistance of an oppressive force which threatens the existence of their respective societies. However, each man expresses this view differently. In an essay examine the approaches to resistance that each man advocates, and explain why these approaches are different.

Oral Response

16. Choose question 4, 10, 12, 14, or 15 or one your teacher assigns you. Take a few minutes to look through the speeches to prepare an oral response to give in class. If necessary, make notes to be clear about the order in which you want to present your answer.

Rubric for Evaluating Extended Responses

0	1	2	3	4
Blank paper Foreign language Illegible, incoherent Not enough content to score	Incorrect purpose, mode, audience Brief, vague Unelaborated Rambling Lack of language control Poor organization	Correct purpose, mode, audience Some elaboration Some details Gaps in organization Limited language control	Correct purpose, mode, audience Moderately well elaborated Clear, effective language Organized (perhaps with brief digressions)	Correct purpose, mode, audience Effective elaboration Consistent organization Sense of completeness, fluency

"**The Fiddle**" by Alan Sillitoe

Open-Book Test

Multiple Choice and Short Answer

Write your answers to all questions in this section on the lines provided.
For multiple-choice questions, circle the letter of the best answer.

1. The cottages on Harrison's Row are described in the opening paragraphs of "The Fiddle" as being "in a ruinous condition, but lived in nevertheless." What sort of mood does this description create?

   _____

   _____

2. The narrator of "The Fiddle" explains the location of Harrison's Row in the town of Nottingham. Select the answer that explains how "Harrison's Row" is described. Explain why the answer you chose is correct.
   a. It is located on an isolated edge of Nottingham.
   b. It is nestled in the center of Nottingham.
   c. It is in a rural section of Nottingham.
   d. It is located in a well-known area of Nottingham.

   _____

   _____

3. What does the story of Ted Griffin illustrate about the setting of Harrison's Row? Cite one or two examples to support your response.

   _____

   _____

4. When Jeff Bignal plays his fiddle, his neighbors listen. Choose the answer that explains the effect of Jeff's fiddle playing on his neighbors in "The Fiddle." Explain why the answer you chose is correct.
   a. "Or they opened the doors and windows so that the sound of his music drifted in . . ."
   b. "Anyone with a wireless would turn it down or off."
   c. "She smiled at seeing everyone occupied, fixed or entranced, and therefore no torment to herself . . ."
   d. "But his face was almost down and lost to the world as he sat on his chair and brought forth his first sweet notes of a summer's evening."

   _____

5. How does the setting of Harrison's Row reflect Jeff's frustrations about his job in "The Fiddle"? Write your response in the chart below.

6. Everyone in the neighborhood listens as Jeff plays his fiddle in "The Fiddle." How does

Details of setting	Effect on Jeff Bignal	Reaction of Jeff Bignal

Jeff's fiddle playing alter the mood of the story? Support your answer with one or two examples from the story.

7. Select the answer that is closest in meaning to the word *harried* as it is used in "The Fiddle." Explain why your answer choice is correct.

a. persuaded   b. commanded   c. begged   d. harassed

8. In "The Fiddle," Jeff decides to sell his fiddle and to use the proceeds from this sale to open a butcher shop. How does the following sentence reflect the reasons for Jeff's decision?

> "All he'd had to do was make up his mind, and he'd done that lying on his side at the pit face while ripping coal out with his pick and shovel."

9. In "The Fiddle," the narrator tells us that the people were disappointed that Jeff sold his fiddle because they missed the sound of his music. What does the fiddle represent to the people who live on Harrison's Row?

10. At the end of "The Fiddle," the reader learns about what ultimately happens to the residents of Harrison's Row. Choose the answer that explains the mood that this account establishes at the end of the story. Explain why your answer choice is correct.

a. The account establishes an atmosphere of resiliency.
b. The account establishes an atmosphere of anger.
c. The account establishes an atmosphere of sadness.
d. The account establishes an atmosphere of hopelessness.

Extended Response

11. In "The Fiddle," the River Leen plays a prominent role as a part of the setting of the story. In one or two paragraphs, explain how the River Leen contributes to the depressing mood of the story. Support your response with examples from the text.

12. Jeff Bignal, the main character in "The Fiddle," sells his fiddle in order to make a new start in life. Earlier in the story, this fiddle is a source of comfort to Jeff as he struggles to manage the difficulties of his job and his life. In one or two paragraphs, analyze Jeff's personality, based on how he uses his fiddle. Support your response with examples from the text.

13. The setting and the mood in "The Fiddle" work together to give the reader an impression of the difficult lives that the people of Harrison's Row lead. In a short essay, explain what details in the story illustrate the poverty of these people.

14. Jeff complains that "it was hard on a man not to see daylight for weeks at a time." In a brief essay, analyze how the interplay between light and darkness works to reflect Jeff's feelings about his life in "The Fiddle."

15. Despite the hardships faced by the people in "The Fiddle," the narrator regards them with a degree of respect. In an essay, analyze how the narrator's attitude is presented in the story.

Oral Response

16. Choose question 5, 6, 11, 14, or 15 or one your teacher assigns you. Take a few minutes to look through "The Fiddle" to prepare an oral response to give in class. If necessary, make notes to be clear about the order in which you want to present your answer.

Rubric for Evaluating Extended Responses

0	1	2	3	4
Blank paper	Incorrect purpose, mode, audience	Correct purpose, mode, audience	Correct purpose, mode, audience	Correct purpose, mode, audience
Foreign language	Brief, vague	Some elaboration	Moderately well elaborated	Effective elaboration
Illegible, incoherent	Unelaborated	Some details	Clear, effective language	Consistent organization
Not enough content to score	Rambling	Gaps in organization	Organized (perhaps with brief digressions)	Sense of completeness, fluency
	Lack of language control	Limited language control		
	Poor organization			

Name _____ Date _____

"The Distant Past" by William Trevor

Open-Book Test

Multiple Choice and Short Answer

Write your answers to all questions in this section on the lines provided.
For multiple-choice questions, circle the letter of the best answer.

1. In "The Distant Past," the Middletons are described as struggling to support themselves. Choose the answer that indicates the cause of their financial demise. Explain why your answer choice is correct.
   a. Maintaining the house wiped out their finances.
   b. Their father mortgaged the estate to support a Dublin woman.
   c. The war wiped out their savings.
   d. The Middletons gave most of their money to their church.

   _____

   _____

2. In "The Distant Past," the Middletons' relationship with the townspeople is not only illustrated by their interactions with them, but it is also represented by the way that their estate is described. How does the description of the estate illustrate the Middletons' connection to the town?

   _____

   _____

3. The brother and sister in "The Distant Past" make "no secret of their continuing loyalty to the past." What social conflict is alluded to in this statement?

   _____

   _____

4. Select the word that is closest in meaning to the word *anachronism* as it is used in the story. Explain why the answer you chose is correct.
   a. a symbol of the present era   c. zealous patriotism
   b. something that is out of its proper time in history   d. a disturbing vision or dream

   _____

   _____

5. How did the town benefit from the end of the war? Support your response with one or two examples from the story.

   _____

   _____

6. The narrator in "The Distant Past" describes items owned by the Middletons which hearken to their family heritage. Among these items is a piece of ancient Irish linen on which is presented the Cross of St. George. What does this item symbolize about the political situation in the story?

   _____

   _____

7. During one of their visits to town, the Middletons discuss the bombing of the post offices in Belfast with Fat Driscoll. Why does Miss Middleton regard this conversation as an example of a "game" that she and her brother play with their neighbors?

_____

_____

8. After hearing the news that British soldiers have landed in Northern Ireland, the townspeople's attitude toward the Middletons changes. Select the answer which explains how and why the townspeople's attitude changes.
   a. The townspeople are no longer friendly to the Middletons. They see the Middletons as a symbol of the landing of the troops.
   b. The townspeople are no longer friendly to the Middletons. They resent the fact that their father had connections to the British armed forces.
   c. The townspeople no longer like the Middletons. They have lost respect for them now that the British troops have landed.
   d. The townspeople no longer like the Middletons. They are jealous of the Middletons' ties to Britain.

_____

_____

9. In "The Distant Past," the Middletons put away many old family mementos. "They did not remove these articles in fear but in mourning for the _modus vivendi_ that had existed for long between them and the people of the town." Explain what you learn about the change in the Middletons' relationship with the townspeople from this quotation.

_____

_____

10. In "The Distant Past," why does Miss Middleton assert that, despite the economic hardships that she and her brother have endured over the years, the _modus vivendi_ had been easy for them, because, "you could take a pride out of living in peace"? What can you conclude from this quotation about what Miss Middleton values? Choose the correct answer. Explain why the answer you chose is correct.
   a. She values material goods over spiritual well-being.
   b. She values her lifestyle over peace.
   c. She values the distant past over the present.
   d. She values her connections to her neighbors over material comforts.

_____

_____

Extended Response

11. "The Distant Past" chronicles both the situation of the Middletons in their Irish village and the political situation in Ireland. In a short essay, explain how the deterioration of the Middletons' relationship with their neighbors parallels the deterioration of the political situation in Ireland and Northern Ireland. Support your response with examples from the story.

12. The deterioration of the Middletons' social position and material wealth occurred many years ago, yet the story is entitled "The Distant Past." In a short essay explain why this title is an appropriate one for the story. Support your response with examples from the story.

13. After she has realized that the friendships she and her brother have forged with the people of the town have been destroyed, Miss Middleton feels that "because of the distant past, they would die friendless. It was worse than being murdered in their beds." In a short essay, evaluate the types of friendships that the Middletons have developed in "The Distant Past" and explain why the Middletons would value them so much. Support your response with examples from the story.

14. "The Distant Past" presents the reader with the Middletons' insistence on remaining devoted to England, even though they live in Ireland. On the herringbone organizer below, use the diagonal lines to list the qualities of the Middletons' personalities. Cite examples from the text to support your findings on the horizontal lines. Then using the information from the organizer, write an essay about the personal qualities of the Middletons that have enabled them to live among people whose beliefs oppose theirs.

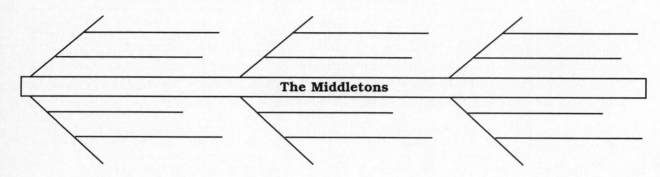

15. In "The Distant Past," visitors to the town remark that "it was a pleasant wonder . . . that old wounds could heal so completely, that the Middletons continued in their loyalty to the past, and that, in spite of it, they were respected in the town." In one or two paragraphs, explain why this comment is ironic.

Oral Response

16. Choose question 2, 5, 8, 12, or 15 or one your teacher assigns you. Take a few minutes to look through the story to prepare an oral response to give in class. If necessary, make notes to be clear about the order in which you want to present your answer.

Rubric for Evaluating Extended Responses

0	1	2	3	4
Blank paper	Incorrect purpose, mode, audience	Correct purpose, mode, audience	Correct purpose, mode, audience	Correct purpose, mode, audience
Foreign language	Brief, vague	Some elaboration	Moderately well elaborated	Effective elaboration
Illegible, incoherent	Unelaborated	Some details	Clear, effective language	Consistent organization
Not enough content to score	Rambling	Gaps in organization	Organized (perhaps with brief digressions)	Sense of completeness, fluency
	Lack of language control	Limited language control		
	Poor organization			

"Follower" and **"Two Lorries"** by Seamus Heaney
"Outside History" by Eavan Boland

Open-Book Test

Multiple Choice and Short Answer

Write your answers to all questions in this section on the lines provided.
For multiple-choice questions, circle the letter of the best answer.

1. In "Follower," Heaney describes a father-son relationship from the son's perspective. Choose the answer which explains how the son feels about his father. Explain why the answer you chose is correct.
    a. The son admires his father.   c. The son is annoyed with his father.
    b. The son is jealous of his father.   d. The son is intimidated by his father.

    _____

    _____

2. The farmer's son, who is the speaker in "Follower," follows his father around the farm, watching him perform the daily chores. Summarize what the son observes the father accomplishing in stanza two.

    _____

    _____

3. Heaney's chooses his words carefully for "Follower." Explain how the words in stanza five of the poem reflect the desire of the speaker to be like his father.

    _____

    _____

4. In the last stanza of "Follower," the speaker tells us that the roles of father and son have been reversed. What does this role reversal represent about the change in the relationship between father and son?

    _____

    _____

5. In the first three stanzas of "Two Lorries," the speaker describes an encounter between his mother and a coal man. What is the speaker's impression of this encounter? Support your response with one or two examples from the poem.

    _____

    _____

6. In stanzas four and five of "Two Lorries," the speaker has a vision that his mother is killed by the explosion of the second lorry. Which lines from the poem prove that this incident occurred in the speaker's imagination? Explain why the answer you chose is correct.
    a. lines 25–27   b. lines 28–30   c. lines 31–34   d. lines 35–37

    _____

    _____

7. What does the speaker's account of the explosion of the second lorry (stanzas 5–6) reveal about his attitude toward violence? Support your answer with one or two examples from the poem.

_____

_____

8. How does the word choice affect the meaning of the following stanza? Explain why the answer you chose is correct.

> As you heft a load of dust that was Magherafelt,
> Then reappear from your lorry as my mother's
> Dreamboat coalman filmed in silk-white ashes.

   a. Words like *reappear*, *dreamboat*, and *filmed* reinforce the unreal quality of the incident of the second lorry.
   b. The word *dreamboat* emphasizes the mother's attraction to the coalman.
   c. "Heft a load of dust" produces an image of the hard work of the coalman.
   d. The word *reappear* serves to remind the reader that the mother and the coalman met twice.

_____

_____

9. In "Outside History," the speaker refers to stars as "outside history" (line 6). How does this choice of words provide a contrast to the speaker's experience? Explain why the answer you chose is correct.
   a. The stars and light from them have no direct impact on the workings of people on Earth, but the speaker decides to become an active maker of history.
   b. While it takes thousands of years for the light of the stars to reach Earth, the speaker decides to work in the darkness.
   c. While the stars' light isn't bright enough to alert the speaker to the dangers on Earth, she is able to recognize them anyway.
   d. While the stars shine light on Earth, the speaker moves to a darker place.

_____

_____

10. In stanzas five and six of "Outside History," the speaker becomes aware of the condition of society. Which answer best summarizes what the speaker realizes? Explain why the answer you chose is correct.
   a. The society is filled with death and destruction.
   b. The society is plunged into darkness.
   c. The society is flooded by rivers.
   d. The society's fields have been destroyed.

_____

_____

Extended Response

11. In "Follower," Seamus Heaney describes a relationship between a farmer and his son. In a short essay, explain how the act of farming, as it is described in the poem, effectively portrays this relationship.

12. "Two Lorries" incorporates the image of a lorry to illustrate two different events—the mother's flirtations with a coalman, and the lorry that explodes and kills the speaker's mother in a dream that he has. In one or two paragraphs, explain how Heaney uses the lorry in these two different contexts to convey his opposition to violence.

13. The poetic structure of "Two Lorries" incorporates the sestina. In a short essay, identify the ideas that Heaney recycles within the sestina and explain what these ideas describe in the poem.

14. In "Outside History," the speaker chronicles the effect of her decision to become more involved in shaping the "ordeal" of history (line 14). Using the Venn diagram below, identify the concrete and abstract images in the poem, and what they represent. Then, in a short essay, explain how Boland uses these concrete and abstract images to illustrate this view of history. Support your response with examples from the poem.

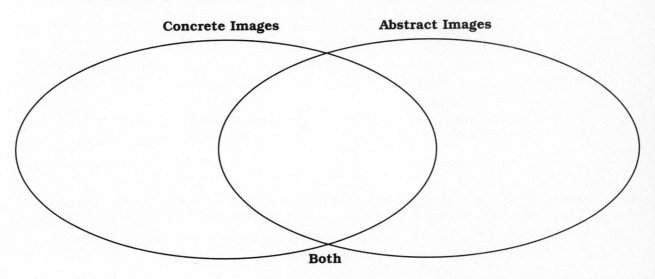

Concrete Images   **Abstract Images**

Both

15. In "Outside History," Boland uses an improvised free verse to structure her poem. In an essay, explain how this structure emphasizes the speaker's assertion that one must become involved in events in order to change them.

Oral Response

16. Choose question 1, 8, 9, 11, or 12 or one your teacher assigns you. Take a few minutes to look through the poems to prepare an oral response to give in class. If necessary, make notes to be clear about the order in which you want to present your answer.

Rubric for Evaluating Extended Responses

0	1	2	3	4
Blank paper Foreign language Illegible, incoherent Not enough content to score	Incorrect purpose, mode, audience Brief, vague Unelaborated Rambling Lack of language control Poor organization	Correct purpose, mode, audience Some elaboration Some details Gaps in organization Limited language control	Correct purpose, mode, audience Moderately well elaborated Clear, effective language Organized (perhaps with brief digressions)	Correct purpose, mode, audience Effective elaboration Consistent organization Sense of completeness, fluency

"**No Witchcraft for Sale**" by Doris Lessing

Open-Book Test

Multiple Choice and Short Answer

Write your answers to all questions in this section on the lines provided.
For multiple-choice questions, circle the letter of the best answer.

1. The Farquars' son, Teddy, and the servant, Gideon, develop a special relationship in "No Witchcraft for Sale." Describe this relationship, citing one or two examples from the story to support your response.

   _____

   _____

2. When Teddy is six years old, he teases Gideon's youngest son. What do Teddy's remarks about Gideon's son reflect about Teddy's views of the native African people? Explain why the answer you chose is correct.
   a. He views the Africans as his equals.   c. He is biased against the Africans.
   b. He views the Africans as his friends.   d. He respects the Africans.

   _____

   _____

3. Gideon remarks that it is "God's will" that the white child will grow up to be a master and the black child will grow up to be a servant. What does this remark reflect about Gideon's view of the social structure in colonial Africa? Explain your answer choice.
   a. It is unknown how this social structure developed.
   b. This social structure was mandated by religious teachings.
   c. The social structure was destined to be this way.
   d. The social structure is something which Africans are unable to control but are forced to accept.

   _____

   _____

4. In "No Witchcraft for Sale" how do Mrs. Farquar and Gideon react when they realize that a poisonous snake has spit in Teddy's eyes? Write your response in the Venn diagram below.

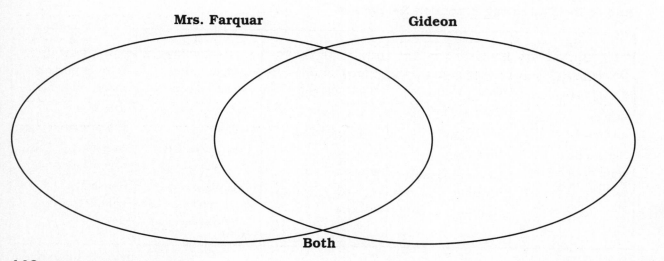

5. In "No Witchcraft for Sale," why does Gideon refuse to show the scientist the location of the plant that he used to heal Teddy's eyes?

_____

_____

6. In "No Witchcraft for Sale," Gideon refuses to reveal the identity of the plant. What does the scientist's reaction to this reveal about the cultural conflict between Europeans and Africans regarding medicine and healing?

_____

_____

7. Choose the answer that contains the definition for the word *incredulously*, as used in the sentence below from "No Witchcraft for Sale." Explain how the information in the sentence helped you to select your answer.

> He spoke incredulously, as if he could not believe his old friends could so betray him.

a. in a doubting manner   c. in a terrified manner

b. in an exaggerated manner   d. in an angry manner

_____

_____

8. In "No Witchcraft for Sale," the Farquars are surprised and angry that Gideon refuses to reveal the location of the plant. Choose the answer that identifies the cultural conflict between the Farquars and Gideon. Explain why the answer you chose is correct.

a. The Farquars see the plant as a potentially valuable asset to the scientific community, while Gideon views the Farquars' insistence about revealing the location of the plant as a symbol of their authority and control over him.

b. While the Farquars see the plant as a valuable asset to science, Gideon is insulted at the idea that the scientists would profit from it.

c. Gideon would have shown the scientists the location of the plant, but the Farquars asked him to do it in a way that is considered impolite by his people.

d. Gideon cannot show the scientist where the plant is located because he has been sworn to secrecy about it.

_____

_____

9. In the final incident of the story, Teddy and Gideon share a joke over Gideon's refusal to reveal the plant to the scientist. How does the last paragraph of "No Witchcraft for Sale" reflect the relationship that Gideon and Teddy have?

_____

_____

10. Based on how he speaks to Gideon in the last two paragraphs of "No Witchcraft for Sale," what can you conclude about the way that Teddy treats Gideon?

_____

_____

Extended Response

11. In "No Witchcraft for Sale," Lessing examines the British colonization of Africa from the perspective of the Farquar family and their servant, Gideon. In a short essay, analyze how the Farquars assert their authority over Gideon, and how Gideon reacts to it.

12. Gideon's relationship to Teddy in "No Witchcraft for Sale" appears to be a caring one—even after Teddy insults Gideon with his racist remark about Gideon's son. In a short essay, explain how this relationship represented British attitudes toward native Africans. Support your response with examples from the story.

13. Although Gideon and the Farquars are separated by a large cultural gap in "No Witchcraft for Sale," their overall coexistence appears to be a relatively peaceful one. In one or two paragraphs, explain how Gideon and the Farquars manage to live together so peacefully for so long.

14. In "No Witchcraft for Sale," the reader learns about many aspects of Gideon's personality, based on his interactions with the Farquars. In a short essay, explain what you have learned about Gideon's personality from this story. Support your response with examples from the story.

15. The scientist in "No Witchcraft for Sale" wants to acquire the plant that Gideon used to treat Teddy's eyes. He wants this plant for both its medicinal and monetary value. In an essay, explain what the scientist's desire for the plant reflects about the goals and attitudes of the British colonizers of Africa. Support your response with examples from the text.

Oral Response

16. Choose question 3, 4, 8, 12, or 13 or one your teacher assigns you. Take a few minutes to look through "No Witchcraft For Sale" to prepare an oral response to give in class. If necessary, make notes to be clear about the order in which you want to present your answer.

Rubric for Evaluating Extended Responses

0	1	2	3	4
Blank paper	Incorrect purpose, mode, audience	Correct purpose, mode, audience	Correct purpose, mode, audience	Correct purpose, mode, audience
Foreign language	Brief, vague	Some elaboration	Moderately well elaborated	Effective elaboration
Illegible, incoherent	Unelaborated	Some details	Clear, effective language	Consistent organization
Not enough content to score	Rambling	Gaps in organization	Organized (perhaps with brief digressions)	Sense of completeness, fluency
	Lack of language control	Limited language control		
	Poor organization			

"The Lagoon" by Joseph Conrad
"Araby" by James Joyce

Open-Book Test

Multiple Choice and Short Answer

Write your answers to all questions in this section on the lines provided.
For multiple-choice questions, circle the letter of the best answer.

1. The narrator in "The Lagoon" describes the environment around Arsat's clearing in great detail. Explain how this description reflects the mood of Arsat's story.

   _____

   _____

2. Tuan's oarsmen are reluctant to spend the night on Arsat's lagoon. Why would the men prefer to sleep somewhere else?

   _____

   _____

3. Arsat recalls how his brother died while assisting him in his efforts to take Diamelen away from the Ruler. Choose the answer that explains how Arsat feels about his brother's death. Explain why the answer you chose is correct.
   a. relief   b. confusion   c. anger   d. guilt

   _____

   _____

4. In "The Lagoon," why does Arsat decide to return to the domain of the Ruler?

   _____

   _____

5. After Diamelen dies, Arsat says, "She has died and now . . . darkness." Choose the quotation from "The Lagoon" that best illustrates why Arsat feels that Diamelen's death has brought him darkness.
   a. " . . . and I remembered the stirring times, and I always remembered you, Tuan, till the time came when my eyes could see nothing in the past, because they looked upon the one who is dying there—in the house."
   b. "But I fed the hunger of my heart on short glances and stealthy words."
   c. "And could I not with her find a country where death is forgotten—where death is unknown!"
   d. "What did I care who died? I wanted peace in my own heart."

   _____

   _____

6. The white man in "The Lagoon" speaks very little throughout the story. He briefly responds to Arsat's questions or comments. Why is the character of the white man necessary to convey Arsat's story to the reader?

   _____

   _____

7. Choose the word that is most opposite in meaning to *imperturbable* in the following sentence. Explain why the answer you chose is correct.

   The other houses of the street, conscious of decent lives within them, gazed at one another with brown imperturbable faces.

   a. flat   b. dark   c. emotional   d. calm

   _____

   _____

8. In "Araby," the narrator has a crush on Mangan's sister. How does the narrator's act of watching this girl leave her house help you to realize how much he likes her?

   _____

   _____

9. After the narrator speaks to Mangan's sister about the bazaar, he tells her that if he goes to Araby, he will bring a gift for her. How does the narrator's behavior at home and in school show how this decision has affected him? Cite one or two examples from "Araby" to support your response.

   _____

   _____

10. When the narrator in "Araby" reaches the bazaar, he finds that many of the stalls are closed, and there is little from which to choose as a gift for Mangan's sister. This discovery leads him to an eqiphany. Choose the answer which best sums up the realization he has at the end of the story. Explain your answer choice.
    a. The futility of finding a gift parallels the futility of winning the girl's affection.
    b. Because there were no gifts to purchase, the narrator feels that he has missed his chance to impress the girl.
    c. The offhanded treatment of the narrator by the salesgirl offends the narrator.
    d. The narrator is annoyed that he didn't have more time to look for a gift.

   _____

   _____

Extended Response

11. In "The Lagoon," Arsat tells Tuan the story of his relationship with Diamelen. In one or two paragraphs, explain why Arsat's emotions change while he tells this story. Support your response with examples from the story.

12. "The Lagoon" contains a story within a story. Arsat gives his own account in the inner story of "The Lagoon." In one or two paragraphs, explain why it is necessary that Arsat, and not another narrator, gives his own account of what has happened to him. Support your response with examples from the story.

13. In "The Lagoon," Arsat chooses his love for Diamelen over his duty to his brother. On the diagonal lines of the herringbone organizer below, list several different aspects of Arsat's personality. On the horizontal lines, cite examples that support the aspects you have listed. Then, in a short essay, use the information that you have compiled to explain why Arsat is an admirable character.

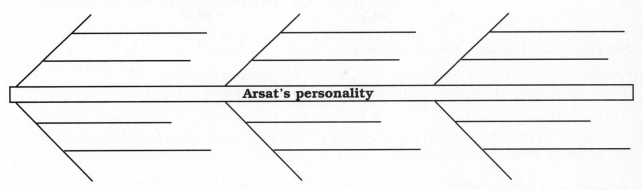

Arsat's personality

14. "Araby" examines how a young boy's crush on a neighborhood girl affects his daily life. In a brief essay, explain how the narrator's fantasies about Mangan's sister serve to heighten his anger at the end of the story.

15. In "Araby," Joyce describes the setting of the story in great detail. In an essay, examine how the setting of the story reflects the emotional condition of the narrator.

Oral Response

16. Choose question 1, 8, 11, 13, or 14 or one your teacher assigns you. Take a few minutes to look through the stories to prepare an oral response to give in class. If necessary, make notes to be clear about the order in which you want to present your answer.

Rubric for Evaluating Extended Responses

0	1	2	3	4
Blank paper Foreign language Illegible, incoherent Not enough content to score	Incorrect purpose, mode, audience Brief, vague Unelaborated Rambling Lack of language control Poor organization	Correct purpose, mode, audience Some elaboration Some details Gaps in organization Limited language control	Correct purpose, mode, audience Moderately well elaborated Clear, effective language Organized (perhaps with brief digressions)	Correct purpose, mode, audience Effective elaboration Consistent organization Sense of completeness, fluency

"The Lady in the Looking Glass: A Reflection" by Virginia Woolf
"The First Year of My Life" by Muriel Spark

Open-Book Test

Multiple Choice and Short Answer

Write your answers to all questions in this section on the lines provided.
For multiple-choice questions, circle the letter of the best answer.

1. In "The Lady in the Looking Glass: A Reflection," the narrator compares her observation of Isabella's house through a looking glass to the work of a "naturalist." Why does the narrator make this comparison?

   _____

   _____

2. The narrator in "The Lady in the Looking Glass: A Reflection" surmises that Isabella went to the lower garden to pick flowers. Why does the narrator think that Isabella would pick "something light and fantastic and leafy and trailing, traveler's joy, or . . . convolvulus that twine around ugly walls"? Explain why the answer you chose is correct.
   a. The narrator suggested to Isabella that she should pick these types of flowers.
   b. The narrator gets the impression that these flowers reflect Isabella's personality.
   c. The narrator found out from Isabella that she prefers these types of flowers.
   d. The narrator saw Isabella picking these flowers through observations made in the looking glass.

   _____

   _____

3. Flowers in Isabella's garden are repeatedly mentioned in "The Lady in the Looking Glass: A Reflection." Choose the answer that explains what the flowers symbolize in this story. Explain why the answer you chose is correct.
   a. The flowers represent the narrator's unproven perceptions about Isabella's personality.
   b. The flowers represent the narrator's knowledge about Isabella's personality.
   c. The flowers represent the beauty of Isabella's garden.
   d. The flowers represent Isabella's interests.

   _____

   _____

4. How well does the narrator know Isabella in "The Lady in the Looking Glass: A Reflection"? Support your answer with examples from the story.

   _____

   _____

5. How do the narrator's perceptions of Isabella, as they are reflected in the looking glass, contrast with the real Isabella in "The Lady in the Looking Glass: A Reflection"? Support your response with one or two examples from the text.

   _____

   _____

6. Based on how *discerned* is used in "The First Year of My Life," choose the correct definition. Explain your answer choice.
   a. heard clearly
   b. recognized as separate
   c. imagined
   d. became confused about

   _____

   _____

7. The narrator of "The First Year of My Life" is a baby who recounts the events of the last months of World War I. How does the narrator account for her storytelling power?

   _____

   _____

8. The baby narrator of "The First Year of My Life" describes the mourning women as "These careless women in black always losing their husbands and their brothers." What does this tell you about the baby's understanding of the war?

   _____

   _____

9. What is the purpose of the poems that are alluded to throughout "The First Year of My Life"? Explain your answer choice with references to the story.
   a. The poems emphasize the contrast between the normal life and growth of the baby and the destruction of war.
   b. The poems show what is in the mind of the adults versus what is in the mind of the baby.
   c. The poems illustrate how the baby's life is related to the events of the war.
   d. The poems reveal the personality of the adults in the baby's world.

   _____

   _____

10. One of the guests at the baby's birthday party in "The First Year of My Life" recites Lord Asquith's remarks after the war had ended. Why does his recitation of this remark cause the baby to smile?

   _____

   _____

Extended Response

11. The narrator of "The Lady in the Looking Glass: A Reflection" forms many conclusions about Isabella based on the observations that she makes in the looking glass of Isabella's house. In one or two paragraphs, explain what the mirror represents in this story. Support your response with examples from the story.

12. In "The Lady in the Looking Glass: A Reflection," Woolf employs a stream-of-consciousness technique when she has the narrator speculate about Isabella's personality and life. In a short essay, analyze how this technique serves to emphasize the contrast between Isabella's imagined and actual lives.

13. The narrator in "The First Year of My Life" is a baby who simultaneously provides an account of her development during the first year of her life and the events of the last months of World War I. In a short essay, evaluate how effectively this contrast emphasizes the horrors of the war. Support your response with examples from the story.

14. The narrator of "The First Year of My Life" describes her first year of life in great detail. In an essay, explain how the baby's physical actions—kicking, scowling, and smiling, for example—represent reactions to news about World War I.

15. Examine the reliability of the narrators in "The Lady in the Looking Glass: A Reflection" and "The First Year of My Life." Using the Venn diagram below, list what makes them believable storytellers, and what makes you skeptical about them. Then write an essay comparing and contrasting the reliability of the two narrators. Based on your analysis, conclude which narrator is more reliable.

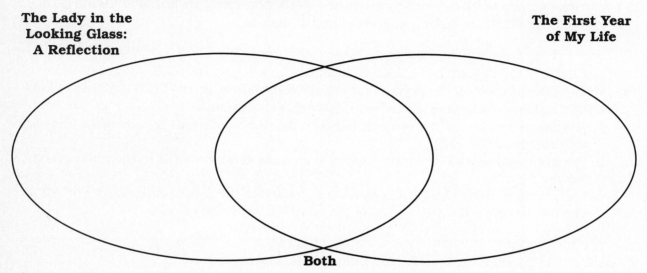

The Lady in the Looking Glass: A Reflection

The First Year of My Life

Both

Oral Response

16. Choose question 4, 9, 11, 13, or 15 or one your teacher assigns you. Take a few minutes to look through the stories to prepare an oral response to give in class. If necessary, make notes to be clear about the order in which you want to present your answer.

Rubric for Evaluating Extended Responses

0	1	2	3	4
Blank paper Foreign language Illegible, incoherent Not enough content to score	Incorrect purpose, mode, audience Brief, vague Unelaborated Rambling Lack of language control Poor organization	Correct purpose, mode, audience Some elaboration Some details Gaps in organization Limited language control	Correct purpose, mode, audience Moderately well elaborated Clear, effective language Organized (perhaps with brief digressions)	Correct purpose, mode, audience Effective elaboration Consistent organization Sense of completeness, fluency

"The Rocking-Horse Winner" by D. H. Lawrence
"A Shocking Accident" by Graham Greene

Open-Book Test

Multiple Choice and Short Answer

Write your answers to all questions in this section on the lines provided.
For multiple-choice questions, circle the letter of the best answer.

1. In "The Rocking-Horse Winner," the mother is described as having no luck even though she "started out with all the advantages." Identify two examples from the text which show that the mother has no luck.

    _____

    _____

2. The narrator of "The Rocking-Horse Winner" describes how the children's toys heard the whisper, "There must be more money." Why is it significant that the toys "hear" this remark?

    _____

    _____

3. In "The Rocking-Horse Winner," what is *luck* to Paul? Explain why your answer choice is correct.
    a. Luck is a concept that is beyond human understanding.
    b. Luck is an idea that only resides in the imagination.
    c. Luck is a tangible object that can be found and used.
    d. Luck is an actual place which a person can visit.

    _____

    _____

4. As Paul rides his rocking-horse, he is somehow able to determine the names of winning racehorses. He bets on these horses and wins money. At the end of "The Rocking-Horse Winner," however, Paul dies as a result of riding his rocking-horse. What does the rocking-horse represent in this story?

    _____

    _____

5. At the end of "The Rocking-Horse Winner," Paul's mother is described as "heart-frozen," she feels "that her heart had gone, turned actually into a stone." Which answer describes the mother's feelings for her son? Explain why your answer choice is correct on the lines provided.
    a. detachment   b. anger   c. annoyance   d. concern

    _____

    _____

6. After Paul dies, his Uncle Oscar tells the mother, "My God, Hester, you're eighty-odd thousand to the good, and a poor devil of a son to the bad. But, poor devil, poor devil, he's best gone out of a life where he rides his rocking-horse to find a winner." How does Uncle Oscar's remark reflect the theme of "The Rocking-Horse Winner"?

_____

_____

7. In "A Shocking Accident," the young Jerome is told by his housemaster that his father was killed when a pig fell on him. Why does the housemaster have such difficulty conveying this news to Jerome?

_____

_____

8. How does Jerome's question "What happened to the pig?" in "A Shocking Accident" suggest Greene's belief that life is basically absurd?

_____

_____

9. Based on how *embarked* is used in the sentence from "A Shocking Accident," select the correct definition for it. Explain your answer choice.

    . . .it pained him when his aunt embarked with strangers on the story
      of his father's death.

a. share an idea   c. disagreed in principle
b. set out to tell   d. changed the subject

_____

10. Why does Jerome rehearse two different versions of the story of his father's death in "A Shocking Accident"? Explain your answer choice.

a. Jerome wants to find a way to minimize the humor in the story of his father's death.
b. Jerome wants to find a version of the story that will contradict his aunt's version.
c. Jerome wants to find a version of the story that will memorialize his father.
d. Jerome wants to hide the true story from Sally.

_____

_____

Extended Response

11. What types of relationships exist among the family members in "The Rocking-Horse Winner," by D. H. Lawrence? What keeps the family members, especially Paul and his mother, connected to each other? In a short essay, support your response with examples from the story.

12. Paul dies at the end of "The Rocking horse Winner" after he takes one last ride on his rocking-horse. In a short essay, identify the theme of this story and explain how the rocking-horse and Paul's connection to it illustrate this theme.

13. After his mother tells him that she has no luck, Paul rides his rocking horse in order to find luck, in order to make enough money to quiet the whispers in the house. In one or two paragraphs, explain how Paul would define the word *luck* in "The Rocking-Horse Winner." Support your response with examples from the story.

© Prentice-Hall, Inc.

14. "A Shocking Accident" recounts the long-term effects that the father's death has on Jerome's behavior. In a brief essay, explain why "A Shocking Accident" is an ironic title for this story.

15. In "A Shocking Accident," Jerome tries to deal with his father's death and move on with his life. Despite his efforts to move on, Jerome still appears as an absurd character. On the diagonal lines of the herringbone organizer list the examples of what Jerome says and does that prove that he is an absurd character. Write the proof for the examples that you have listed on the horizontal lines. Using the information from the herringbone organizer, write an essay in which you explain how Greene uses the character of Jerome to illustrate his belief that human existence is irrational.

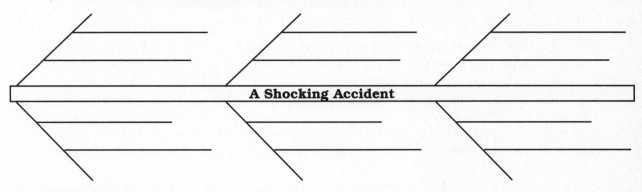

A Shocking Accident

Oral Response

16. Choose question 4, 6, 11, 13, or 14 or one your teacher assigns you. Take a few minutes to look through the stories to prepare an oral response to give in class. If necessary, make notes to be clear about the order in which you want to present your answer.

Rubric for Evaluating Extended Responses

0	1	2	3	4
Blank paper Foreign language Illegible, incoherent Not enough content to score	Incorrect purpose, mode, audience Brief, vague Unelaborated Rambling Lack of language control Poor organization	Correct purpose, mode, audience Some elaboration Some details Gaps in organization Limited language control	Correct purpose, mode, audience Moderately well elaborated Clear, effective language Organized (perhaps with brief digressions)	Correct purpose, mode, audience Effective elaboration Consistent organization Sense of completeness, fluency

"Do Not Go Gentle into That Good Night" and **"Fern Hill"**
by Dylan Thomas
"The Horses" and **"The Rain Horse"** by Ted Hughes

Open Book Test

Multiple Choice and Short Answer

Write your answers to all questions in this section on the lines provided.
For multiple-choice questions, circle the letter of the best answer.

1. Dylan Thomas's use of certain poetic devices helps create a distinctive voice. What poetic devices does he use in stanza two of "Do Not Go Gentle into That Good Night"? Explain why your answer choice is correct.
   a. phrases run into each other; alliteration is used to emphasize emotions within the poem
   b. phrases lack punctuation; rhyme is repeated in other stanzas
   c. phrases continue with the same image; rhyme is used to emphasize the importance of the image
   d. phrases lack appropriate punctuation; last line is used as a refrain

   _____

   _____

2. In "Do Not Go Gentle into That Good Night," the speaker addresses his dying father. Why does he beg the father to "Curse me, bless me now with your fierce tears"? (line 17)

   _____

   _____

3. In "Fern Hill," the speaker reflects on how he has dealt with the passage of time. How does the speaker use nature to establish the happy mood of his youth in the first three stanzas? Support your response with one or two examples from the poem.

   _____

   _____

   _____

4. How does the speaker in "Fern Hill" suggest that Time, and not he, controls the course that his life has taken? Explain your answer choice.
   a. The speaker has been forced by Time to remain on the farm.
   b. The speaker explains that he is the child of Time.
   c. The speaker describes his fight against Time for control of his life.
   d. The speaker states that Time has allowed him to enjoy his youth.

   _____

   _____

   _____

5. In "Fern Hill," the speaker looks back on the days of his youth and concludes his reminiscences with the lines "Time held me green and dying/Though I sang in my chains like the sea" (lines 54–55). How does the mood of the first five stanzas contrast with the mood established in these last two lines of the poem? Explain why the answer you chose is correct.
   a. The mood shifts from confused to happy.
   b. The mood shifts from happy to melancholy.
   c. The mood shifts from carefree to enraged.
   d. The mood shifts from wistful to confused.

   _____

   _____

6. In "The Horses," the speaker presents his observations to the reader in densely grouped descriptive phrases. How does this structure, as it is used in stanza four, prepare the reader for the speaker's sighting of the horses?

   _____

   _____

7. Hughes contrasts the gray color of the horses with the intense colors of the environment in which he finds them in "The Horses." How does this color contrast convey the speaker's impression of the horses?

   _____

   _____

8. In lines 35–38 of "The Horses," the speaker asserts, "In the din of the crowded streets, going among the years, the faces,/May I still meet my memory in so lonely a place/Between the streams and the red clouds, hearing curlews,/Hearing the horizons endure." What message about the importance of his memory of the horses does the speaker convey through these lines?

   _____

   _____

9. What is the meaning of the word *transfiguring*, as it is used in the following passage from "The Rain Horse":
   > Not that he had looked forward to any very transfiguring experience. But he had expected something, some pleasure, some meaningful sensation, he didn't know quite what.

   How does the context of these sentences assist you in determining the meaning?
   a. changing the appearance of   c. explaining the existence of
   b. manipulating the emotions of   d. denying the validity of

   _____

   _____

10. In "The Rain Horse," the man takes a walk on the land that he had left twelve years earlier. What do the choice of words and use of sound devices in paragraph two of the story convey about what the man sees and feels?

   _____

   _____

Extended Response

11. In "Do Not Go Gentle into That Good Night," the speaker attempts to persuade his father to fight against death. In a short essay, analyze how the speaker tries to persuade his father not to give in to dying. Support your response with examples from the poem.

12. In "Fern Hill," the speaker contemplates the passage of time and its effect on him. In a short essay, examine the speaker's feelings about the passage of time and why he feels this way. Support your response with examples from the poem.

13. The speaker in "The Horses" describes his awe-struck observation of horses during an early morning walk in the woods. In a short essay, analyze how his sense of awe about the horses is conveyed through Hughes's choice of words and construction of phrases.

14. The man in "The Rain Horse" struggles to overcome both his feelings of isolation from the land and his feelings about the attack of the horse. Use the diagonal lines on the herringbone organizer below to list ways the speaker deals with both issues. Use the horizontal lines to list examples supporting the speaker's behavior. Then write an essay explaining the man's relationship to the land and how it affects his reaction to the horse.

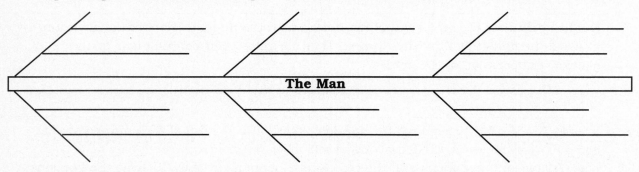

15. Both "Fern Hill" and "The Horses" employ images of the natural world to convey the speaker's thoughts about life. In a short essay, identify the main idea in each poem, and contrast how the natural imagery in each poem is used to illustrate its respective main idea.

Oral Response

16. Choose question 5, 10, 11, 13, or 14 or one your teacher assigns you. Take a few minutes to look through the poems and story to prepare an oral response to give in class. If necessary, make notes to be clear about the order in which you want to present your answer.

Rubric for Evaluating Extended Responses

0	1	2	3	4
Blank paper Foreign language Illegible, incoherent Not enough content to score	Incorrect purpose, mode, audience Brief, vague Unelaborated Rambling Lack of language control Poor organization	Correct purpose, mode, audience Some elaboration Some details Gaps in organization Limited language control	Correct purpose, mode, audience Moderately well elaborated Clear, effective language Organized (perhaps with brief digressions)	Correct purpose, mode, audience Effective elaboration Consistent organization Sense of completeness, fluency

"An Arundel Tomb" and **"The Explosion"**
by Philip Larkin
"On the Patio" by Peter Redgrove
"Not Waving but Drowning" by Stevie Smith

Open-Book Test

Multiple Choice and Short Answer

Write your answers to all questions in this section on the lines provided.
For multiple-choice questions, circle the letter of the best answer.

1. The speaker in "An Arundel Tomb" describes the tomb of the dead couple in stanza one. Select the answer that explains the narrator's first impression of the tomb. Explain why the answer you chose is correct.

   a. The narrator thinks that the tomb is typical of many others he has seen.

   b. The narrator cannot believe how ridiculous the tomb looks.

   c. The narrator is impressed with the carvings of the tomb.

   d. The narrator dislikes the decorative sculptures on the tomb.

   _____

   _____

2. Larkin uses iambic pentameter to structure the rhythm of "An Arundel Tomb." However, he occasionally breaks this rhythm when discussing certain ideas in the poem. What does the variation of the rhythm in stanza two suggest about the speaker's feelings about the carving on the tomb?

   _____

   _____

3. In the last stanza of "An Arundel Tomb," the speaker forms a judgment about the way in which the earl and countess are presented in the sculpture. Why does the speaker feel that "Time has transfigured them into/Untruth" (lines 37–38)?

   _____

   _____

4. In stanzas 1–4 of "The Explosion," Larkin describes the miners. Select the answer which states the impression of the miners presented in these stanzas. Explain why the answer you chose is correct.

   a. The miners are happy and carefree.   c. The miners are exhausted and bitter.

   b. The miners are coarse and ignorant.   d. The miners are serious and hardworking.

   _____

   _____

5. How does Larkin manipulate the rhythm of the poem in stanza five to prepare the reader for the tragic news of the deaths of the miners in "The Explosion"?

   _____

   _____

6. In "The Explosion," Larkin divides one sentence among the last stanzas of the poem. How does this division serve to clarify the image of the dead men and their wives' memory of them?

_____

_____

7. In "On the Patio," why is it significant for the speaker to note that "the rain eats everything except the glass/Of spinning water that is clear down here" (lines 9–10)? Select the answer that explains the meaning of these lines. Explain why your answer choice is correct.
   a. The rain has a destructive power, except for its ability to replenish the water in the drinking glass.
   b. The rain is being likened to a wild animal who drinks from a glass to quench its thirst.
   c. The rain symbolizes the angry mood of the poem.
   d. The rain and the speaker are engaged in a symbolic battle over the glass.

_____

_____

8. In "On the Patio," the speaker describes how the heavy rainstorm fills a wineglass with water. How is the rain represented by the physical structure of the lines in the poem?

_____

_____

9. In "Not Waving but Drowning," what might the title represent to the speaker? Support your answer with one or two examples from the poem.

_____

_____

10. Select the answer that is closest in meaning to *larking* as it is used in "Not Waving but Drowning." Explain why the answer you chose is correct.
   a. thinking   b. swimming   c. lighthearted fun   d. bird watching

_____

_____

Extended Response

11. Write an essay contrasting the impression that the tomb creates in "An Arundel Tomb" with what the speaker suggests the couple were really like when they were alive. Support your response with examples from the poem.

12. Examine the shift in mood in the poem "The Explosion." List details that convey the mood before the explosion, after the explosion and in the last line. Then write an essay based on your notes. What feeling does the final line of the poem leave with the reader?

13. The rain in "The Patio" is described as "transferring its might into a glass" (line 12), which the speaker then drinks from. In a short essay, analyze how the speaker's action illustrates the struggle for power over nature.

14. In a short essay, explain how the free verse structure of the poem "Not Waving but Drowning" underscores the emotional chaos of "the dead man." Examine the poetic device of using varying line lengths. How does this technique support the idea that the "dead one" was "much too far out all my life" (line 11)?

15. In both "An Arundel Tomb" and "Not Waving but Drowning," the speakers show how the life of a person can be misconstrued after death. Compare and contrast how the subjects of each poem are presented. Then, in an essay analyze how each poet presents the idea that one's view of a person's life can be altered by the person's death.

Oral Response

16. Choose question 2, 8, 9, 11, 13, or 15 or one your teacher assigns you. Take a few minutes to look through the poems to prepare an oral response to give in class. If necessary, make notes to be clear about the order in which you want to present your answer.

Rubric for Evaluating Extended Responses

0	1	2	3	4
Blank paper Foreign language Illegible, incoherent Not enough content to score	Incorrect purpose, mode, audience Brief, vague Unelaborated Rambling Lack of language control Poor organization	Correct purpose, mode, audience Some elaboration Some details Gaps in organization Limited language control	Correct purpose, mode, audience Moderately well elaborated Clear, effective language Organized (perhaps with brief digressions)	Correct purpose, mode, audience Effective elaboration Consistent organization Sense of completeness, fluency

"**B. Wordsworth**" by V. S. Naipul

Open-Book Test

Multiple Choice and Short Answer

Write your answers to all questions in this section on the lines provided.
For multiple-choice questions, circle the letter of the best answer.

1. In "B. Wordsworth," the narrator explains how beggars called at his house, asking for money and food. However, he describes B. Wordsworth differently than he does these beggars. What impression of B. Wordsworth does the narrator present in his initial description of the poet?

   _____

   _____

2. How does Naipul convey the impression that the narrator in "B. Wordsworth" is telling a story about an experience he had as a young boy?

   _____

   _____

3. In "B. Wordsworth," the narrator is puzzled by Wordsworth's request to watch the bees in the gru-gru palm trees. What reason does Wordsworth give for wanting to observe the bees? Explain your answer choice.
   a. Watching is an excuse for selling a poem to the narrator's mother.
   b. Wordsworth is interested in meeting other people who are interested in bees.
   c. Since he is unemployed, Wordsworth has nothing better to do.
   d. Observing nature serves as Wordsworth's inspiration for writing poetry.

   _____

   _____

4. The boy and Wordsworth develop a friendship and meet regularly. What is the significance of this friendship to the boy? Support your response with one or two examples from the poem.

   _____

   _____

5. Wordsworth takes the boy on long walks all over Port of Spain. What is Wordsworth's purpose for taking the boy on these walks? Explain your answer choice.
   a. Wordsworth is lonely and needs a companion for these walks.
   b. Wordsworth is preparing the boy to become a poet.
   c. Wordsworth is trying to keep the boy out of trouble.
   d. Wordsworth is helping the boy to avoid confrontations with his mother.

   _____

   _____

6. What does the following sentence from "B. Wordsworth" reveal about Wordsworth's personality? Explain your answer choice.

    He did everything as though he were doing some church rite.
    a. Wordsworth is a religious man.
    b. Wordsworth is a cautious man.
    c. Wordsworth takes the time to value life experiences.
    d. Wordsworth is confused about his role in life.

    _____

    _____

7. The first-person narrator in "B. Wordsworth" is a young boy who recounts his friendship with an older man. How does the narrator's view of Wordsworth affect your impression of the poet? Support your response with one or two examples from the story.

    _____

    _____

8. During the last half of "B. Wordsworth," the narrator repeatedly asserts that Wordsworth is growing older. Why does the narrator repeat this statement? Support your response with one or two examples from the story.

    _____

    _____

9. Select the word that is closest in meaning to *keenly*. Explain how the context of the sentence assists you in understanding the meaning of the word.

    And then— I felt it so keenly, it was as though I had been slapped by my mother.
    a. sharply   b. suddenly   c. strangely   d. softly

    _____

    _____

10. Before the narrator leaves Wordsworth's house for the last time in "B. Wordsworth," he tells the reader that Wordsworth says all the stories about his life are not true. Wordsworth's voice cracks when he makes this statement. What impression about Wordsworth do you form based on this information?

    _____

    _____

Extended Response

11. In "B. Wordsworth," Wordsworth tells the boy that he is in the process of writing "the greatest poem in the world." However, he only writes one line each month, and he expects to finish the poem in twenty-two years. In one or two paragraphs, explain what this poem represents to Wordsworth, and why he is taking so long to complete it. Support your answer with examples from the story.

12. Wordsworth teaches the boy how the power and value of observation lead to writing poetry in "B. Wordsworth." One year after Wordsworth dies, the boy returns to Alberto Street, where the poet lived. He describes what he sees there. In a brief essay, analyze how the last two paragraphs of the story reflect what the boy has learned from Wordsworth's lessons about the value of observation.

13. In "B. Wordsworth," the boy develops a special friendship with the old poet. In the chart below, list the qualities of B. Wordsworth that the narrator admires in the left column. In the right column, cite examples from the stories that support these qualities. Write a short essay discussing B. Wordsworth's qualities and why the boy admires them.

Wordsworth's Admirable Qualities	Examples

14. Though "B. Wordsworth" is mainly about the boy's reflections on his friendship with the poet, the reader also learns about the boy's character. In a short essay, analyze the boy's personality and the way his experiences with Wordsworth shaped it. Support your response with examples from the story.

15. In "B. Wordsworth," what is Wordsworth really looking for when he requests permission to observe the bees in the boy's yard? Answer this question in an essay.

Oral Response

16. Choose question 7, 4, 11, 12, or 14 or one your teacher assigns you. Take a few minutes to look through the story to prepare an oral response to give in class. If necessary, make notes to be clear about the order in which you want to present your answer.

Rubric for Evaluating Extended Responses

0	1	2	3	4
Blank paper Foreign language Illegible, incoherent Not enough content to score	Incorrect purpose, mode, audience Brief, vague Unelaborated Rambling Lack of language control Poor organization	Correct purpose, mode, audience Some elaboration Some details Gaps in organization Limited language control	Correct purpose, mode, audience Moderately well elaborated Clear, effective language Organized (perhaps with brief digressions)	Correct purpose, mode, audience Effective elaboration Consistent organization Sense of completeness, fluency

"The Train from Rhodesia" by Nadine Gordimer

Open-Book Test

Multiple Choice and Short Answer

Write your answers to all questions in this section on the lines provided.
For multiple-choice questions, circle the letter of the best answer.

1. In "the Train from Rhodesia," the second paragraph of the story describes the environment in and around the train station. What can you conclude about the lifestyles of the people who live there?

    _____

    _____

2. The bargaining between the old man and the young woman is described in "The Train from Rhodesia." The narrator tells the reader that "The old man held it up to her, still smiling, not from the heart, but at the customer." What does this sentence suggest about the old man's bargaining position?

    _____

    _____

3. How is the conflict between blacks and whites at the station captured in the following quotation from "The Train from Rhodesia"?

    > Those sitting inside looked up: suddenly different, caged faces, boxed in, cut off, after the contact of outside.

    _____

    _____

4. The wife rejects the wooden lion after her husband buys it for less money than the old man initially asked for it. Why does this conflict between the husband and wife develop? Explain your answer choice.
    a. The wife feels that the husband exploited the old man by forcing him to sell the wooden lion for a much lower price.
    b. The wife feels that the husband should have bargained for an even lower price than the one he paid for the lion.
    c. The wife has changed her mind; she no longer wants the lion, and she is annoyed that her husband insisted on purchasing it.
    d. The wife feels that the lion represents her husband's domination of her life.

    _____

    _____

5. Explain what point Gordimer is trying to illustrate by contrasting the description of the wooden figures with the description of the begging children in "The Train from Rhodesia."

    _____

    _____

6. In "The Train from Rhodesia," a man walks along the train platform, "past the dogs; glancing up at the dining car where he could stare at the faces, behind glass, drinking beer, two by two, on either side of a uniform railway vase with its pale dead flower." What does "the glass" in this sentence represent? Explain your answer choice.
   a. The glass represents the past.
   b. The glass represents the distance that white people put between themselves and the black people.
   c. The glass indicates that this is a dream sequence.
   d. The glass represents how the white people are unable to do anything to help the black people outside.

   _____

   _____

7. The young woman suddenly understands the significance of her encounter with the old man in "The Train from Rhodesia." What does she mean when she says, "But he is not part of the unreality; he is for good now"?

   _____

   _____

8. In "The Train from Rhodesia," the woman is shocked that her husband paid only one-and-six for the wooden lion. Select the answer which explains why the phrase "one-and-six" is repeated four times at the end of the story. Explain your answer choice.
   a. The woman cannot believe that her husband bought the wooden lion for such a good price.
   b. She needs to remember the price to tell her friends.
   c. The woman is annoyed because she feels that her husband still paid too much for the lion.
   d. She thinks the price that the husband paid for the wooden lion represents the inequality that exists between white and black people.

   _____

   _____

9. "A weariness, a tastelessness, the discovery of a void made her hands slacken their grip, atrophy emptily, as if the hour was not worth their grasp." Based on how *atrophy* is used in this sentence from "The Train from Rhodesia," select the answer that contains a synonym for the word. Explain your answer choice.
   a. drop   b. squeeze   c. deteriorate   d. relax

   _____

   _____

10. The arrival and departure of the train in "The Train from Rhodesia" are described in the same way. The narrator states that the train whistle "calls out to the sky, I'm coming, I'm coming." Why is there no answer to the train's whistle?

   _____

   _____

Extended Response

11. In many places in the story "The Train from Rhodesia," Gordimer alludes to the inequality between blacks and whites in Africa. In a short essay, explain how the train represents this inequality throughout the story. Support your response with examples from the story.

12. In "The Train from Rhodesia," the train is described in terms that are normally associated with a living organism. Use the sunburst organizer below to list the ways in which the train is described as a living thing. Then, write an essay explaining why Gordimer describes the train in this way, citing the examples that you have compiled to support your points.

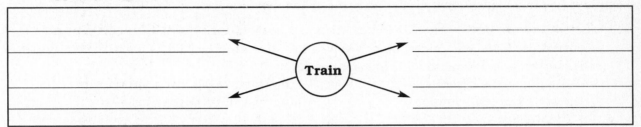

13. In "The Train from Rhodesia," how has the young woman become aware of the differences between blacks and whites in Africa? Answer this question in one or two paragraphs, supporting your points with examples from the story.

14. The wooden lion appears at many points in the story of "The Train from Rhodesia." In an essay, explain what this wooden lion represents. Support your response with examples from the story.

15. The image of the stationmaster's wife is twice repeated in "The Train from Rhodesia." In an essay explain how the description of this image and its placement within the story serve to underscore the separation of blacks and whites at the train station. Support your response with examples from the text.

Oral Response

16. Choose question 5, 7, 11, 12, or 13 or one your teacher assigns you. Take a few minutes to look through the story to prepare an oral response to give in class. If necessary, make notes to be clear about the order in which you want to present your answer.

Rubric for Evaluating Extended Responses

0	1	2	3	4
Blank paper Foreign language Illegible, incoherent Not enough content to score	Incorrect purpose, mode, audience Brief, vague Unelaborated Rambling Lack of language control Poor organization	Correct purpose, mode, audience Some elaboration Some details Gaps in organization Limited language control	Correct purpose, mode, audience Moderately well elaborated Clear, effective language Organized (perhaps with brief digressions)	Correct purpose, mode, audience Effective elaboration Consistent organization Sense of completeness, fluency

from Midsummer, XXIII and **from *Omeros*, Chapter XXVIII**
by Derek Walcott
"From Lucy: Englan' Lady" by James Berry

Open-Book Test

Multiple Choice and Short Answer

Write your answers to all questions in this section on the lines provided.
For multiple-choice questions, circle the letter of the best answer.

1. The speaker in *Midsummer*, XXIII describes the season during which the Brixton riots occurred. He says "the midsummer's leaves race to extinction" (line 2) like which of the following choices? Explain your answer choice.
    a. changing of the seasons   c. the water hoses used in the riots
    b. the scurry green lemmings   d. the roar of the Brixton riot

    _____

    _____

2. Walcott compares the Brixton rioters to "Boer cattle under Tory whips" in *Midsummer*, XXIII (line 7). Why does he make this comparison?

    _____

    _____

3. "'But the blacks can't do Shakespeare, they have no experience.'"/This was true. Their thick skulls bled with rancor/ when the riot police and the skinheads exchanged quips/you could trace to the Sonnets or the Moor's eclipse" (lines 13–16). In this section of *Midsummer*, XXIII, what does Walcott suggest about Shakespeare's subject matter, and the qualifications of blacks to play Shakespeare?

    _____

    _____

4. What are the emotions of the speaker as reflected in his account of the Brixton riots in *Midsummer*, XXIII?

    _____

    _____

5. Based on how *rancor* is used in line 14 of *Midsummer*, XXIII, select the answer that contains the antonym for this word. Explain your answer choice.
    a. love   b. hate   c. blood   d. disgust

    _____

    _____

6. In *Omeros* Chapter XXVIII, Walcott envisions a *griot* who recounts how slavery brought Africans to the Caribbean. How does Walcott use this history to parallel the present situation of black people in the Caribbean?

    _____

    _____

186 Open-Book Test

7. The bodies of those people who were enslaved in Africa and brought to the Caribbean are described as containing "seeds," "pods," and "fronds" (lines 10 and 14) in *Omeros* XXVIII. Why are these people described in these terms?

    _____

    _____

8. How does Walcott illustrate the way in which slavery destroyed the slave's ability to claim a heritage and a community, in the last stanza of *Omeros* Chapter XXVIII?

    _____

    _____

9. From the context of the poem "From Lucy: Englan' Lady," it is evident that the speaker is relaying her impressions of England and its queen based on her observations of London and the behavior of the people there. Select the answer which explains what conclusion Lucy has drawn about the Queen. Explain why the answer you chose is correct.
    a. Lucy is impressed, but she feels sorry for the Queen.
    b. Lucy feels that the Queen is lucky to have such a respected position among her people.
    c. Lucy doesn't understand why people don't expect more from the Queen.
    d. Lucy is impressed with the Queen, but is annoyed by her willingness to tolerate so much public criticism.

    _____

    _____

10. Based on Lucy's account of London and her impression of the Queen in "From Lucy: Englan' Lady," what can you conclude about the life that Lucy has left behind in Jamaica?

    _____

    _____

Extended Response

11. The title of the poem *Midsummer*, XXIII, and the images in the first eight lines contain references to nature and a season's change. Write an essay explaining the significance of these references to nature and the season. Support your response with examples from the poem.

12. In *Midsummer*, XXIII, Walcott alludes to several literary works when he describes the events of the Brixton riots. In one or two paragraphs, explain how these literary references relate to the present-day conflicts between blacks and whites in Britain. Support your response with examples from the poem.

13. *Omeros* Chapter XXVIII recounts how the enslaved peoples of Africa were brought to the Caribbean islands. In a short essay, explain how Walcott views the effects of slavery on the people of the Caribbean today.

14. The speaker's voice in "From Lucy: Englan' Lady" reflects her natural, conversational tone. In an essay, explain how the speaker's voice reflects her feelings about life in England.

15. Both *Midsummer*, XXIII and "From Lucy: Englan' Lady" deal with the speaker's experiences as a Caribbean immigrant living in Britain. Using the Venn Diagram below, compare and contrast the experiences of the speakers in each poem. Then in an essay analyze why and how the speakers' experiences in Britain are similar and different. Support your response with examples from each poem.

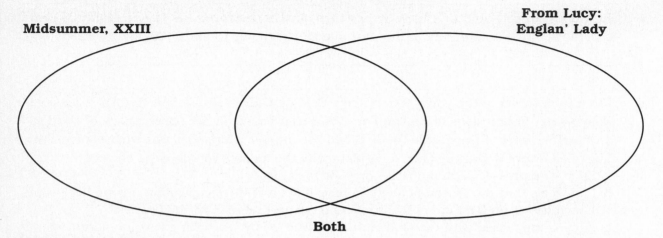

Midsummer, XXIII

From Lucy: Englan' Lady

Both

Oral Response

16. Choose question 3, 4, 11, 12, 13, or 15 or one your teacher assigns you. Take a few minutes to look through the poems to prepare an oral response to give in class. If necessary, make notes to be clear about the order in which you want to present your answer.

Rubric for Evaluating Extended Responses

0	1	2	3	4
Blank paper Foreign language Illegible, incoherent Not enough content to score	Incorrect purpose, mode, audience Brief, vague Unelaborated Rambling Lack of language control Poor organization	Correct purpose, mode, audience Some elaboration Some details Gaps in organization Limited language control	Correct purpose, mode, audience Moderately well elaborated Clear, effective language Organized (perhaps with brief digressions)	Correct purpose, mode, audience Effective elaboration Consistent organization Sense of completeness, fluency

"A Devoted Son" by Anita Desai

Open-Book Test

Multiple Choice and Short Answer

Write your answers to all questions in this section on the lines provided.
For multiple-choice questions, circle the letter of the best answer.

1. The neighbors in "A Devoted Son" are impressed by Rakesh's scholastic success, but they are even more impressed by the respectful way that he treats his father. Why do the neighbors approve of the way that Rakesh bows down and touches his father's feet? Explain your answer choice.
   a. Despite his success, Rakesh is still humble enough to show his father respect.
   b. The neighbors have never heard of anyone's son doing such a thing.
   c. Rakesh still shows his father respect in this way, even though he is no longer required to do so.
   d. Rakesh has never done this before, and the neighbors are impressed that he has begun to show respect in this old-fashioned way as an adult.

   _____

   _____

2. In the first half of "A Devoted Son," how does Rakesh's father feel about the way his son treats him?

   _____

   _____

3. " . . . He pursued his career in the most prestigious of all hospitals and won encomiums from his American colleagues which were relayed to his admiring and glowing family." Based on how *encomiums* is used in the sentence above, from "A Devoted Son," select the answer that best defines the word. Explain why your answer choice is correct.
   a. awards   b. praise   c. scholarships   d. offers

   _____

   _____

4. Rakesh's progression in his career is chronicled in "A Devoted Son." Based on the account of Rakesh's achievements, why might he appear to be a dynamic character at this point in the story?

   _____

   _____

5. Rakesh's progress is also noted by his neighbors in "A Devoted Son." How do the neighbors view Rakesh's achievements? Support your response with one or two examples from the story.

   _____

   _____

6. After he retires from his position in the kerosene dealer's depot, Varma "went to pieces." How does Varma's personality change at this point in the story? Support your response with one or two examples from "A Devoted Son."

_____

_____

7. In "A Devoted Son," Rakesh restructures Varma's diet, explaining that Varma's illness stems from the rich foods that he prefers to eat. Explain the larger conflict that develops from Rakesh's decision to change his father's eating habits.

_____

_____

8. What does the conversation between Bhatia and Varma reveal about how Rakesh's treatment of his father is viewed by the older generation? Explain your answer choice.
   a. Rakesh's control of Varma's diet is considered to be disrespectful.
   b. Rakesh's control of Varma's diet is in accordance with tradition.
   c. Rakesh's control of Varma's diet is tolerated even if it goes against tradition, because he does it out of love for his father.
   d. Rakesh's control of Varma's diet is part of the new tradition and should be respected.

_____

_____

9. At the end of "A Devoted Son," Varma has decided that he no longer wants to submit to Rakesh's treatments. Select the answer which explains why Varma has made this decision. Explain why the answer you chose is correct.
   a. Varma has decided to use an alternative treatment suggested to him by Bhatia.
   b. Varma knows that Rakesh's treatment will have no positive effect on his health.
   c. Varma wants to find a more modern treatment for his illness.
   d. Varma feels that he can no longer tolerate the decrease in the quality of his lifestyle since Rakesh has restricted his diet and activities.

_____

_____

10. How has Varma's view of his son changed by the end of "A Devoted Son"? Support your answer with one or two examples from the story.

_____

_____

Extended Response

11. "A Devoted Son" chronicles Rakesh's efforts to care for his father, Varma—even if Varma doesn't want his son to care for him. In one or two paragraphs, explain why the title of this story is ironic. Support your response with examples from the story.

12. Although it is Rakesh who goes away to school to become a doctor, he is the most static character of "A Devoted Son." In a short essay, analyze how and why Rakesh is a static character. Support your response with examples from the story.

13. In "A Devoted Son," Varma struggles in vain to maintain his sense of independence from Rakesh. In a short essay, analyze the change in Varma's personality and explain what experiences in his life cause him to change.

14. Rakesh maintains that he is only fulfilling his duty to Varma by caring for him in "A Devoted Son." In an essay, explain how Rakesh uses tradition to control his father.

15. Although Rakesh shows his respect for his father in a number of ways in "A Devoted Son," the reader gets the impression that Rakesh has a low opinion of Varma. In an essay, explain why you can draw this conclusion based on how Rakesh speaks to and treats Varma.

Oral Response

16. Choose question 5, 6, 10, 11, 12, or 13 or one your teacher assigns you. Take a few minutes to look through the story to prepare an oral response to give in class. If necessary, make notes to be clear about the order in which you want to present your answer.

Rubric for Evaluating Extended Responses

0	1	2	3	4
Blank paper	Incorrect purpose, mode, audience	Correct purpose, mode, audience	Correct purpose, mode, audience	Correct purpose, mode, audience
Foreign language	Brief, vague	Some elaboration	Moderately well elaborated	Effective elaboration
Illegible, incoherent	Unelaborated	Some details	Clear, effective language	Consistent organization
Not enough content to score	Rambling	Gaps in organization	Organized (perhaps with brief digressions)	Sense of completeness, fluency
	Lack of language control	Limited language control		
	Poor organization			

Name _____ Date _____

from "We'll Never Conquer Space" by Arthur C. Clarke

Open-Book Test

Multiple Choice and Short Answer

Write your answers to all questions in this section on the lines provided.
For multiple-choice questions, circle the letter of the best answer.

1. In "We'll Never Conquer Space," Clarke asserts, "we have forgotten—and our descendants must learn again, in heartbreak and loneliness" that human beings will never conquer space. Explain your answer choice.
   a. Recent events have distorted the view of what is possible to accomplish in space.
   b. People will never develop the technological ability to travel in space.
   c. People still need to conquer parts of the earth before space can be tackled.
   d. Our ancestors have tried space exploration and failed.

   _____

   _____

2. Clarke structures his argument in "We'll Never Conquer Space" to persuade the reader to adopt his opinion. What is the most frequent persuasive technique that Clarke uses in this essay? Explain why the answer you chose is correct.
   a. analysis of current events
   b. quotations of expert opinions
   c. emotional descriptions
   d. analogies to past and present events and ideas

   _____

   _____

3. In "We'll Never Conquer Space," Clarke maintains a bleak outlook on man's ability to travel to all the corners of space. What statement about humanity's technological capabilities does Clarke make by taking this position?

   _____

   _____

4. Clarke discusses his view on the possibility of mapping our solar system in "We'll Never Conquer Space." How does Clarke feel about this possibility? Support your answer with a line from the essay.

   _____

   _____

5. "And again they are wrong, for they have failed to grasp the great lesson of our age— that if something is possible in theory, and no fundamental scientific laws oppose its realization, then sooner or later it will be achieved." How does Clarke reconcile this statement from "We'll Never Conquer Space" with his assertion that human beings will never map all of space?

   _____

   _____

6. Although Clarke maintains that people will not dominate space in the way that they dominate the earth, what does he predict that man will accomplish in "We'll Never Conquer Space"? Select the answer which accurately states Clarke's prediction. Explain why the answer you chose is correct.
   a. Human beings will eventually explore and settle many parts of the galaxy.
   b. Human beings will devise a way to travel at the speed of light.
   c. Human beings will find life on another planet.
   d. Human beings will be able to maintain connections with those people who will settle in other parts of the galaxy.

   _____

   _____

7. In "We'll Never Conquer Space," Clarke asserts that "all the star-borne colonies of the future will be independent, whether they wish it or not." How does he feel about his claim that relationships between those on Earth and in deep space will not exist? Support your answer with one or two examples from the essay.

   _____

   _____

8. Clarke declares that "Space can be mapped and crossed and occupied without definable limit; but it can never be conquered." How does Clarke define the word *conquered* in "We'll Never Conquer Space"?

   _____

   _____

9. "When you are next outdoors on a summer night, turn your head towards the zenith." Based on how the word *zenith* is used in "We'll Never Conquer Space," select the answer which best defines it. Explain why the answer you chose is correct.
   a. the central area   b. the moon   c. the horizon   d. the highest point

   _____

   _____

10. What does Clarke mean when he concludes "We'll Never Conquer Space" with the statement: "For no man will ever turn homewards from beyond Vega, to greet again those he knew and loved on the earth?"

   _____

   _____

Extended Response

11. In "We'll Never Conquer Space," Clarke predicts that humans will settle in space, but they will not conquer it. He evaluates the qualities of human beings that will enable them to colonize space to some extent. In a short essay, explain what you can conclude about how Clarke views human nature, based on what he predicts humans will achieve. Support your response with examples from the essay.

12. Clarke structures his argument very carefully in "We'll Never Conquer Space." He wants to persuade his readers that conquering space is an impossible feat. Using the sunburst organizer below, list the methods that Clarke uses to persuade his readers to adopt his position on this issue. Then write a short essay evaluating the effectiveness of the methods you have found. Support your response with examples from the essay.

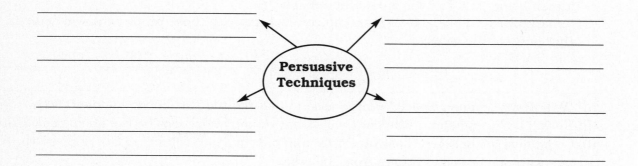

13. Identify some statements in "We'll Never Conquer Space" that are debatable. In one or two paragraphs, explain why these statements are open to debate. Explain whether you agree or disagree with these statements and why.

14. In "We'll Never Conquer Space," Clarke reveals his views about life in the future. In an essay, evaluate Clarke's view of the future. Support your response with examples from the text.

15. In an essay, identify what Clarke believes humans value the most. Citing examples from the text explain how he presents his views.

Oral Response

16. Choose question 5, 7, 8, 10, 11, or 13 or one your teacher assigns you. Take a few minutes to look through "We'll Never Conquer Space" to prepare an oral response to give in class. If necessary, make notes to be clear about the order in which you want to present your answer.

Rubric for Evaluating Extended Responses

0	1	2	3	4
Blank paper Foreign language Illegible, incoherent Not enough content to score	Incorrect purpose, mode, audience Brief, vague Unelaborated Rambling Lack of language control Poor organization	Correct purpose, mode, audience Some elaboration Some details Gaps in organization Limited language control	Correct purpose, mode, audience Moderately well elaborated Clear, effective language Organized (perhaps with brief digressions)	Correct purpose, mode, audience Effective elaboration Consistent organization Sense of completeness, fluency

ANSWERS

Unit 1: From Legend To History (449–1485)

from "The Seafarer"
translated by Burton Raffel

from "The Wanderer"
translated by Charles W. Kennedy

from "The Wife's Lament"
translated by Ann Stafford

Open-Book Test (p. 1)

Multiple Choice and Short Answer

1.d Explanation: Students may say that the speaker gives an account of his suffering and is neither praising nor overly emotional.

2.c Explanation: Student may write: "Orchards blossom, the towns bloom, / Fields grow lovely as the world springs fresh."

3.c Explanation: Students may quote lines 39-43, beginning "But their isn't" or lines 68-70, beginning "No man has."

4. Sample answer: To be exiled is to be permanently removed from loved ones. The practice of exile was more common historically than it is today. Understanding the sorrow of permanent separation from loved ones takes on more intese meaning when you recognize how much people had to deal with it.

5. Sample answer: Students may say that the speaker sadly misses his friends and the joyful life he shared with other warriors and his lord. They may cite evidence from lines 26 to 51, for support.

6. Sample answer: Students should note that the wife mourns the loss of her husband, friends, and family. She grieves when her husband first leaves her, and she lives in exile, longing for her loved ones. An elegy is a solemn and formal lyric poem about death. It reflects on the tragic.

7.a Explanation: The poem has a rhythm; the wife does not possess heroic qualities or overcome fate; she is not a commoner.

8.a,c Explanation: caesura—Each line contains a sound break.

9.b,c Explanation: The wife expresses intense emotion and ill will toward the man. She shows no happiness or pity for him.

10. Sample answer: The picture should show a winter storm that batters a high wall with serpents drawn on its face. Students might say that the wall symbolizes the fleetingness of life or the unimportance of temporary glory.

Questions are classified in these categories:

Comprehension	10 (A)
Interpretation	1 (A), 3 (A), 5(A)
Literary Analysis	6 (A), 7 (A), 8 (A)
Reading Strategy	4 (A)
Vocabulary	2 (E), 9 (C)

E=Easy, A=Average, C=Challenging

Extended Response

11. (Average) Students should use appropriate reasons and examples to support their opinion. They may include such references as the desolate weather, the wall's deteriorated condition, the deaths of the warriors, images of war, the role of fate, and the poem's tone.

12. (Challenging) The speaker has learned that a person who is lost in sorrow does not have the strength to succeed in life. Now the speaker no longer speaks about his troubles and tries to use wisdom and experience to guide his actions. Students should use examples and reasons from the text to elaborate on these points.

13. (Average) Students should use reasons and examples from "The Seafarer" to focus on a seaman's fears, pains, and desires. Their discussion should include the lure and punishment of the sea.

14. (Average) Students may write about why the seafarer will turn away from the advice. They may say that the seafarer has a strong faith in God and use evidence from the selection to support their opinion.

15. (Average) Students may use evidence from the text to show that the wife has no choice or that fate has dictated her plight. They should also discuss the wife's anger, loneliness, and fear.

Oral Response

16. In their oral responses, students should substantiate their presentations and expand on their earlier responses by citing specific passages from the poems.

from *Beowulf*
translated by Burton Raffel

Open-Book Test (p. 4)

Multiple Choice and Short Answer

1. Sample answer: Grendel is impatient with the music and celebration of Hrothgar's men; his home is a hell on earth; he was born in slime; his parents are the children of Cain, who were exiled by God; he is family to "a thousand forms of evil," who angrily fight against God.

2. Sample answer: The word *reparation* means "making up for wrong or injury." Reasons may include: Grendel loves the conflict; he continues the feud; he will not accept a truce.

3. Sample answer: The watchman thinks Beowulf

is self-confident and honest. Beowulf comes "openly," not in secret; he acts as if he doesn't need permission to enter the territory; the watchman has seen no one greater; Beowulf carries weapons not owned by commoners.

4.c Explanation: The underlined words are a noun phrase describing Beowulf.

5.b Explanation: *Affliction* means "pain and suffering."

6. Sample answer: Beowulf does not want to die and go to a place he does not know.

7.a Explanation: The line includes a break in the middle.

8. Sample answer: Students should list two kennings and show whom or what each names. They might say a kenning adds creativity and interest to a writer's work.

9. Sample answer: Beowulf may mean that the Danish people and their nation are no longer a dominant power. He says, "Fate has swept our race away"(line 836).

10. Sample answers: The timeline should include the following battles: Grendel attacks Hrothgar's men at Herot; Beowulf kills Grendel at Herot; Beowulf kills Grendel's mother in her battle hall under the lake; A dragon beats Beowulf at the entrance to the dragon's tower; Beowulf and Wiglaf kill the dragon, but Beowulf dies from his wounds. Students may say the fight between Beowulf and Grendel is most important because it symbolizes the struggle between good and evil. This battle also reveals Beowulf's virtues and the characteristics of an epic hero.

Questions are classified in these categories:

Comprehension	1 (E)
Interpretation	3 (C), 9 (C), 10 (A)
Literary Analysis	4 (A), 5 (E), 7 (A), 8 (A)
Reading Strategy	6 (A)
Vocabulary	2 (E)

E=Easy, A=Average, C=Challenging

Extended Response

11. (Easy) The Venn diagram and written response may show that both men have royal blood, inherited wealth, brave, loyal, and honorable characteristics, leadership positions, and belief in God and fate. Students may say that Beowulf is older and a greater lord than Wiglaf.

12. (Challenging) Student essays should use examples and references from *Beowulf* to show that Beowulf and Wiglaf held the characteristics of an epic hero, which may include qualities such as bravery and loyalty; belief in both fate and God; participation in noble battles symbolic of good versus evil; representative of cultural, social, and religious values; and part of legend or hero tale.

13. (Easy) Students may say Grendel will return to fight Beowulf again. They may note that Grendel is determined to battle humans and the forces of good. He is also a strong, proud, and brave monster used to winning his battles.

14. (Challenging) Students may write about good versus evil, the virtues of the epic hero, the military role, belief in God and fate, or social and cultural values. They should support their opinions with appropriate evidence from the text.

15. (Average) Students should use reasons, examples, and quotations to show the Danes' acceptance of, or resignation to, fate. They may say that Beowulf believed he was destined to fight the monsters, and he accepted his victory or death as predetermined. For example, in talking about the upcoming battle with Grendel, he says, "Fate will unwind as it must" (line 284).

Oral Response

16. In their oral responses, students should substantiate their presentations and expand on their earlier responses by citing specific passages from the epic.

from *A History of the English Church and People*
by Bede

from *The Anglo-Saxon Chronicle*
translated by Anne Savage

Open-Book Test (p. 7)

Multiple Choice and Short Answer

1. Sample answer: Students may say *innumerable* means "countless."

2. Sample answer: Students may say Bede was not present to hear a direct quotation from the Scots, and the people who preserved the history may have been biased and wished to make the Scots look friendly and helpful.

3.a Explanation: *The Anglo-Saxon Chronicle* is a history of events. It does not focus on battles, and it does not have a persuasive or lively style.

4. Sample answer: Students may say that *stranded* means "driven onto the shore or hopeless."

5.a Explanation: Bede lived his whole life in the monastic school of Jarrow.

6.c Explanation: Students may say the Scots wanted the Pict royal line to have Scot blood.

7. Sample answer: The forces in East Anglia and Northumbria greatly harassed Wessex along the south coast with raiding bands. The force was comprised of Vikings, and the king was King Alfred.

8.c Explanation: "The land has rich veins of many metals including copper, iron, lead, and silver."

9. Sample answer: Students may write the following events on the timeline: Alfred, king of England for 28 1/2 years, dies; Alfred's son Edward becomes king; Aethelwald, Alfred's nephew, takes Wimbourne and Christchurch without permission; King Edward confronts Aethelwald at Wimbourne; Aethelwald escapes to Northumbria; King Alfred rescues a nun Aethelwald has captured.

10. Sample answer: journals, diaries, histories, letters, church documents, public documents, folk tales, legends, literature, and interviews.

Questions are classified in these categories:

Comprehension   9 (E)
Interpretation   5 (C), 6 (E)
Literary Analysis   2 (C), 3 (A)
Reading Strategy   7 (A), 8 (A), 10 (A)
Vocabulary   1 (E), 4 (E)

E=Easy, A=Average, C=Challenging

Extended Response

11. (Challenging) Students may say the speaker believes social status should determine who is listed in the chronicle. Because of this, he may fail to name men who could be included or leave out other relevant information. Historians will check other sources to confirm and add more information to the story.

12. (Challenging) Students may discuss the historian's attention to British geography in the first paragraph, the history of Britain through migration and the folktales of the Irish.

13. (Average) Facts for *A History of the English Church and People* may include: The Pict tradition of settling disputes exists in Bede's day; under their leader Reuda, the Scots migrated to Britain; Ireland is larger than Britain; Ireland's natural resources include honey, fish, birds, deer, and goats. Opinions may include: Ireland has a superior climate; in Ireland, it is unnecessary to stable animals or store hay for the winter; reptiles die when they breathe Irish air; almost everything in Ireland is immune to poison. Student paragraphs should summarize the facts listed in the chart.

14. (Average) Students may suggest resources from areas like transportation, communication, technology, and science. Examples from the text should accompany their opinions. For example, historians could use pocket calculators to quantify natural resources and determine distances.

15. (Easy) Students should use examples from the text to support reasons, such as these: Bede describes the geography, climate, and natural resources; he adds quotations to lend a storybook quality; details, like the qualities of coal, are instructive; Bede's friendly, informative tone keeps a listener's interest.

Oral Response

16. In their oral responses, students should substantiate their presentations and expand on their earlier responses by citing specific passages from the selection.

The Prologue from *The Canterbury Tales*
by Geoffrey Chaucer

Open-Book Test (p. 10)

Multiple Choice and Short Answer

1. Sample answer: Who: Narrator and pilgrims; What: spending the night; Where: hostelry; When: one night; Why: on pilgrimage; How: by horse.

2. b Explanation: Sample quotations: He loved a morning sop of cake in wine (line 344); He lived for pleasure and had always done (line 345).

3. c Explanation: Students should point to what the nun says about how she spends her time and what she's willing to overlook or pardon in exchange for gifts.

4. a Explanation: Students may say that a friar forgives people for their sins.

5. Sample answer: Direct characterization: Students may say the cook has a sore on his knee. Indirect characterization: Students may say the cook is unsanitary and contaminates the food with bacteria from his sore.

6. Sample answer: Direct characterization: "Whatever money from his friends he took / He spent on learning or another book" (lines 309-310). Indirect characterization: "The thread upon his overcoat was bare" (line 300).

7. Sample answer: "In all the parish not a dame dared stir / Towards the altar steps in front of her, / And if indeed they did, so wrath was she / As to be quite put out of charity" (lines 459-462). The Wife of Bath gets angry if another woman draws attention away from her. "Her hose were of the finest scarlet red / And gartered tight; her shoes were soft and new / Bold was her face, handsome, and red in hue." (lines 466-468). The wife likes to attract and flirt with men.

8. Sample answer: Students may say the speaker is humble and honest. He may be trying to ingratiate himself and win the listeners' trust.

9. Sample answer: Students may say the Miller wins the prize ram at wrestling contests, and he can tear a door off its hinges.

10. Sample answer: Students should list three characters representative of various social classes, from the noble knight to the lowly plowman. They may say that the reader receives a more realistic and intriguing look at medieval life with Chaucer's depiction.

Questions are classified in these categories:

Comprehension	10 (A)
Interpretation	8 (A), 9 (A)
Literary Analysis	5 (C), 6 (A), 7 (C)
Reading Strategy	1 (A), 3(A)
Vocabulary	2 (E), 4 (E),

E=Easy, A=Average, C=Challenging

Extended Response

11. (Challenging) Students may discuss Chaucer's use of wit, allusion, irony, and innuendo to draw his complex characters. He presents the qualities, frailties, values, and motivations of the pilgrims, several of which students should illustrate in their essays.

12. (Average) Both knight and squire value military skill and share the code of chivalry. The father has gained respect through his military action, which he performs with honor, wisdom, and humility. His son is more of a courtly lover, dancing, composing poetry, and jousting in tournaments.

13. (Average) Students should say the parson is the more devoted Christian because he is holy, virtuous, and compassionate. He does not take from the poor but lives among them, serving as a model for Christian service. The nun's courtly manner suggests she is more concerned with appearances and impressing people with her position in higher society.

14. (Easy) Students may say doctors used astrology to diagnose and treat patients. They made charms and magic effigies to balance the four humors.

15. (Challenging) Students should use details from the text to show the monk easily fits into the hunter's lifestyle while shunning books and hard labor. For example, he "spared for no expense" (line 196) in pursuing his sport. Students may also add that the monk is a man of wealth who indulges in his appetites. He spends extravagantly on his wardrobe, and he wears a "lover's knot" to attract female attention.

Oral Response

16. In their oral responses, students should substantiate their presentations and expand on their earlier responses by citing specific passages from the poem.

"The Nun's Priest's Tale" and "The Pardoner's Tale" from *The Canterbury Tales* by Geoffrey Chaucer

Open-Book Test (p. 13)

Multiple Choice and Short Answer

1. Sample answer: Students may say the widow is a dairy-woman who leads a sad and poor life, making ends meet through hard work. Sample quotations: "Sooty her hall, her kitchen melancholy, / And there she ate full many a slender meal (lines 12-13); And all her physic was a temperate diet, / Hard work for exercise and heart's content" (lines 18-19).

2.b Explanation: Rhetorician, chronicle, Notable Remarks.

3. Sample answer: Students may say *timorous* means "timid." Poltroon, cowardice.

4.c Explanation: Peretelote is scornful when she speaks to Chanticleer.

5.b Explanation: In lines 120-125, the narrator extols the virtue of the writer Cato.

6.d Explanation: The old man knows that the gold will lead the men to their own deaths, but he pretends to be helping them by pointing them toward Death.

7.b Explanation: Though a short stroy may teach a lesson, it does not have to. An *exemplum*, however, is used to teach a moral through a story that serves as an example.

8. Sample Answer: Students may note that the appetite of the men drove them to live for each other only when it eas to their own personal advantage (getting the gold). In the end, they were divieded by their greed. Though they died, they did not die *for* the others; rather, *because* of the others.

9.c Explanation: The three rioters are chattering and bragging arrogantly about their ability to destroy Death.

10.c Explanation: The Pardoner appears to assert that living a greedy life is worse than death itself; in fact, greed will lead to death.

Questions are classified in these categories:

Comprehension	1 (E)
Interpretation	6 (A), 10 (A)
Literary Analysis	7 (C), 8 (A), 9 (C)
Reading Strategy	2 (A), 3 (A), 5 (A)
Vocabulary	4 (A)

E=Easy, A=Average, C=Challenging

Extended Response

11. (Easy) Students may discuss the characteristics unique to each animal. For example, a rooster is cocky, vain, and admired. A fox is cunning and conniving. They may also say the animals are appropriate for Chaucer's mock-heroic style.

12. (Average) Students may cite the use of Macrobius, Bishop Bradwardine, Boethius, and others to exemplify respect for Roman and Christian authority. They may say Chaucer wants to show how his characters add importance to their actions, and he points out the humorous exaggeration in the conflict between a rooster and a fox.

13. (Average) Student charts should include Fate, God, astrology (or astronomy), and magic while citing appropriate examples from the text. Students may say the English are in a transition from pagan beliefs to faith in God.

14. (Challenging) Students may agree that the men received their due and support it by giving evidence of the men's selfishness and greed in their betrayal of each other. Others may disagree that the men received their due and argue that Death is the greater traitor.

15. (Average) Students should use details to show that the dialogue exibits the characteristics of the three men and the other characters. For example, the bragging comments of the three men show that they may be easily deceived through their pride and greed. The old man's milder words show that he may be more thoughtful and clever.

Oral Response

16. In their oral responses, students should substantiate their presentations and expand on their earlier responses by citing specific passages from the poem.

from *Sir Gawain and the Green Knight*
translated by Marie Borroff

from *Morte d'Arthur*
by Sir Thomas Malory

Open-Book Test (p. 16)

Multiple Choice and Short Answer

1. Sample answer: The crowd's response is realistic; people are amazed, fearful, curious, and courteous. The green knight is supernatural. He and his horse shine green, and some people think he is a phantom or fairy.

2. Sample answer: Students may say Arthur is confident, courteous, and commanding. He shows no fear, plays host to the Green Knight, and deals firmly with this guest.

3. Sample answer: A challenger strikes the Green Knight with an ax. If the Green knight dies, the other knight keeps the Green Knight's ax. If the Green Knight lives, the challenger must travel to the Green Knight's home in a year and a day. There the Green Knight will strike the warrior with his ax.

4.c Explanation: Students may say Sir Gawain is earnest, solemn, sincere, or trusting.

5.c Explanation: The Green Knight is decapitated by Sir Gawain, but he picks up his head, which continues to speak. The poem says, "Yet all who saw it say 'twas a wonder past compare."

6.d Explanation: The speaker retells the events with detail but little emotion.

7.b Explanation: Sample quotation: King Arthur says of Sir Mordred, "For I in no wise trust him."

8.d Explanation: King Arthur is sad over the loss of his men and angry that Sir Mordred caused their deaths.

9. Sample answer: Some students may say the sword symbolizes courage, honor, and respect. Others may say Excalibur signals King Arthur's upcoming death. Each student should use appropriate details and quotations for support.

10. Sample answer: Details may include: The explanation of Arthur's death is majestic and lamentable; mournful and wailing queens carry Arthur on a barge to his deathbed; the queens are compassionate and attentive to Arthur; Bedivere feels lost without Arthur's leadership; Arthur is humble and resigned to God's plan; Arthur is entombed under the keeping of a hermit.

Questions are classified in these categories:

Comprehension	7 (A)
Interpretation	2 (C), 6 (A)
Literary Analysis	1 (A), 9 (A), 10 (A)
Reading Strategy	3 (C), 5 (E), 8 (A)
Vocabulary	4 (E)

E=Easy, A=Average, C=Challenging

Extended Response

11. (Average) Students should identify the characteristics of a medieval hero and show how they are exemplified in Gawain. They should also discuss the fearful, deceptive side of Gawain's personality with examples like his courtship of the Green Knight's wife and his possession of the green girdle.

12. (Challenging) Sample responses: "A knight obeys his king." Arthur's knights fight to their death against Sir Mordred's men. "This noble duke [Lucan] so die for my sake." Knights are trustworthy. "Take thou [Bedivere] here Excalibur my good sword." Students should elaborate on the code of conduct in their essays.

13. (Easy) Some students may say no because the Green Knight is arrogant, opposes authority, and has supernatural powers. Others may say yes because he is strong, courageous, forgiving, and faithful to God. All essays should include relevant details to support their position.

14. (Average) Students can point to Arthur's dream, Sir Gawain's warning, Arthur and Mordred's

distrustful attitudes, a knight's poisonous snakebite, the drawn sword, and Arthur's comment, "Alas, this unhappy day!"

15. (Challenging) Some students may say Sir Gawain believes that God guides his actions, he fights on God's side, and God has sent him to warn Arthur. Others may say Gawain meets the definition of the medieval hero, who should embody a devout faith in God. Students should then explain how Gawain's faith is representative of English culture.

Oral Response

16. In their oral responses, students should substantiate their presentations and expand on their earlier responses by citing specific passages from the selections.

**The Letters of Margaret Paston
"Lord Randall," "The Twa Corbies," "Get Up and Bar the Door," and "Barbara Allan,"**
Anonymous

Open-Book Test (p. 19)

Multiple Choice and Short Answer

1. c Explanation: Students may say Margaret Paston describes how the Duke's forces took Hellesdon. Heveningham and Wingfield are already allied with the Duke. Margaret Paston does not belittle the Duchess or ask pity from her husband.

2. Sample answer: The word *certify* means "to endorse officially."

3. c Explanation: The word "mother" is a direct address.

4. Sample answer: Students may use the footnote that accompanies the ballad to define *hussyfskap* as "household duties."

5. Sample answer: "But never a word would one of them speak."

6. Sample answer: Students may say the bell signals the young man's death and symbolizes Barbara Allan's sorrow.

7. a Explanation: Students may say the lines are written in a Scottish-English dialect, or the messenger speaks in the language particular to the people in the ballad.

8. c Explanation: Sample response: The poem lacks repeating lines. The four-line stanzas have rhyming second and fourth lines, and the two ravens converse about the dead knight.

9. Sample answer: She tells her husband that one of their homes has been seized; she expresses worries about finances; She is frustrated by her son's lack of response; she shows great courage. Students should support their ideas in a paragraph.

10. Sample answer: Students may say none are there: the hound is hunting, the hawk is catching dinner, and the lady has left for another man.

Questions are classified in these categories:
Comprehension   10 (E)
Interpretation   1 (A), 6 (A)
Literary Analysis   3 (A), 8 (C), 9 (C)
Reading Strategy   4 (E), 5 (A), 7 (A)
Vocabulary   2 (A)

E=Easy, A=Average, C=Challenging

Extended Response

11. (Average) Students may say "Lord Randall" is a narrative; the author is unknown; the second and fourth lines in the four-line stanzas rhyme; the ballad uses a refrain, dialogue, and repetition. Students should use specific examples from the ballad to support their reasoning.

12. (Challenging) Sample response: In matters of war and law, women are expected to defer to men. However, they should be strong, intelligent, capable, honorable, and loyal. For example, Barbara Allan has the resolve to discuss matters with Heveningham, but she intends to comply with her husband's decision when she says, "I pray you send me word how I shall act" in light of Hellesdon's destruction. Barbara Allan also asks her son for help in leading soldiers who do not respect her as their commander.

13. (Challenging) Students may cite examples of dialogue, conflict, and style from the ballad to show its humorous tone. They may prove the cynicism by discussing character motivation, disrespect for property, and disregard for life.

14. (Average) Students may say yes because Barbara Allan is at Graeme's side when he dies, the dead-bell cries her "woe," and she will die for Graeme's love. Others will say no because she is cold, inconsiderate, and vindictive. All essays should include appropriate reasons and examples from the text for support.

15. Sample answer: Both ballads portray a graphic and gruesome picture of death. The reader is aware there is tragedy coming, but the lyric quality and lack of striking detail do not give the reader a sense of dread until the fourth stanzas. At this point, the tone becomes dark and futile.

Oral Response

16. In their oral responses, students should substantiate their presentations and expand on their earlier responses by citing specific passages from the selections.

Sonnets 1, 35, and 75
by Edmund Spenser

Sonnets 31 and 39
by Sir Philip Sidney

Open-Book Test (p. 22)

Multiple Choice and Short Answer

1.d Explanation: The meaning is made clear by the parallel with "lines" in line 5 and "rhymes" in line 9, with all three ("leaves, lines, and rhymes") summed up in line 13. Choice a is not supported by the context, which does mention lilies but only to help us picture the beloved's hands holding the leaves of the books. Choices b and c are verb meanings also not supported by the context.

2. Sample answer: All of the world's glory seems vain to me; and, except for my beloved, everything in the world seems like a shadow, lacking substance or value.

3.d Explanation: The answer is supported by the opening lines, where the speaker indicates that no matter how much his eyes behold his beloved (the "object of their pain"), it will not suffice. Choices a and c suggests that the speaker is conceited, but in fact he seems to have low self-esteem. Choice b is not supported in any way by the details of the poem or the information in the footnote.

4. Sample answer: "conceited" and "futile."

5.a Explanation: The end rhyme in a Spenserian sonnet is *ababbcbc cdcdee*, the *ee* indicated a rhymed couplet at the end. That final rhyme is illustrated by "alone/none" in Sonnet 1, "me/she" in Sonnet 35, and "subdue/renew" in Sonnet 75. Choice b is a possible rhyme scheme for a Petrarchan, not a Spenserian, sonnet. Choice c is inaccurate; a sonnet by definition is a fourteen-line poem. Choice d is inaccurate and is not illustrated in the three sonnets by Spenser. In Sonnet 1, for example, a break in meaning occurs before the final couplet, which sums up the rest of the poem.

6.a Explanation: Details in the sonnets, such as the final two lines in Sonnet 1, support this response. Choice b applies only to Sonnet 1 and is not the main purpose of even that poem. Choice c is contradicted by the details in the sonnets, especially Sonnet 75. Choice d applies only to Sonnet 35 of the three sonnets presented.

7.c Explanation: The answer is supported by the description of the moon in lines 1-12 and the state of the speaker's love that can be inferred from the questions in lines 10-14. Choices a and d are contradicted by the details of the poem. Choice b is not supported by details in the poem.

8. Sample answer: something that soothes or eases woe.

9.b Explanation: This is the only choice that the words and their sequence can convey. Choices a, c, and d are not supported by the language of these lines.

10.d Explanation: This statement is supported by the textbook definition of a Petrarchan sonnet and the Petrarchan sonnets by Sidney. Choice a is incorrect, because the last two lines occasionally do rhyme, as in the two Petrarchan sonnets by Sidney. Choice b is inaccurate; a Spenserian sonnet has a different rhyme scheme and does not always break into an octave and a sestet. Choice c is inaccurate; a sonnet by definition is a fourteen-line poem.

Questions are classified in these categories:

Comprehension	7 (E)
Interpretation	1 (A), 6 (A)
Literary Analysis	3 (A), 8 (C), 9 (C)
Reading Strategy	2 (A), 5 (A)
Vocabulary	4 (A)

E=Easy, A=Average, C=Challenging

Extended Response

11. (Average) Students should cite details from the poems to support general statements about the attitude toward the beloved that the speakers express. They should recognize that in Sonnets 35, 31, and to a lesser extent Sonnet 39, the speaker seems to suffer from unrequited love, but that in Sonnet 75 and particularly Sonnet 1, the speaker simply celebrates or pays tribute to his beloved.

12. (Average) Students should use quotations or paraphrases from Sonnet 75 and the other two poems by Spenser to support their opinions of Elizabeth's likely reactions.

13. (Easy) Students should provide a modern conversation that accurately reflected the attitudes expressed by the speaker and his beloved. Students' conversations should use correct capitalization and punctuation and should begin a new paragraph each time the speaker changes.

14. (Average) Images and ideas that students list might include "the certain knot of peace," "the baiting place [place for refreshment] of wit," "the balm of woe," "the poor man's wealth," "the prisoners release," and "the indifferent judge between the high and low." Students should discuss the meaning of each image or idea in terms of how it relates to sleep and should then consider the overall impression of sleep made by all of the images or ideas taken together.

15. (Challenging) Students should discuss the use of apostrophe in the three sonnets and consider the effects it has on the immediacy, emotional

level, and/or tone of the poems. Students should indicate that in Spenser's Sonnet 1, the speaker addresses the leaves (of the book of sonnets), lines, and rhymes; in Sidney's Sonnet 31, the speaker addresses the moon; and in Sidney's Sonnet 39, the speaker addresses sleep.

Oral Response

16. In their oral response, students should cite specific information from the sonnets that substantiates their presentations and expands on their earlier responses.

Sonnets 29, 106, 116, and 130
by William Shakespeare

Open-Book Test (p. 25)

Multiple Choice and Short Answer

1.b Explanation: This answer is supported by such phrases as "in disgrace," "all alone beweep my outcast state," and "curse my fate." Choice a is not supported by the details of the poem. Choices c and d do not apply to the specified lines 1-9 of the sonnet—the love between the speaker and the person he addresses is not introduced until line 10.

2.d Explanation: This answer is supported by the reason given in line 13. Choices b, c, and d are not supported by the details in the poem.

3. Sample answer: "Chronicle of wasted time" might mean history or past literature in which writers describe their beloved. It seems like "wasted time" to the speaker because writers and others from the past lived their lives without experience the bliss of knowing the speaker's beloved.

4.a Explanation: This answer is supported by the attitude the speaker expresses toward his beloved. Choices b, c, and d are not supported by the details of the poem.

5. Sample answer: Love is the unchanging and eternal joining of two kindred spirits. Details that support this definition include "marriage of true minds," "Love is not love which alters when it alteration finds," "It is an ever-fixed mark," it "is never shaken," and "Love's not Time's fool . . . / But bears it out even to the edge of doom."

6.c Explanation: An existing prior marriage would clearly be an obstacle to love and marriage and thus shows an understanding of the meaning of the word *impediment*. Since a love letter is an expression of love, choice a does not show understanding of the meaning of *impediment*. Since a marriage license would be a requirement for marriage, choice b does not show understanding of the meaning of *impediment*.

Since the clergy member performs marriages, choice d does not show understanding of the meaning of *impediment*.

7. Sample answer: The speaker describes his beloved in realistic terms.

8.d Explanation: The words "and yet" introduce a contrast, and the speaker's saying that he finds his beloved "as rare/As any she belied with false compare" indicate the very positive view he has of his beloved, in contrast to the realistic and not all that glowing remarks he makes about her in lines 1-12. Choices a, b, and c are not supported by the details of the poem.

9.a Explanation: This theme is supported by the details of the poem, especially the concluding remark in lines 13-14. The themes in choices b and d are not supported by the details of the poem. The theme in choice c is contradicted by the details of the poem.

10.c Explanation: The last two lines in a Shakespeare sonnet always rhyme, as indicated in the Literary Analysis and illustrated in the four sonnets. Choice a is inaccurate; a Shakespearean sonnet consists of four quatrains and a couplet. Choice b is inaccurate; a sonnet by definition is a fourteen-line poem. Choice d is inaccurate. The usual meter of a Shakespeare (or other English-language) sonnet, as illustrated by the four sonnets, is iambic pentameter, in which there are five iambic feet to a line.

Questions are classified in these categories:

Comprehension	10 (E)
Interpretation	1 (A), 6 (A)
Literary Analysis	3 (A), 8 (C), 9 (C)
Reading Strategy	4 (E), 5 (A), 7 (A)
Vocabulary	2 (A)

E=Easy, A=Average, C=Challenging

Extended Response

11. (Average) Students should cite details from the poem to support general statements about the speaker of the poem they choose. They should recognize the speaker's change in mood in Sonnet 29, his exaggerated love in Sonnet 106, his idealistic view of love in Sonnet 116, and his honesty and affection in Sonnet 130.

12. (Average) Students should state what they consider to be the speaker's view of time in Sonnets 106 and 116 and then support their statements with specific details from the poems. They should recognize that in Sonnet 29 the speaker indicates that true love does not change over time and that in Sonnet 106 the speaker suggests that loves of times past do not equal the love he has for his beloved.

13. (Easy) Students should accurately complete the chart with information from the sonnet of their choice. They should then use the points they list

in a brief essay examining how the sonnet's form reflects its content.

14. (Average) Students should identify one sonnet, state a point about love that they feel the sonnet makes, and then react to that idea. They should use examples and logical arguments to support their opinion.

15. (Challenging) Students should explain how the speaker's realistic and honest depiction of the beauty of his beloved differs from the exaggeration of a typical love poem and should cite details from the poem as examples of differences. They should then decide whether this realistic approach makes the poem more or less effective in conveying the speaker's love, and explain why.

Oral Response

16. In their oral response, students should cite specific information from the sonnets that substantiates their presentations and expands on their earlier responses.

from *Utopia*
by Sir Thomas More

Elizabeth's Speech Before Her Troops
by Queen Elizabeth I

Open-Book Test (p. 28)

Multiple Choice and Short Answer

1.c Explanation: This answer is supported by the details in the opening sentences. Choice a is incorrect. More says nothing bad about a monarch who lives comfortably, as long as he works for the good of his or her subjects. Choice b is the exact opposite of what More says with his analogy in the second sentence. Choice d is not supported by the details of the selection.

2. Sample answer: Governing rich men would show that Fabricius was an effective ruler and would contribute to peace in his realm and support for his rule.

3.b Explanation: This choice shows an understanding that *sloth* means "laziness." Choices a, c, and d do not show an understanding of the meaning of *sloth*.

4. Sample answer: Who disturbs the public peace more than those who are poor or otherwise dissatisfied?

5.b Explanation: This point is supported by all the details in the selection. Choice a is not supported by any details in the selection. Choice c is not supported and is somewhat contradicted by the remark by Fabricius, which implies that there is little benefit to a monarch himself or herself being rich. Choice d is directly contradicted by the details of the selection.

6.d Explanation: This example shows an understanding that *treachery* means "betrayal of trust, faith, or allegiance." The examples in choices a, b, and c do not show an understanding of the meaning of *treachery*.

7. Sample answer: Though persuaded to watch my safety, I do not mean to show distrust for my subjects.

8.a Explanation: This answer is supported by details such as Elizabeth's reference to "the loyal hearts and good will of my subjects," her promise "to lay down, for my God, and for my kingdom, and for my people, my honor and my blood, even the dust," her observation that "I have the heart of a king, and of a king of England, too," her remark that she thinks "foul scorn that Parma or Spain, or any prince of Europe, should dare to invade the borders of my realms," her praise for "your valor in the field," and her prediction that "we shall shortly have a famous victory over the enemies of my God, of my kingdom, and of my people." Choice b is contradicted by the details in the speech. Choice c is only mildly touched upon in the remark about others daring to "invade the borders of my realms." Choice d is not supported by the details in the speech.

9. Sample answer: She is not a tyrant but instead has always ruled for the benefit of her subjects, relying on their loyalty and good will for her own strength and safety.

10.a Explanation: This answer is supported by the remarks about being a woman but also being a king and by other details in the selection. Choice b draws a false conclusion. Elizabeth believes her people's love comes from the way she has ruled, not from her gender. Choice c is directly contradicted by the details in the speech. Choice d is mentioned only in passing toward the end of the speech and is not the main point Elizabeth wants to convey on this subject.

Questions are classified in these categories:

Comprehension	10 (E)
Interpretation	1 (A), 6 (A)
Literary Analysis	3 (A), 8 (C), 9 (C)
Reading Strategy	4 (E), 5 (A), 7 (A)
Vocabulary	2 (A)

E=Easy, A=Average, C=Challenging

Extended Response

11. (Easy) Students should cite details from the selection to support general statements. They should recognize that More respects a monarch who is responsive to the needs of the people, works for their benefit, and governs a prosperous and peaceful land. Their character sketch of Elizabeth should also reflect similar

values, as well as her courage, determination, sense of duty, and patriotism.

12. (Average) Students should sum up the argument in a way that reflects the idea that a ruler must put his people's needs first if he wants his rule to succeed and the nation to be peaceful and stable. They should then provide concrete examples as they consider how More's argument applies to political leaders today.

13. (Average) Students should write a reaction to Elizabeth's speech from the point of view of one of her subjects. They should discuss their reaction to the message and the feelings that her message inspires. They should cite examples from the speech to support general statements.

14. (Challenging) Students should makes a general statement about the persuasiveness of Elizabeth's speech and then support it with examples. Examples of word choices they might discuss include "safeguard," "loyal," "resolved," "honor," and "victory," all of which have positive connotations; and "tyrant," "foul scorn," and "dishonor," which have negative connotations. Examples of word repetition they may cite include "people," "king," and "I myself." Examples of parallel structure include "to live or die amongst you; to lay down . . . , " "for my kingdom, and for my people," "my honor and my blood," "I have but the body of a weak and feeble woman; but I have the heart of a king, and of a king of England too," "I myself will take up arms; I myself will be your general," and "of my God, of my kingdom, and of my people."

15. (Average) Students may suggest that More's purpose was to offer advice and help improve society. They may suggest that his primary audience was the current and future monarchs as well as others holding high political office. In discussing how persuasive the selection would be to its targeted audience, students might examine More's arguments, examples, and emotional appeals.

Oral Response

16. In their oral response, students should cite specific information from the selections that substantiates their presentations and expands on their earlier responses.

from *The King James Bible*
Open-Book Test (p. 31)
Multiple Choice and Short Answer

1.a Explanation: A psalm is by definition a sacred song or lyric poem in praise of God, and this answer is also supported by the details in the selection. Choice b is incorrect because the shepherd is mentioned merely as a metaphor for God. Choice c and d are not supported by any

details in the psalm, which makes no mention of the speaker's beloved and only mentions the speaker's enemies in passing.

2.c Explanation: This choice is supported by the many details indicating the speaker's closeness with God and the remark "he leadeth me in the paths of righteousness." Choice a is incorrect; the speaker does not live far from the world's woes but is brought through them by the Lord (in verse 4). Choice b is incorrect; the Lord helps the speaker triumph over his enemies, but this is not the focus of the psalm, nor is vengeance mentioned. Choice d is incorrect. The simple rural life is part of the extended metaphor of the Lord being a shepherd and does not apply literally to the speaker.

3.a Explanation: Though the psalm initially refers to the Lord as "He," the pronoun shifts in verse 4, where the speaker now addresses the Lord directly. This shift is supported by the details beginning in verse 4, including "thy rod and thy staff they comfort me," which extends the metaphor of the Lord as shepherd. Choices b, c, and d do not make sense in the context of the psalm.

4. Sample answer: My joy in God knows no bounds; my righteous life is full of joy.

5.b Explanation: A sermon is by definition a speech, and this is the only choice that applies to the selection. Choice a is incorrect because a sermon is not written to be set to music. Choice c is incorrect because the sermon, unlike a dialogue, is not a discussion between two or more people. Choice d is incorrect because the sermon, unlike a parable, does not tell a story to make its point.

6. Sample answer: The two "masters" are God and wealth (or money personified as a false god). This is made clear in the last sentence of verse 24, "Ye cannot serve God and mammon," and by the points and examples that follow.

7.b Explanation: This choice is supported by the opening and closing points. Choice a is incorrect because, among other things, beauty and ugliness are not touched on in the passage. Choice c is incorrect because hard work is not touched on in the passage and the fowls and lilies are nurtured by God, not people. Choice d states the opposite of the point being made in the passage.

8.b Explanation: The elder brother himself points out to his father, "Lo, these many years do I serve thee, neither transgressed I at any time thy commandment," and his father agrees. Choice a is inappropriate, since the elder brother is working in the field when his younger brother returns and has apparently all his life served his father. Choice c is inappropriate because the elder brother at first protests his father's generosity. Choice d is inappropriate from what we know of elder brother, who is positively contrasted with his prodigal brother. Though he initially cites the unfairness of his father's generosity toward the prodigal, nowhere does the parable indicate that the elder son is motivated by greed.

9. Sample answer: It is important to forgive people and allow them to make a fresh start.

10.d Explanation: This choice shows an understanding that *prodigal* means "addicted to wasteful expenditure." Choices a, b, and c do not reflect an understanding of the meaning of *prodigal.*

Questions are classified in these categories:

Comprehension	10 (E)
Interpretation	1 (A), 6 (A)
Literary Analysis	3 (A), 8 (C), 9 (C)
Reading Strategy	4 (E), 5 (A), 7 (A)
Vocabulary	2 (A)

E=Easy, A=Average, C=Challenging

Extended Response

11. (Easy) Students should recognize that Psalm 23 encourages a life of piety and righteousness in which a human being puts his or her faith in the Lord, and they should cite examples from the psalm to support this point.

12. (Average) If students choose Psalm 23, they should explain the central metaphor of "The Lord is my shepherd," recognizing that it portrays the Lord as leader and caretaker, just as a shepherd leads and cares for his flock. They should then explain how other details in the psalm—for example, "he maketh me lie down in green pastures," "he leadeth me beside the still waters," "he leadeth me in the paths of righteousness," "thy rod and they staff they comfort me"—extend the figurative comparison. If students choose the passage from the Sermon on the Mount, they should explain how the figurative examples—the remarks about the fowls of the air and the lilies of the field—support the main idea about not serving mammon (or caring overmuch for material possessions) but instead relying on the Lord to sustain us.

13. (Challenging) Students may say that one brother is dutiful, hard working, and stay-at-home while the other is a disobedient, wandering sinner only just come home to the fold. They may say that the elder brother's attitude is largely one of respect and self-righteousness while the younger brother's is largely one of regret and repentance. They may suggest that both brothers have in common their family heritage and their father's love. Students should cite details from the selection to support these interpretations.

14. (Average) Students may say that the father is loving, forgiving, generous, understanding, and pious and should cite examples to support these views. They may suggest that he is motivated by love and pious obedience to the teachings of his faith.

15. (Average) Students should give a reasonable statement of the advice in one of the selections and should then react to it. They should use examples and logical reasons to support their ideas.

Oral Response

16. In their oral response, students should cite specific information from the selections that substantiates their presentations and expands on their earlier responses.

The Tragedy of Macbeth, Act I
by William Shakespeare

Open-Book Test (p. 34)

Multiple Choice and Short Answer

1.b Explanation: The answer is supported by the opening setting label, the characters (and the real-life historical figures on which some are based), and such details as the castles, swords, and armor. Choices a, c, and d are not supported by the details in the selection.

2.a Explanation: In Shakespeare's day plays were performed in daylight because their was no artificial lighting, and sets were kept to a bare minimum. Choice b is incorrect because most performers clearly had to be able to read to learn their roles. Choice c is incorrect. No such section of stage directions exists. Choice d is incorrect. Shakespeare wrote his plays for performance in his own time and would not have omitted valuable instructions for some future generations' benefit.

3. Sample answer: After the previous Thane of Cawdor is found guilty of treason, Duncan bequeaths his title on Macbeth in gratitude for Macbeth's courage in battle.

4. Sample answer: Two remarks proving true serve as forerunners of the third prediction about the regal event of my becoming king.

5.a Explanation: Only this choice shows an understanding that *valor* means "great courage or bravery." Choices b, c, and d do not show an understanding of the meaning of *valor.*

6. Sample answer: She begins planning Duncan's murder. Supporting details include her many about catching "the nearest way" in line 18 of Scene v, as well as the speeches in Scene v beginning "The raven himself is hoarse/That croaks the fatal entrance of Duncan/Under my

battlements" and "O, never/Shall sun that morrow see!"

7.b Explanation: Lady Macbeth is overly ambitious for her husband. She wants Macbeth to be king, even if it means Duncan must die. Choice a is not specifically supported by any details in the play. Choice c is incorrect because Macbeth has shown himself to be brave in battle—in fact, it is for that reason that Duncan names him Thane of Cawdor. Choice d is incorrect because nowhere is there evidence that the Macbeths do not love each other. Quite the contrary, they seem to have a close, loving relationship in which they share their innermost thoughts and secret ambitions.

8. Sample answer: Duncan's initial remarks in lines 1-3 and portions of Banquo's response in lines 3-10.

9. Sample answer: Macbeth is Duncan's subject and kinsman, and so owes the king his loyalty. In addition, he is Duncan's host, and it is against all laws of hospitality to fail to protect a guest and especially to allow a guest to come to harm at the host's own hands.

10.d Explanation: Lady Macbeth remains firmly behind the plan to murder Duncan while her husband, in contrast, is far more hesitant. Choice a is incorrect. In Act I, she seems less kind and gentle than he does. Choice b is incorrect. Lady Macbeth begins thinking of the murder of Duncan as soon as she reads his letter about the witches' predictions, which include the remark about Macbeth being "king hereafter." Choice c is incorrect. While her husband recognizes the possible dangers of killing Duncan, Lady Macbeth does not foresee any problems.

Questions are classified in these categories:

Comprehension	10 (E)
Interpretation	1 (A), 6 (A)
Literary Analysis	3 (A), 8 (C), 9 (C)
Reading Strategy	4 (E), 5 (A), 7 (A)
Vocabulary	2 (A)

E=Easy, A=Average, C=Challenging

Extended Response

11. (Average) Students should recognize that the remark indicates that things are not what they seem and sets the stage for the Macbeths' disloyalty and other actions that contradict what they pretend to be and what Duncan and others think they are. Students may also feel that the comment underscores the eerie supernatural flavor that runs through the play, owing to the witches' predictions. Students should cite examples from the play to support their ideas.

12. (Average) Students should recognize that Macbeth's discovery that he is indeed Thane of

Cawdor makes him believe that the witches' other predictions must also be accurate. Students may also feel that Macbeth accepts the witches' predictions because he is a superstitious man in a superstitious age and/or because the predictions give him a pretext for doing what he already was wont to do (because of his excessive ambition). Students should support their ideas with details from the play as well as logical reasons.

13. (Easy) Students might mention courage, fighting ability, and a belief in the supernatural as qualities that Macbeth and Banquo have in common. Among the differences they may mention are Macbeth's ambition and Banquo's loyalty.

14. (Average) Students' essays might focus on such qualities in Lady Macbeth as her ambition, manipulative nature, firmness of purpose, inability to foresee consequences, love for her husband, and seeming willingness to abandon the softer feminine virtues associated with women in her day. Students should cite details from the play to illustrate each quality they name.

15. (Challenging) Examples of dramatic irony that students may mention include: Duncan's elevating Macbeth to Thane of Cawdor as a reward for his loyalty and bravery when, unbeknownst to him, Macbeth soon seems willing to betray and murder Duncan; the fact that the previous Thane of Cawdor was guilty of treason but Macbeth is actually planning treason too; Duncan's remarks about the lovely Macbeth castle when in fact it may be the site of Duncan's murder; and Duncan's remarks showing his love for and trust in the Macbeths when in fact the Macbeths are planning to kill him. In discussing how the dramatic irony adds to the play's effectiveness, they may say that it underscores the innocence and goodness of Duncan and builds suspense for the audience.

Oral Response

16. In their oral response, students should cite specific information from the play that substantiates their presentations and expands on their earlier responses.

The Tragedy of Macbeth, Act II
by William Shakespeare

Open-Book Test (p. 37)

Multiple Choice and Short Answer

1.b Explanation: This choice shows an understanding that *augment* means "to make greater; to enlarge" and also accurately reflects

Macbeth's prime motives. Choices a and c do not list items that Macbeth seeks to *augment*— at least, not according to the details in the play thus far. Choice d shows a misunderstanding of the meaning of *augment*.

2.d Explanation: Macbeth's remarks show his reluctance to take Duncan's life and recognition that such an act could have dangerous consequences. Choice a does not accurately reflect Macbeth's attitude. He does not hate the king; he merely kills Duncan to satisfy his own ambitions. Choice b suggests the opposite of Macbeth's situation. The fact that he is contemplating killing the king is a tremendous act of *dis*loyalty. Choice c does not accurately reflect Macbeth's attitude. He does not seem happy to kill the king; rather, he seems nervous and expresses second thoughts.

3. Sample answer: He suggests that the bell is like a church bell tolling Duncan's death and summoning him to heaven or perhaps to hell.

4.a Explanation: With its long lines, occasional breaks in meter, and usual lack of end rhyme, blank verse generally captures the sound of spoken English. Choice b is incorrect because blank verse does not as a rule rhyme. Choices c and d are incorrect because blank verse uses iambic pentameter lines, which have five feet to a measure and tend to be of similar and fairly long length.

5. Sample answer: By killing Duncan as he sleeps, Macbeth commits a terrible crime that will trouble his conscience and for which he must live in fear of punishment, and both the guilty conscience and his fear may keep him from sleeping restfully in future.

6. Sample answer: She could not kill the sleeping Duncan because in sleep he resembled her father. She expresses this reason in II, ii, 12-13.

7.a Explanation: Choice a reflects a careful and accurate reading of the lines of blank verse. Choices b, c, and d show inaccurate readings of the lines of blank verse.

8.d Explanation: This choice shows an understanding that *palpable* means "capable of being touched or felt." Choice a is incorrect because the dagger is one that Macbeth envisions, not a real dagger. Choices b and c do not reflect an understanding of the meaning of *palpable*.

9.c Explanation: The porter speaks in prose; for example: "Here's a knocking indeed! If a man were porter of hell gate, he should have old turning the key. . . . " Choices a, b, and d are incorrect because all of these characters speak most of the time in unrhymed lines of iambic pentameter, or blank verse.

10. Sample answer: They leave because they fear that, as close male relatives of Duncan's with strong claims to the Scottish throne, they will be targets of whatever person murdered Duncan. However, their suspicious flight allows the Macbeths to suggest that they are behind Duncan's murder, as Macduff's remark in lines II, iv, 24-27 indicates.

Questions are classified in these categories:

Comprehension	10 (E)
Interpretation	1 (A), 6 (A)
Literary Analysis	3 (A), 8 (C), 9 (C)
Reading Strategy	4 (E), 5 (A), 7 (A)
Vocabulary	2 (A)

E=Easy, A=Average, C=Challenging

Extended Response

11. (Easy) Students should cite specific examples of dialogue that clarifies the setting and contributes to the mood, which they should identify as some combination of eerie, somber, and violent. Examples they may cite include the exchange between Banquo and Fleance and then Banquo and Macbeth in II, i; the descriptions of night by Lennox in II, iii; and the details provided by the old man and Ross in II, iv.

12. (Average) Students may say that the scene helps forward the plot because it marks the arrival of Macduff. They should recognize that the scene is ironic and occurs at a tense moment in the action, providing comic relief for the audience. Students should cite details from the scene to support general statements about it.

13. (Average) Students should recognize that both Macbeth and Lady Macbeth are motivated by ambition and willing to kill to gain power and status but that Macbeth is more hesitant and/or more able to see possible future dangers. Students should recognize that Lady Macbeth helps egg on Macbeth and fix his resolve. Students should cite details from Act II to support their statements about both characters.

14. (Average) Most students are likely to say that Macbeth has a good imagination. Supporting this view are his powerful language, with its imaginative metaphors, and his ability to envision the possible negative consequences of his actions. Students who feel that he does not have a good imagination should cite details to support that view.

15. (Challenging) Students should choose a single character's speech of five or more lines and discuss how its language and rhythm work together to convey the character's thoughts and feelings. Students should make clear what those thoughts and feelings seem to be. They should also make clear how they think characters should speak their lines, and why.

Oral Response

16. In their oral response, students should cite specific information from the play that substantiates their presentations and expands on their earlier responses.

The Tragedy of Macbeth, Act III
by William Shakespeare

Open-Book Test (p. 40)

Multiple Choice and Short Answer

1.c Explanation: This view is clearly reflected the remark "I fear/Thou play'dst most foully for 't" (III, I, 2-3). Choice a is not supported by any details in Banquo's speech, and choices b and d are contradicted by what he says.

2. Sample answer: Because Malcolm and Donalbain fled Scotland, suspicion fell on them as the ones behind the murder of King Duncan. Macbeth, a more distant relative, was then able to claim the throne.

3.a Explanation: This choice shows an understanding that *dauntless* means "fearless." Choices b, c, and d do not show an understanding of the meaning of *dauntless*.

4. Sample answer: The witches' predictions indicated that Banquo's descendants will be rulers of Scotland, a situation that Macbeth sees as a threat to his dynasty and the disappointment of all he risked in killing Duncan. By killing Banquo's son, he hopes to ensure that this prediction will not come true.

5.b Explanation: This response shows an understanding that Lady Macbeth's remarks in III, ii, 4-7 apply to her and her husband and also recognize the implications of her question, "Why do you keep alone, /Of sorriest fancies your companions making. . . . ?" (III, ii, 8-9). Choice a is directly contradicted by her remarks in III, 4-5. Choice c is directly contradicted by her question "Why do you keep alone. . . . ?" Choice d is not supported by the details in Act III—for example, they do not quarrel— and is belied by such details as Macbeth's use, in addressing his wife, of the term of endearment "chuck" in III, ii, 45.

6.c Explanation: This choice is made clear in the Third Murderer's comments "There's but one down; the son is fled" (III, iii, 20) and one of the murderer's remarks to Macbeth, "Most royal sir, Fleance is 'scaped." (III, iv, 21). Choices a, b, and d do not accurately reflect the events of the play.

7.b Explanation: This choice reflects an understanding that an *infirmity* is a physical or mental illness. Choices a, c, and d do not reflect

an accurate understanding of the meaning of *infirmity*.

8. Sample answer: He is lying, since he knows Banquo is dead, on Macbeth's own orders. Then his wishes are granted—at least in his own mind—in the humorously macabre way, when Banquo does appear—as a gruesome ghost.

9.d Explanation: This response shows an understanding that an internal conflict is a struggle that takes place in a character's mind or conscience. Choices a, b, and c are incorrect because they all point to struggles with outside forces, or *external* conflicts.

10.d Explanation: Only this statement reflects a clear understanding of the content of Act III. Choice a is inaccurate—Macbeth's seeing Banquo's ghost because he feels guilty is an example of an internal conflict in Act III. Choice b is inaccurate—the struggle to kill Banquo and remove those suspicious of Duncan's murder is an example of an external conflict in Act III. Choice c is inaccurate—the play is clearly continuing to build to a climax, with more murders likely to come until Macbeth finally meets his doom.

Questions are classified in these categories:

Comprehension	10 (E)
Interpretation	1 (A), 6 (A)
Literary Analysis	3 (A), 8 (C), 9 (C)
Reading Strategy	4 (E), 5 (A), 7 (A)
Vocabulary	2 (A)

E=Easy, A=Average, C=Challenging

Extended Response

11. (Average) Student should mention Macbeth's fear of Banquo's suspicions about his involvement in Duncan's murder, his desire to remove someone who was present when the witches' prophesies were made, and his attempt to prevent the fulfillment of the prophesy about Banquo's descendants becoming kings. They should cite details from Act III—especially the comments of Macbeth and Banquo—to support their conclusions.

12. (Average) Among the theories students may offer is that the third character is a new character that the other murderers added to their number in order to carry out the crime; that the third murderer is Macbeth or another character in disguise; or that third murderer is a mistake on Shakespeare's part or an inconsistency resulting from some carelessly dropped portion of the play. Students should support their ideas with logical reasons, details from the play, and/or examples from outside experience.

13. (Average) Students should recognize that the play seems to be teaching that those who do evil to gain political power will never really be happy

and will always live in fear of punishment or of someone else doing evil to them. They should cite examples and reasons to support their general statement of the theme.

14. (Easy) Students should recognize that the supernatural elements help establish the play's eerie atmosphere, where "fair is foul and foul is fair," or things are not what they seem. They should also recognize the role that the witches' prophesies play in tempting the Macbeths to commit murder, which is central to the conflicts of the play.

15. (Challenging) Students may mention that the play flatters James simply by being about Scotland, bringing something from James's background to English audiences. They may feel that its portrayal of Scottish heroes like Banquo, Malcolm, and Macduff and, more specifically, of the help that England gave the good heirs of Duncan, is flattering to Scotland and so to James. They may also mention that the elements involving the supernatural catered to a perceived interest of James's.

Oral Response

16. In their oral response, students should cite specific information from the play that substantiates their presentations and expands on their earlier responses.

The Tragedy of Macbeth, Act IV
by William Shakespeare

Open-Book Test (p. 43)

Multiple Choice and Short Answer

1.b Explanation: This is the only choice that accurately sums up the imagery in the chant. Choice a is incorrect because the images are generally negative and often disgusting. Choice c is incorrect because some of the images ("bubble, bubble," for example, and "fire burn") also appear to the senses of sound, touch, and smell. Choice d is incorrect because only a few of the images appeal to the sense of smell.

2.a Explanation: The witch refers to something wicked approaching, and right thereafter, Macbeth enters. Choices b, c, and d do not reflect the actions of the characters.

3. Sample answer: They appeal most strongly to the sense of sight.

4. Sample answer: He believes that they can never come true—he does not think it possible for there to be a person "not of woman born" or for "Birnam wood to come to Dunsinane."

5.a Explanation: Only this answer reflects the whimsical remarks of the boy ("as birds do, mother") and obvious affection he has for his

mother. Choices b, c, and d are not supported by the text, their negative qualities quite contrary to the impression the son gives.

6. Sample answer: He claims to be worse than Macbeth and uninterested in helping to free Scotland from Macbeth's tyranny. He does so because he is in fact plotting against Macbeth and does not initially trust Macduff, since Macbeth has sent others to spy on him and he thinks Macduff may actually be such a spy.

7.d Explanation: The image of sinking beneath the yoke appeals to the sense of sight and perhaps touch; the weeping appeals to the sense of sound; and the new gash added to the wounds appeals to touch and sight. Choices a, b, and c are incorrect because they mention taste, smell, or both, and none of the images in those lines appeal to those senses.

8.c Explanation: Examples include Lady Macduff's many remarks about flying and birds in IV, ii, 1-13; the exchange between son and mother in IV, ii, 32-36; and Malcolm's poignant remark in IV, iii, 218-219. The bird imagery stresses that Macduff's home is a nurturing place, like a nest; that Macduff had to flee his "nest" and leave it unprotected; and, most especially, Lady Macduff and her children's innocence, physical weakness, and lack of protection, thereby underscoring the horror of Macbeth having them killed.

9.d Explanation: This choice shows an understanding that *pernicious* means fatal or deadly. Malcolm and Macduff believe Scotland is in trouble. Malcolm says "I think our country sinks beneath the yoke." Choice a is incorrect because *judicious* means "showing good judgment" and is the opposite of the kinds of adjectives that the two men would ascribe to Macbeth's rule. Choice b is incorrect because *sundry* means "various; miscellaneous" and is not an adjective that would apply to the two men's view of Macbeth's rule. Choice c is incorrect because *credulous* means "tending to believe too readily." It is not the adjective that the two men would most likely apply to Macbeth's rule, especially now that Macduff and others no longer seem to believe Macbeth but, rather, regard his rule as tyranny.

10. Sample answer: Ross's images of "sighs and groans, and shrieks that rent the air" in line 168 and of the knell in line 170 both appeal to the sense of sound.

Questions are classified in these categories:
Comprehension   10 (E)
Interpretation   1 (A), 6 (A)
Literary Analysis   3 (A), 8 (C), 9 (C)
Reading Strategy   4 (E), 5 (A), 7 (A)
Vocabulary   2 (A)

E=Easy, A=Average, C=Challenging

Extended Response

11. (Easy) Students should cite examples of images, indicate the sense or senses to which each image appeals, and then consider how all the negative images work together to create a mood they are likely to describe as eerie, horrid, and/or evil. Among the many images they may cite are the harpier cries of line 3 (sound), the poisoned entrails thrown into the caldron in line 5 (sight), the toad under cold stone in line 6 (touch, sight), and the two images in the refrain of "fire burn and caldron bubble" (touch, sight, and sound).

12. (Average) Students should recognize that the chant, unlike blank verse, uses end rhyme and that the lines are shorter than blank verse's iambic pentameter (five-beat) lines. They may speculate that Shakespeare uses this form because a witches' chant should by its nature be more musical and should not try to approximate the sound of spoken English (the way blank verse does) and that the strong, repetitious rhythm and rhyme adds to the lulling sense of the supernatural spell.

13. (Challenging) Students should recognize that the murder of Duncan is motivated by ambition; the murder of Duncan's guards, by self-preservation; the murder of Banquo and attempted murder of his son, in part by ambition or pride (about his future descendants) and in part (in Banquo's case) by fear and the desire for self-preservation; and the murder of the Macduff family, by some combination of anger and revenge and the hope of sending out a warning to other would-be traitors. They should recognize that Macbeth's fears are becoming less and less rational. They should also recognize that all the murders are great evils—killing Duncan betrays the king to whom he has sworn loyalty, as well as a kinsman and a guest in his home; killing the grooms is an attempt at escaping the consequences of one's own acts by harming others; killing Banquo betrays a friend and comrade-in-arms; the killing Fleance and particularly the Macduff family seems like irrational overkill, with the killing of an innocent woman and her young children a particularly heinous act for a king (who vows to protect his subjects) and former soldier. Students are likely to say that the events show that violence seems to bring not happiness but only fear, isolation, insecurity, and more violence, and that as time goes on it seems to become easier and easier to commit violence with fewer and fewer pangs of conscience.

14. (Average) Students should evaluate this praise based on the details of Act IV. They should focus on the behavior of Macbeth, Malcolm, Macduff,

Lady Macduff and her son, and Ross and point out that their behavior and attitudes seem realistic. They should also explain that Shakespeare's knowledge of human nature holds up across the centuries. Students may disagree with this premise, as long as they support their opinions with textual details.

15. (Average) Students are likely to predict that what seems impossible will in fact happen, since "Fair is foul and foul is fair," and the unexpected has been happening all along. They may also point out that the supernatural characters are not friends of Macbeth (or any other human being) and that they seem bent on spreading evil and creating mischief. In discussing how the seemingly impossible predictions will actually come to pass, students' speculations will of course vary and need only show a reasonable understanding of the predictions themselves (none of women born will harm Macbeth; Macbeth won't be harmed until Birnam wood comes to Dunsinane).

Oral Response

16. In their oral response, students should cite specific information from the play that substantiates their presentations and expands on their earlier responses.

The Tragedy of Macbeth, Act V
by William Shakespeare

Open-Book Test (p. 46)

Multiple Choice and Short Answer

1.d Explanation: "All of the above" is the correct response. Choice a is applicable as Duncan is the "old man" to whom she refers in line 40. Choice b is applicable since she recalls the appearance of Banquo's ghost in lines 63-65. Choice c is applicable because she recalls Lady Macduff, the slain wife of the Thane of Fife, in lines 43-44.

2. Sample answer: "Will all great Neptune's ocean wash this blood/Clean from my hand?" (II, iii, 59-60).

3.c Explanation: Her remarks about Duncan and Lady Macduff and her belief that she cannot wash the blood from her hands are evidence of her guilty conscience. Choice a is incorrect; lust for power no longer seems to animate her. Choice b is incorrect; she says nothing about hating Macbeth and still seems to show concern for him. Choice d is not supported by any details in the scene.

4.a Explanation: The doctor himself tells Macbeth that Lady Macbeth must cure herself of her "mind diseased." Choice b is illogical. The fact that one person sleepwalks does not show that people in the Middle Ages were more prone to sleepwalking than they are today, and it makes little sense that they would be. Choice c is contradicted by the details in the play. Shakespeare's depiction of Macbeth, Lady Macbeth, and Macduff—among others—shows a vast understanding of emotional distress. Choice d is not supported by any details in the play.

5.b Explanation: This answer is supported by details expressing hopeless attitudes, such as "And all our yesterdays have lighted fools/The way to dusty death" and "It [life] is a tale/Told by an idiot, full of sound and fury/Signifying nothing." Choices a, c, and d are not supported by the details in the soliloquy.

6.d Explanation: This answer shows an understanding that a *harbinger* is a "forerunner," or "something that comes before to signal something else." Choices a, b, and c do not show an understanding of the meaning of *harbinger*.

7. Sample answer: Macbeth is indeed killed by someone "not of woman born"—apparently, Macduff was delivered in a Caesarian section and so, in an era when this medical procedure was uncommon, seems not to be "born" in the usual biological way. Macbeth is also killed when Birnam wood comes to Dunsinane, since the soldiers attacking Dunsinane camouflage themselves with tree boughs that make it look like Birnam wood is approaching.

8.a Explanation: Macbeth faces Macduff bravely in the play's final scenes. Choice b in incorrect because Macbeth is introduced as a brave soldier, and he faces battle bravely at the end. Choice c is incorrect because Macbeth has not made wise choices in his life. Choice d is incorrect because Macbeth, as a murderer, has sinned greatly and does not repent.

9.d Explanation: Swords are mentioned throughout, including in the close combat between Macbeth and Macduff at the end. Choice a is contradicted by the details. Macduff and Macbeth do face each other one on one. Choice b is contradicted by the details. The attacking army does camouflage itself, with the tree branches—that is how "Birnam Wood" seems to be coming to Dunsinane. Choice c is not supported by the details. The characters seem to rely mainly on human messengers, and these other inventions (in fact, from the nineteenth century) appear nowhere in the play.

10. Sample answer: Macbeth's flaw is his excessive ambition, or willingness to do anything (even commit murder) to succeed.

Questions are classified in these categories:

Comprehension	10 (E)
Interpretation	1 (A), 6 (A)
Literary Analysis	3 (A), 8 (C), 9 (C)
Reading Strategy	4 (E), 5 (A), 7 (A)
Vocabulary	2 (A)

E=Easy, A=Average, C=Challenging

Extended Response

11. (Easy) Students should choose one recurring image in the play and trace it throughout the play, citing concrete examples to illustrate its use. They should discuss the characters, character traits, values, and/or emotions with which they feel it is associated.

12. (Average) Students should identify Macbeth's tragic flaw and then evaluate Macbeth as a tragic hero, considering whether he is a noble enough figure to qualify as a typical tragic hero. Students should support their ideas with details from the play.

13. (Average) Students should recognize that Lady Macbeth, who initially persuades her husband to murder and does not seem guilt-ridden over murderous acts, has come to be deeply troubled by them and mentally unstable as a result. Macbeth, on the other hand, who is initially hesitant and troubled by the acts, has become less mentally troubled and more firm of purpose. Students may speculate about why this reversal may have occurred and what it reveals about each character's personality and ability to foresee the future.

14. (Challenging) Students should choose one saying, explain what it means, and then cite examples from the play to show that the idea expressed by the saying is one of the play's themes. They should recognize that saying (a) focuses on the ideas of excessive political ambition and tyranny, (b) on violence leading only to more violence, (c) on the idea of justice and legal or moral law, (d) on the importance of considering future consequences, and (e) on the ideas that things are not always what they appear to be.

15. (Average) Students should explain why they think Macbeth has endured as a classic and cite examples from the play to support their opinions. They may focus on what they consider to be the play's universal themes, on its understanding of human behavior and the universals of human nature, or on its brilliant use of poetic and memorable language.

Oral Response

16. In their oral response, students should cite specific information from the play that substantiates their presentations and expands on their earlier responses.

Unit 3: A Turbulent Time (1625–1798)

Works of John Donne
Open Book Test (p. 49)

Multiple Choice and Short Answer

1.d Explanation: A *paradox* is something that appears to be a contradiction. Since death is described as having the ability to die, it can be inferred that death is alive— hence the paradox. No such contradictions exist in the other answer choices. Answers (a), (b), and (c) describe death.

2. Sample answer: The speaker does not view death as a terrible event (lines 1–2). Rather, he views death as a sleep from which one awakens into eternal life (line 13–14).

3. Sample answer: The speaker loves his beloved (line 1) and wishes to console her over their separation (lines 13–16). Other lines in the poem may also be cited to support these ideas.

4.c Sample Answer: The speaker suffers emotional pain becaouse of the beloved's reaction to him. His motivation is to tell her of his pain.

5. Sample answer: Viewing parting as sleeping reinforces the idea that the separation is only temporary. One wakes up after one sleeps, just as the beloved will "awaken" by losing her sadness when the speaker returns to her.

6.b Explanation: The speaker views himself and the beloved as one unit, and his parting will not cause a division (breach) between them (lines 22–24).

7. Sample answer: The conceit is found on lines 25–36. The relationship between the speaker and his beloved is compared to "twin compasses" (line 26). The beloved is the fixed foot of the compass, and the speaker is the foot of the compass that draws the circle. The beloved's stability brings the speaker back to her after they part, just as the fixed foot of the compass enables the other foot to make a perfect circle and return to its starting point.

8.c Explanation: The analogy is made explicit within "Meditation 17." This answer is supported by evidence from the poem: "The bell doth toll for him that thinks it doth; and though it intermit again, yet from that minute that that occasion wrought upon him he is united to God."

9. Sample answer: Whatever occurs in the church affects all of its members. For example, Donne states that the baptism of a child is an event that affects him because it signals that child's entrance into the church community, which is also his community.

10.a Explanation: Mankind is compared to a volume or set of books. Man's spiritual ascent to heaven after death is compared to the way the words of

a book may be translated into another language. The other answers are not correct because they do not contain any such comparisons. Answer (b) is incorrect because it is a statement of Donne's beliefs; no comparison is made within it. Answer (c) is incorrect because it is a rhetorical question that Donne is using to persuade his readers to agree with his views. Answer (d) is incorrect because it contains a simile—not a conceit.

Questions are classified in these categories:

Comprehension	2 (E)
Interpretation	5 (A), 8 (A)
Literary Analysis	1 (C), 7 (C), 10 (A)
Reading Strategy	3 (E), 4 (A), 6 (A)
Vocabulary	9 (A)

E=Easy, A=Average, C=Challenging

Extended Response

11. (Average) Students should use quotations from "Holy Sonnet 10" to support that the speaker does not fear death because he does not see it as a terrible event (lines 1–2). They should also locate evidence from the sonnet to show the speaker sees death as inevitable and as a period that one must pass through in order to reach eternity (for example, lines 4–5 and 13–14).

12. (Average) Students should cite and explain evidence from "Song" to show that the time of separation is described as a brief period. While the speaker laments his inability to control time (lines 17–20), the parting of the lovers is described as being shorter than the rising and setting of the sun (stanza 2), and the time it takes to sleep the night away (lines 37–38). The speaker explains the passage of time in this manner in order to console his beloved and to make her realize that he will be back soon.

13. (Challenging) Venn diagram: Circle with "Song" only: The speaker tries to console his beloved about their impending separation (lines 14–16). He reaffirms his love for her (lines 1–4), and he refers to his beloved as "you," implying that he does not share her incredible sadness. The beloved is distraught over the departure of the speaker (lines 25–28). Circle with "A Valediction: Forbidding Mourning" only: The speaker is assured that his beloved feels the same way that he does about their separation—that it is only temporary. He uses the pronouns "we" and "us" to signal this agreement. He also states that he and the beloved have faith in each other (line 19). The beloved is more calm than aggrieved about the speaker's impending departure; instead of trying frantically to calm her, the speaker talks about how other couples don't deal as well as they do with absence (lines 13–16).Intersecting space (both): in both poems, the separation is viewed as a temporary one.

Essay should focus on why and how the reactions of the speakers and beloveds in each poem differ over a temporary separation. Citations from each poem should be used to support the ideas stated in the essay.

14. (Average) Students should use quotations or paraphrases from "Meditation 17" to support that Donne views suffering, or "affliction," as a "treasure," and that suffering helps one to focus on how a relationship with God may provide security during this painful time. Such contemplation takes one's attention away from earthly troubles and instead focuses it on spiritual matters, which Donne believes are more important. Awareness of other people's afflictions is also a valuable means through which one may be persuaded to think about one's own impending death and one's relationship with God.

15. (Easy) Students may select examples about baptism and death and explain how these examples support Donne's belief about how membership within the church community necessarily connects people.

Oral Response

16. In their oral response, students should cite specific information from the works of Donne that substantiates their presentations and expands their earlier responses.

"On My First Son," "Song: to Celia," and "Still to Be Neat"
by Ben Jonson
Open-Book Test (p. 52)

Multiple Choice and Short Answer

1. Sample answer: The speaker's son was seven years old when he died suddenly. Jonson uses the metaphor of a loan to describe this sudden death of a child. The child was "lent" to the speaker, who as the recipient of his son, "repays" this loan when "fate" takes the child away (lines 3–4).

2. Sample answer: Because his son's untimely death prevents the son from suffering worldly harm, physical pain, and aging, the speaker feels that he should not regret his son's death (line 2).

3. Sample answer: Jonson has learned a painful lesson about tempering his love for another person— in this case, his son. His unlimited love for his son has caused him great sorrow (line 2).

4.a Explanation: In line 10, Jonson asserts that he is the speaker of this poem. Answer (b) is incorrect because there is no evidence to support this answer. Answer (c) is incorrect because, while line 1 gives us the idea that the

speaker is a father, it is more specifically Jonson who is speaking as the father of the dead child (line 10). Answer (d) is incorrect because there is no evidence to support this answer.

5. Sample answer: In "Song: To Celia," the speaker exhorts his beloved to pledge her fidelity to him by looking at him in a loving way. This looking is represented in the poem by the act of drinking (line 1). In return, the speaker pledges to do the same (line 2).

6.b Explanation: Lines 11–12 support this answer. Answer (a) is incorrect because the speaker states that this was not his purpose in line 10. There is no evidence in the poem to support answers (c) and (d).

7. Sample answer: The speaker is deeply in love with the beloved, and as a result, he idealizes her. When the wreath is returned to the speaker, he asserts that because the beloved breathed on the wreath (line 13), the wreath not only flourishes (line 15) but also smells of the beloved (lines 15–16).

8. Sample answer: The speaker views the lady's preparations—her dressing, powdering, and perfuming—as a means of hiding her true appearance. She may not be as pretty as she makes herself out to be (lines 4–5).

9.d Explanation: "Sweet neglect" is the twist in these lines. The speaker implies that natural beauty— beauty that is attained without artifice—is what he considers to be most attractive about a woman.

10. Sample answer: The word "still" means "always" in this poem. "Still" begins phrases that describe the steps in a lady's beauty regimen (lines 1, 3). The speaker is suspicious of a woman who always needs to create an artificial facade (line 6) and who will not let people see what she looks like without such beauty preparations. These suspicions are contrasted with what the speaker does feel is attractive about a woman, which is a natural, unadulterated beauty (stanza 2).

Questions are classified in these categories:

Comprehension	10 (E)
Interpretation	1 (A), 6 (A)
Literary Analysis	3 (A), 8 (C), 9 (C)
Reading Strategy	4 (E), 5 (A), 7 (A)
Vocabulary	2 (A)

E=Easy, A=Average, C=Challenging

Extended Response

11. (Easy) The response should indicate that while Jonson is saddened by his son's loss (line 1), he realizes that his pain is due to the fact that he loved his son too much (line 2). While he is not sure that he wants to be a father (line 5), Jonson does comfort himself about his son's untimely death. Jonson concludes that his son is better off dead because the son has escaped

earthly suffering, illness, and the pain of aging (lines 7–8). Rather than mourn his son's death, Jonson thinks that he should envy it (line 6). Jonson makes peace with his son's death and vows never to love someone that much again (lines 9, 12).

12. (Challenging) The speaker uses romantic images to depict his love for the beloved. Drinking to someone is usually done to celebrate that person in some way. The speaker's use of drinking to symbolize a loving look from the beloved also represents a celebration of their love (lines 1–2). The speaker's thirst in line 5 represents his desire to be with the beloved. He views their love as something special, since he speaks of it in terms of being a "drink divine" (line 6). The speaker's description of how his beloved kept a wreath of flowers from being "withered" (line 12) reveals his admiration of the beloved's vitality. He credits her with preventing the wreath of roses from dying by permeating it with her own breath (lines 13, 15–16).

13. (Challenging) The response should indicate that the second-person narrator serves to give the poems an intimate feeling. The reader gets the impression that he or she is eavesdropping on a private talk or reading a private letter between the speaker and his subject. Because the speaker is addressing a specific person directly, the content of these poems seems more realistic. For example, in "On My First Son," the reader feels the speaker's pain acutely when he states, "My sin was too much hope of thee, loved boy" (line 2). The reader can visualize the speaker paying his final respects to his dead son by uttering these words. In "Song: To Celia," the romantic tone of the poem and the speaker's passionate feelings for the beloved are emphasized by lines such as ""Drink to me only with thine eyes, / And I will pledge with mine. . ." (line 1–2). Lines such as these, where the speaker speaks directly with the beloved, lend credence to the love he is unafraid of expressing to her.

14. (Average) Venn diagram: "On My First Son" : Type of love: paternal love (lines 1–2). How this love is presented in the poem: The father is paying his final respects to his dead son, lamenting his loss and comforting himself that his son is in a better place. The speaker has learned that he must temper such love if he does not want to be hurt by it through another loss (line 3–4). "Song: To Celia": Type of love: Romantic love (lines 1–2). How this love is presented in the poem: This romantic love is presented in a figurative manner through the act of drinking and the presentation of a wreath. In both of these images, the reader gets the impression that this love will last eternally. In stanza 1, the speaker's love is presented as

arising from the soul (line 5), and his beloved's affection is described as a "drink divine" (line 6). In stanza 2, the speaker's breath is credited with keeping a wreath of roses alive (lines 13–16). Here, love appears to conquer even death. The essay should use the information gathered in the Venn diagram to show that Jonson portrays two very different types of love and the results that these two kinds of love have on the people involved in them. In "On My First Son," Jonson talks about how love is temporary; in "Song: To Celia" Jonson shows the reader that love can conquer even death.

15. (Challenging) The ideas presented in these poems appear at first glance to go against common sense; however, on reflection, the reader discovers that the poems express a truth. For example, in "On My First Son," the speaker vows that next time he loves someone, he will not "like too much" (line 12). Initially, one is puzzled. How can one love, but not like, since these terms connote similar feelings? Upon reflection, one realizes that Jonson means that when one does love someone, one should temper one's love in order to avoid heartache if the love should ever end. In "Still To Be Neat," the speaker explains that the beauty of "sweet neglect" (line 10) is what he finds most attractive about a woman. The term "sweet neglect" appears to be a contradiction in terms, but within the context of the poem, the reader understands that this phrase refers to natural beauty and not a beauty of artifice. "Song: To Celia" is memorable for its imagery ("Drink with me only with thine eyes") and its universal theme of unrequited love.

Oral Response

16. In their oral responses, students should cite specific information from the poems that substantiates their presentations and expands on their earlier responses.

"To His Coy Mistress"
by Andrew Marvell

"To the Virgins, to Make Much of Time"
by Robert Herrick

"Song"
by Sir John Suckling

Open-book Test (p. 55)

Multiple Choice and Short Answer

1. Sample answer: The speaker asserts that, if he were able, he would spend a great deal of time with his mistress. He emphasizes this point by exaggerating how much time he would spend admiring and loving her. Lines 13–14 illustrate one such example of this point, but there are various examples within the poem.

2.b Explanation: Lines 25-27 state the speaker's opinion that if the mistress wastes any more time in making her decision to enter into a relationship with him, she will lose her beauty. This statement implies that she is beautiful since she is able to lose her beauty. Also lines 13–17, and lines 33–34 reveal the speaker's belief that his beloved is beautiful.

3.a Explanation: *Amorous* means "full of love." Based on the context of the poem, the speaker suggests that he and the mistress should act aggressively to use what time they have to love each other (lines 39–40)—hence the image of a pair of loving, yet aggressive birds is used to illustrate this idea.

4. Sample answer: The flowers and "rosebuds" (line 1) in this poem represent youth. Through his reference to the brief lifespan of freshly picked flowers, the speaker advises young women to make the most of their youth.

5.b Explanation: The speaker advises the young women not to be overly flirtatious, but to enter a permanent relationship with a man through marriage. Answer (a) is incorrect because it states the speaker's opinion that youth is the best time of life, not his ideas about how it should be spent. Answer (c) is incorrect because it explains the transiency of youth. Answer (d) is incorrect because it explains what happens if the speaker's advice isn't followed.

6. Sample answer: The speaker first proves that time, and, consequently, youth, pass by quickly. Stanzas 1 and 2 explain how time passes quickly by presenting images of fading flowers and of the setting sun. In stanza 3, the speaker directly asserts that youth is the best time of a woman's life, and that life becomes more tedious as one grows older. In stanza 4, the speaker offers his advice and the consequences of not following it.

7. Sample answer: The speaker's questions about the toll that the lover's efforts have taken on him emphasizes the futility of the lover's efforts to get the attentions of a woman who has no interest in him.

8.d Explanation: The speaker is impatient with the lover. The last three lines of the poem signal this impatience because they imply that the lover should give up in his efforts to win the beloved's affections. The exclamation mark at the end of this phrase also suggests the speaker's impatience. There is no evidence to support answers (a), (b), or (c).

9.d Explanation: In this quotation, the speaker suggests that the lover seize the opportunity to move on with his life by leaving the beloved alone. Answers (a), (b), and (c) are incorrect because they are questions that the speaker

poses to the lover in an effort to make the lover see the terrible effect that his efforts to win the beloved have had on him.

10.a Explanation: The speaker in "To His Coy Mistress" wants to persuade his mistress to enter into a relationship with him, while the speaker in "Song" wants to persuade the lover to discontinue his efforts to win the affections of his beloved.

Questions are classified in these categories:

Comprehension	10 (E)
Interpretation	1 (A), 6 (A)
Literary Analysis	3 (A), 8 (C), 9 (C)
Reading Strategy	4 (E), 5 (A), 7 (A)
Vocabulary	2 (A)

E=Easy, A=Average, C=Challenging

Extended Response

11. (Average) The essay response should demonstrate that in stanza 1, the speaker first establishes that he would not mind conducting this relationship at a slower pace if he had the time to do so. Possible lines of the poem to support this idea are lines 7–8 and lines 13–14. In stanza 2, the speaker attempts to stir the beloved into action by explaining how rapidly a person moves toward death. Possible lines of the poem that support this statement are lines 25 and 31–32. Now that he has alarmed the beloved by reminding her of her short time on earth, the speaker exhorts her to make the most of the time they have together. Possible lines of the poem to support this idea are lines 37–40. The students may cite lines of the poem other than those listed to support the points they make in their essay.

12. (Easy) The image of fading flowers and the setting sun should be discussed. The response should indicate that the fading flowers represent how beauty and youth fade with the passage of time. The setting sun represents how quickly time passes and how making the most of one's youth is likened to a race against time.

13. (Challenging) The response should indicate that the speaker in "Song" serves as an impartial witness to the effect that the lover's futile efforts to win his beloved have on the lover. In stanzas 1 and 2, the speaker describes how the lover has been physically and emotionally destroyed by these efforts. The speaker's impartial description makes his advice to the lover in stanza 3 seem sensible. Various lines in the poem may be used to support these statements.

14. (Average) Venn diagram: Circle with "To His Coy Mistress" only: images of love and consequences of not pursuing it are more aggressive (lines 27–32, 38–40). Circle with "To the Virgins, to Make Much of Time" only: images of love and consequences of not pursuing it are more

romantic and sensual (stanza 1, lines 9–10)
Intersecting space (both): In both poems, love is
described as an emotion that belongs to the
young; making the most of youth by falling in
love illustrates the carpe diem theme in both
poems. Evidence of this idea in "To His Coy
Mistress" is found in lines 41–46. Evidence of
this idea in "To the Virgins, to Make Much of
Time" is found in lines 13–16. Essay responses
should be based on the information that is
compiled in the Venn diagram.

15. (Challenging) Responses to this answer will
depend on the work that the students have
selected to analyze. Students should support
their answers with specific examples from the
poem they have selected.

Oral Response

16. In their oral response, students should cite
specific information from the poems that
substantiates their presentations and expands
on their earlier responses.

Poetry of John Milton

Open-Book Test (p. 58)

Multiple Choice and Short Answer

1. Sample answer: The speaker acknowledges that
he has aged physically with the passage of time;
however, he does not feel that he has matured
intellectually or emotionally in a comparable
manner.

2. Sample answer: Time has stolen upon the
speaker and has taken away his youth—he is
now in the "late spring" of his life (line 4). He
has no control over the passage of time, and,
consequently, no control over the aging process.

3.a Explanation: Lines 11–13 support this assertion.
The speaker has to trust in God to help him
deal with the aging process.

4. Sample answer: The speaker feels a sense of
inadequacy. He is unready to face adulthood
(lines 4–6).

5. Sample answer: The speaker refers to the loss of
his eyesight when he tells of how his "light is
spent" before half his days on earth have passed
(lines 1–2). He also states that he is living in a
dark world (line 2), which implies that he is
blind.

6.b Explanation: In the sestet of "Sonnet XIX," the
second speaker tells the first speaker that he
can still serve God by coping with and accepting
his blindness (line 11).

7. Sample answer: *Illumine* means "to light up." In
lines 22–23, the word illumine is opposed with
what is dark in the speaker. The pattern of pairing
opposites is established in the line that follows,
"what is low raise and support. . ." (lines 22–23).

8. Sample answer: This section of *Paradise Lost* is
told from Satan's perspective. By his own
admission, Satan (who represents evil) is
defeated by God (who represents good) (lines
249–250) and has fallen from "the happy realms
of light" (line 85), or Heaven. The devil expresses
his intentions to wreak havoc in opposition to
God's efforts to create goodness at various
points in the poem (lines 162-165, for example).

9. Sample answer: The main clause in lines in
lines 81–83 is "Satan thus began." Satan, the
archenemy of heaven, breaks the silence and
begins speaking to Beelzebub.

10. Sample answer: Although Satan is tormented by
defeat (lines 55–56), he composes himself (lines
246–250) and resigns himself to creating his
own kingdom in Hell (line 264).

Questions are classified in these categories:

Comprehension	10 (E)
Interpretation	1 (A), 6 (A)
Literary Analysis	3 (A), 8 (C), 9 (C)
Reading Strategy	4 (E), 5 (A), 7 (A)
Vocabulary	2 (A)

E=Easy, A=Average, C=Challenging

Extended Response

11. (Easy) The response should indicate that Time
and "the will of Heaven" control the development
of the speaker's life (line 12). The speaker leaves
the resolution of this conflict to the will of God,
who is referred to as his "Taskmaster" (line 14).

12. (Average) The first speaker in "Sonnet XIX" is
grappling with a problem over which he has no
control: the onset of his blindness. Because he
has no control over this problem, the speaker
feels that he has no way to resolve it. Frustrated
by his inability to serve God through his work,
the speaker questions God about his condition
(lines 5–7). The second speaker is necessary to
present the divine solution to this problem and
to remind the first speaker that some problems
are necessarily out of his control. The second
speaker explains to the first speaker that to
serve God he need not strive to produce "work
or his own gifts" (line 10). Rather, the second
speaker counsels the first speaker to serve God
by bearing his "mild yoke" of blindness (line 11),
declaring, "they also serve who only stand and
wait" (line 14).

13. (Challenging) The rhyme scheme of the sestet in
"Sonnet VII" is abcbac, while the rhyme scheme
of "Sonnet XIX" is abcabc. The sestet in "Sonnet
XIX" contains a more regular rhyme pattern that
reinforces the comforting message of the second
speaker. The irregular rhyme pattern of "Sonnet
VII" reflects the speaker's uncertainty about the
way that he has resolved his problem; He
wonders "if [he has] the grace to use it so" (line

13) when he wonders if he has the faith to let his "Taskmaster" (line 14), or God, control the direction of his development.

14. (Challenging) Milton uses Hebrew allusions as a parallel to Greek allusions that are usually found in epic poems in order to emphasize the grand scale of the subject he is presenting to the reader. He also uses allusions to reconcile the religious nature of his poem with the classical format of the epic poem, in which, among other things, the speaker calls on a Muse for aid. Examples of such allusions are found on lines 7, 12,17, and 198–202, though students may locate and use other examples from the poem.

15. (Average) Qualities of Satan that would be written on the diagonal line include the following: frustrated (lines 84–88), stubborn (lines 157–165); angry (lines 215–221); heroic (lines 250-271). Students will utilize the information they compiled in the graphic organizer to write an essay about these qualities, citing specific lines from the poem to support their assertions. (Note: The examples supporting these qualities that would appear on horizontal lines appear in parentheses immediately after the qualities they substantiate.)

Oral Response

16. In their oral responses, students should cite specific information from the sonnets or from *Paradise Lost* that substantiates their presentations and expands on their earlier responses.

from "Eve's Apology in Defense of Women"
by Amelia Lanier

"To Lucasta, on Going to the Wars" and "To Althea, from Prison"
by Richard Lovelace

Open-Book Test (p. 61)

Multiple Choice and Short Answer

1. Sample answer: Lanier portrays Eve's gift of the apple to Adam as an act of love (lines 25–28); Eve never meant to harm Adam (lines 26-27), and Adam never reproved Eve for her actions (line 29).

2. Sample answer: Possible student responses on diagonal lines would include the following:
1. Adam is inherently weak (lines 3, 6–7);
2. Adam knew the consequences but still took the apple (lines 11–14); 3. Adam blames Eve for his mistake (lines 18–21); No one forced Adam to take the apple (lines 23–24); Adam wanted the knowledge that the apple promised, despite his knowledge of the consequences (lines 29–32). (Note: Examples substantiating these assertions are provided in parentheses.)

3. Sample answer: Since the idea of equality for men and women was a radical concept during the years when Lanier was alive, presenting her ideas on this subject in a medium that was as familiar and non-threatening as the story of Adam and Eve makes Lanier's views more understandable and allows her to reach a wide range of people.

4.c Explanation: This answer is supported by lines 11–12 of the poem.

5. Sample answer: Lovelace himself was a member of the army of King Charles I and fought against the anti-Royalists.

6. Sample answer: The speaker feels elated. He describes Althea as "my divine Althea" (line 3) and declares that there is no better freedom than when he is "tangled in her hair" (line 5) and staring into her eyes (line 6).

7. Sample answer: In stanza 4, the speaker voices his unconditional support for the King. He views the king as sweet, merciful, majestic, and good (lines 19 and 21).

8. Sample answer: This poem shows the reader that the speaker is willing to go to prison for his Royalist beliefs, giving up his beloved (Althea) and his freedom. The speaker's optimistic attitude about restoring the King to the throne is not dampened by his confinement. The poem is a powerful statement of loyalty to the Royalist cause.

9.b Explanation: The speaker demonstrates that he is unafraid to suffer for his beliefs (lines 25–26). He describes how he deals with separation and confinement in each stanza in a way that suggests that he feels free.

10. Sample answer: In the last line of each stanza, the speaker concludes that his visits from and drinks with Althea, his desire to sing about the King, and the meditation that he is able to do in prison all contribute to a sense of liberty. He is determined not to let his imprisonment depress him.

Questions are classified in these categories:

Category	
Comprehension	10 (E)
Interpretation	1 (A), 6 (A)
Literary Analysis	3 (A), 8 (C), 9 (C)
Reading Strategy	4 (E), 5 (A), 7 (A)
Vocabulary	2 (A)

E=Easy, A=Average, C=Challenging

Extended Response

11. (Challenging) During the period in which Lanier wrote her poem, tensions rose between Protestants and Catholics, and conflict between Royalists and anti-Royalists became more pronounced after Charles I was beheaded by the anti-Royalists. The victors of these conflicts persecuted their enemies. It was a time of great

instability; therefore, Lanier's proposal for equal rights for men and women, while radical, was another example of how established social, religious, and political institutions were being questioned and sometimes overthrown.

12. (Easy) The response should indicate that the speaker assures his beloved that it is necessary that he go to war (lines 7–8). He is also eager to fight in the war; he states, "To arms I fly" (line 4). He sees his participation in the war as a means of entering another type of relationship (lines 5–8). Through this relationship with war, the speaker believes that he can prove his honor (lines 11–12).

13. (Average) Student responses should indicate that the speaker associates his confinement with references to divine beings, animals, and forces of nature that are associated with freedom. He compares his visit from Althea to the eternal frolicking of the gods (line 6), thus making a brief prison visit appear to last an eternity. He presents drinking with Althea as a celebratory event, complete with unlimited toasts and drinks (line 13), making him feel freer than fish that swim in the ocean (line 15). Voicing his loyalty for the King makes the speaker feel as free as the wind (line 23). Finally, the speaker views his imprisonment not as a confinement, but as a place for meditation, which frees his soul to fly like the angels (lines 25–30).

14. (Challenging) Possible responses to this question may include that the speaker has a strong and uncompromising character. He would rather accept imprisonment than renounce his allegiance to the King, and strives to keep his spirits up by refusing to let his depressing circumstances cause him to lose hope.

15. (Average) In "To Lucasta, on Going to the Wars," the speaker offers the perspective that war is the place to prove his honor, which he needs in order to maintain his relationship with his beloved. (lines 7–8, 11–12). He offers this view to comfort his beloved about his departure and possible death on the battlefield. In "To Althea, from Prison," the speaker views his imprisonment as an opportunity to meditate and enrich himself spiritually (stanza 4).

Oral Response

16. In their oral responses, students should cite specific information from the poems that substantiates their presentations and expands on their earlier responses.

from *The Diary*
by Samuel Pepys
from *A Journal of the Plague Year*
by Daniel Defoe
Open-Book Test (p. 64)

Multiple Choice and Short Answer

1. Sample answer: Pepys records the names of friends and acquaintances who were victims of the bubonic plague. The recording of these names and Pepys's reactions to the deaths of these people show how personally this epidemic affected Pepys.

2. Sample answer: Pepys was a member of the upper class. The names of his colleagues are preceded by titles such as "Lord" and "Sir." In addition, Pepys and his colleagues seem to have a degree of political clout in London, as evidenced by their decision to allow a child who was smuggled out of a plague-infested house into Greenwich to remain in Greenwich.

3.a Explanation: Pepys states that he found his "money and plate. . . all safe at London." He also writes that there is a "decrease of 500 and more" deaths from the plague. Though he is happy about this news, he is still worried about the proximity of the plague to his house and the alarming number of people who are infected with it.

4.d Explanation: Pepys awakens and moves his belongings in the early morning hours because he is worried that his house and his possessions will be consumed by the fire. The other answers are simply observations of the fire. They do not convey Pepys's growing concern.

5. Sample answer: Pepys values his money and possessions. This value is shown through his concern about these things. Knowing that his money and possessions are safe during the plague cheers him up. He also carts away all of his "money, plate, and best things" during the Fire of London.

6. Sample answer: The narrator describes the reactions of the people affected by the plague in vivid detail. For example, he recounts the "shrieks of women and children at the windows and doors of their houses where their dearest relations were dying or perhaps just dead." Students may use other examples from the text to support their response.

7. Sample answer: Citing the number of people who died from the plague emphasizes the catastrophic scale of the disease.

8.c Explanation: This meaning can be determined from the context of the sentence. So many people died that there were not enough coffins in which to bury them.

9. Sample answer: Defoe writes the journal in the first person and further personalizes it by describing the burial he witnesses. The narrator not only recounts this experience, but also records his emotional reaction to it.

10. Sample answer: Both authors describe the plague's devastating impact on the population and everyday life. Pepys's account of the child who was smuggled to Greenwich, and the narrator's eyewitness account of the father who watched the burial of his own family in *A Journal of the Plague Year* are examples that illustrate how the plague destroyed families.

Questions are classified in these categories:
Comprehension   10 (E)
Interpretation   1 (A), 6 (A)
Literary Analysis   3 (A), 8 (C), 9 (C)
Reading Strategy   4 (E), 5 (A), 7 (A)
Vocabulary   2 (A)

E=Easy, A=Average, C=Challenging

Extended Response

11. (Easy) Pepys's account shows the reader how a wealthy member of English society during this period may have coped with the advent of the plague and the fire. In *The Diary*, Pepys describes how he saves his money and valuables, watches the fire spread, and notes the deaths of people he knows; he himself does not appear to have experienced the loss of a loved one from the bubonic plague or the fire. As a result, the emotional impact of such recorded experiences is blunted.

12. (Average) Possible responses to this question could include the lack of a systematized means for dealing with catastrophic events, and the close quarters in which people lived in order for the plague and the fires to spread so rapidly.

13. (Challenging) The story map should be filled in as follows:

Conflict: Narrator wants to gain access to church yard in order to satisfy his curiosity about the burial pit and to watch the burial of the bodies.

Rising Action:

1. The Narrator asks the sexton for permission to enter the church yard.

2. The sexton attempts to persuade him not to go.

3. After the narrator insists that he must go, the sexton yields to him, but warns the narrator that it might be a shocking experience.

4. The narrator enters the church yard.

Climax:

5. The narrator witnesses the grief-stricken reaction of a father who watches the careless manner in which his entire family is buried.

Falling Action:

6. The father is led away and cared for.

7. The narrator is greatly affected by what he has witnessed.

8. The narrator is also shocked at the condition of the corpses that are being unloaded from the cart and buried in a common grave.

Resolution: The narrator fully realizes the calamity of the plague after he witnesses the mass burial. Setting: London, 1660's.

Major characters: The narrator.

After they have completed the story map, students will use this information to write their essay. The response should indicate that *A Journal of the Plague Year* has a definite narrative structure, which points to the fact that it is not an authentic journal and that Defoe wrote it with the intent of publishing it.

14. (Average) In *The Diary*, Pepys discussed the fire and the bubonic plague by describing the effects that each event had on his life. The details, such as names of friends lost to the plague, his opinion of the Lord Mayor, and the walk to the alehouse after watching the spread of the fire, are what make *The Diary* so valuable as a record of how these events affected an individual living during that time. Through these details, one discovers insights into the opinions and values of Pepys with respect to these events, not just an accounting of timeliness and events.

15. (Easy) The diary form personalizes the historical events that are being described by the writer. From the writer, one gets not only an explanation of the events that occurred, but also how these events affected real people such as Pepys in the way that they lived their everyday lives. Students may cite various examples from both works to substantiate their answers.

Oral Response

16. In their oral responses, students should cite specific information from the diary excerpts that substantiates their presentations and expands on their earlier responses.

from *Gulliver's Travels*
by Jonathan Swift

Open-Book Test (p. 67)

Multiple Choice and Short Answer

1.c Explanation: It is ridiculous to impose a harsh penalty merely for breaking eggs in a certain way. Here, Swift implies that the religious conflict in England is petty.

2. Sample answer: Swift views England and France as two empires entrenched in a conflict at the expense of forming political relationships with other nations and dealing more effectively with wider world issues.

3. Sample answer: The small size of the Lilliputians and the Blefescudians represents their small-mindedness in refusing to end this conflict. Because he is a giant and therefore "above" the Lilliputians and Blefuscudians, both literally and figuratively, in this quarrel, Gulliver is easily able to change the course of the conflict by capturing the Blefuscudians' ships and averting bloodshed.

4. Sample answer: Gulliver was morally offended by the king's request. He could not bring himself to be an "instrument of bringing a free and brave people into slavery."

5.b Explanation: The King laughs at what Gulliver considers to be examples of the greatness of English politics and society.

6. Sample answer: The King's huge size represents his greater understanding of how ridiculous and dangerous some aspects of English politics and society are.

7.a Explanation: The King is shocked at the pointlessly violent and dishonorable behavior of the English.

8. Sample answer: This remark by Gulliver tells the reader that he is a reliable narrator. The reader needs to believe Gulliver's account of his storytelling and the King's reaction to it in order to understand that Swift is basing the satire on the King's reactions to Gulliver's stories, and Gulliver's confusion about the King's reactions.

9.c Explanation: The King states, "I cannot but conclude the bulk of your natives to be the most pernicious race of little *odious* vermin that nature ever suffered to crawl upon the surface of the earth." *Odious* is associated with "pernicious" and "vermin," words that also have negative connotations.

10. Sample answer: Swift is against war. The King's view, as it is described in detail, represents Swift's view of this issue.

Questions are classified in these categories:

Comprehension	10 (E)
Interpretation	1 (A), 6 (A)
Literary Analysis	3 (A), 8 (C), 9 (C)
Reading Strategy	4 (E), 5 (A), 7 (A)
Vocabulary	2 (A)

E=Easy, A=Average, C=Challenging

Extended Response

11. (Average) Responses should include the use of the egg-breaking conflict as the symbol for the religious rift in England; the size of the Lilliputians and Blefescudians as representative of the pettiness of the quarrels; and the description of the six rebellions and the emperors' losses of life and crown as references to the impact that the religious conflict had had on England.

12. (Average) Student responses should indicate that Gulliver's stories about England introduce the elements of actual English society that Swift satirizes, and that the King's emotional responses are Swift's commentary on these issues.

13. (Challenging) Responses to this question may vary. Possible responses may show that the King shows a keen apprehension of the issues that are raised in Gulliver's stories, or that he is a humane ruler based on his reaction to the more violent aspects of Gulliver's stories and by the way that he treats Gulliver.

14. (Easy) Student responses to the question will vary since they are allowed to choose one work to analyze.

15. (Challenging) In Lilliput, Gulliver's large size gave him the ability to decide conflicts and control outcomes. For example, Gulliver captured the naval fleet of the Blefuscudians and averted a war between the Lilliputians and Blefuscudians. Gulliver's small size reduced him to the role of a pet while he was at the court of Brobdingnag. Gulliver's small size in relation to the King's huge stature emphasizes the small-mindedness of Gulliver's views of England. In each piece, size is used to contrast what Swift considers to be petty or dangerous ideas and behaviors in England (represented by small size) with Swift's own views of the direction that English society should take (represented by large size).

Oral Response

16. In their oral response, students should cite specific information from *Gulliver's Travels* that substantiates their presentations and expands on their earlier answers.

from *An Essay on Man* and from *The Rape of the Lock* by Alexander Pope

Open-Book Test (p. 70)

Multiple Choice and Short Answer

1.b Explanation: The poem lists the conflicting behaviors that an individual (represented by the word "he") possesses.

2. Sample answer: An isthmus is a narrow strip of land that connects two larger bodies of land. A human being is viewed by Pope to be the link between the heavenly and the material worlds. As Pope declares, a person is "Created half to rise, half to fall" (line 15).

3. Sample answer: These contrasts are intended by Pope to show the variety of conflicting behaviors that are present in an individual.

4.c Explanation: Lines 10–14 deal with a person's ability to think. One can conclude that *disabused* has something to do with the thought process.

5.a Explanation: The subjects of this conversation include unimportant matters such as parties (line 12) and furniture (line 14).

6. Sample answer: Lines 19–23 describe the life and death matters that take place in the courts, and the transaction of business. These events contrast with the self-absorption involved with keeping up one's appearance (line 24).

7. Sample answer: The objective of omber is described in terms of conquest (line 27–28). The faces of the cards are described as soldiers (lines 39–44). The cards of Belinda's opponents in this game are described as "armies" (line 65). The capture of cards is described in terms of war casualties (lines 69–74).

8. Sample answer: Clarissa gives the baron a pair of scissors (lines 127–130). The baron attempts to cut a lock of hair from behind Belinda's head while Belinda bends over to sip a cup of coffee (lines 133–134). He makes three attempts to cut her hair; each time, because of the distractions of sprites, Belinda looks over her shoulder just as the baron is about to cut the lock from her hair (135–138). On his fourth attempt, the baron successfully cuts the lock of hair from Belinda's head because the sylph does not prevent it (lines 144–154).

9. Sample answer: The conversation emphasizes the preposterous nature of the conflict between Belinda and the baron. They speak to each other as if they are at war with each other (lines 50–59).

10. Sample answer: The heavenly ascent of the lock mocks the romantic intrigues around which Belinda's life has revolved (lines 83–88).

Questions are classified in these categories:

Comprehension	4 (E)
Interpretation	5 (A), 10 (A)
Literary Analysis	2 (C), 3 (C), 7 (A)
Reading Strategy	1 (A), 8 (E), 9 (A)
Vocabulary	6 (A)

E=Easy, A=Average, C=Challenging

Extended Response

11. (Challenging) Pope sees the human condition as idiosyncratic. He thinks that many contradictory qualities exist in a human being, and he becomes perplexed (and amused) as a result. Pope's view of the inconsistency of human nature is summed up by the last line of the poem; man is "The glory, jest, and riddle of the world" (line 18).

12. (Easy) Student responses should indicate that in the same way that a true epic involves gods and goddesses, Pope incorporates sylphs and sprites into his mock epic. To further imitate the elevated style of the true epic, Pope also

describes the card game in terms of a bloody battle and portrays Belinda's actions as heroic. Examples cited should support these elements.

13. (Average) Responses to this question may vary, but possible segments of the poem that may be analyzed for humor are Belinda's antic conquests during the game of omber (lines 28-29), Belinda's reaction to the baron's winning hand (lines 89–92), the baron's cry of triumph after he cuts the lock of Belinda's hair (lines 161–178), or the ascent of the lock to the heavens (lines 69–88).

14. (Average) The lock represents the pettiness of English society. He expresses his disdain for this pettiness through his mocking descriptions of the commotion made over the theft of the lock, the baron's obsession with it, and the lock's ascent to heaven.

15. (Challenging) Students may say *The Rape of the Lock* is more hopeful because of its humorous style, and because the lock asends upward to the "lunar sphere." They may say *An Essay on Man* is hopeful, because it describes man's best impulses; or that it is not hopeful, because it acknowledges his worst impulses.

Oral Response

16. In their oral responses, students should cite specific information from the poems that substantiates their presentations and expands on their earlier responses.

from *The Preface to A Dictionary of the English Language* and from *A Dictionary of the English Language*
by Samuel Johnson

from *The Life of Samuel Johnson*
by James Boswell

Open-Book Test (p. 73)

Multiple Choice and Short Answer

1.a Explanation: Johnson describes the lexicographer as the "slave of science, pioneer of literature, doomed only to remove rubbish and clear obstructions from the paths through which learning and genius press forward to conquest and glory."

2. Sample answer: Based on the information in this preface, people view the lexicographer critically. As Johnson writes, the lexicographer only hopes "to escape reproach."

3.b Explanation: Johnson states that when he began this process, he found "our speech copious without order and energetic without rule; wherever I turned my view, there was perplexity to be disentangled and confusion to be regulated. . ."

4. Sample answer: Johnson defends his efforts in creating this dictionary by saying that he tried his best to create a comprehensive dictionary—something no one else has ever done.

5. Sample answer: In the column labeled "K," students might list the structure of the dictionary—specifically, the use of famous quotes from literary works and authors. Under the column labeled "W," students may list questions such as, "How are analogies used to define the words?" or "What sort of organizational system is evident in Johnson's dictionary?" Under the column labeled "L," students should list the answers to any questions that they found. For example, students may respond to the first questions listed above by writing that the analogies are used to clarify the meaning and use of a word within a context that would be familiar to users of Johnson's dictionary.

6. Sample answer: The definition for *patron* not only clarifies the meaning of the word; it also reflects Johnson's disdain for this group of people. In the definition, he refers to patrons as wretches although his more neutral definition includes supporters and protection.

7. Sample answer: Johnson stated that he wanted to organize the meanings and uses of words in the English language; in his dictionary, Johnson has ordered words alphabetically, and illustrated their grammatical and colloquial uses through the use of literary examples.

8. Explanation: Boswell describes an instance where Johnson spoke sarcastically in "Boswell meets Johnson." He describes Johnson's tendency to be sarcastic in milder terms in "Johnson's Character."

9. Sample answer: Religious faith and loyalty to the king were two of the qualities held in high esteem by Johnson and the society of his time. Students should cite details to support their comments.

10. Sample answer: *Credulity* is readiness or willingness to believe, especially on slight or uncertain evidence. Although the word "superstition" suggests a belief that goes against the laws of nature or science, the quotation suggests that Johnson was not so superstitious as to believe outlandish ideas.

Questions are classified in these categories:

Comprehension	10 (E)
Interpretation	1 (A), 6 (A)
Literary Analysis	3 (A), 8 (C), 9 (C)
Reading Strategy	4 (E), 5 (A), 7 (A)
Vocabulary	2 (A)

E=Easy, A=Average, C=Challenging

Extended Response

11. (Easy) Student responses should indicate that Johnson discusses his achievement in terms of the difficulty of the task, the hardships that he has suffered, and the acceptance of a high risk of failure. Johnson's explanations of the mental, emotional, and physical difficulties of his experience are meant to evoke the reader's sympathy for Johnson's efforts. Examples from the text should support these points.

12. (Challenging) Johnson has definite opinions about the people and things that certain words represent. For example, the definition for "shall-I-shall-I" reflects Johnson's contempt for procrastinators, while the word "willow" reflects Johnson's romantic view of the tree.

13. (Average) Johnson wanted to order the English language; however, since no one had ever accomplished this feat, he had to create his own system for doing so. He used excerpts from famous literary works and authors to "illustrate any word or phrase." He established rules for word usage "as experience and analogy suggested to me." These two methods for structuring the dictionary are evident in the entries.

14. (Average) Boswell portrays Johnson positively. Even when he discusses a potentially negative aspect of Johnson's personality, Boswell qualifies it. For example, Boswell writes that Johnson "had many prejudices; which, however, frequently suggested many of his pointed sayings that rather show a playfulness of fancy than any settled malignity." Various other examples showing Boswell's positive portrayal of Johnson may be cited in support of this assertion.

15. (Challenging) The response should indicate that Boswell appears to let friendship color his assessment of the subject of his work, his persistence in pursuing relationships that he considers to be important, and his high esteem for famous persons such as Johnson.

Oral Response

16. In their oral responses, students should cite specific information from the works by Johnson and Boswell that substantiates their presentations and expands on their earlier responses.

"Elegy Written in a Country Churchyard"
by Thomas Gray

"A Nocturnal Reverie"
by Ann Finch, Countess of Winchilsea

Open-Book Test (p. 76)

Multiple Choice and Short Answer

1.b   Explanation: The landscape glimmers and fades from sight in the twilight, and the air seems to hold still as if waiting for something, creating a mood of expectation and suspense.

2.   Sample answer: "Neither the morning breezes, the singing of the birds, the rooster's call, nor the echoes of a horn will revive those who are buried in the churchyard."

3.   Sample answer: The speaker imagines that some of these people were poor, simple farmers (stanzas 7–8).

4.   Sample answer: The speaker imagines what an old man would say about him because he is contemplating his own death, and, just as he contemplates the lives of those buried in the churchyard, he hopes others will speak about how they viewed him while he was still alive (lines 93-96).

5.   Sample answer: This is the speaker's epitaph. Lines 115–116 reveal this answer to the reader. These lines, spoken by the imaginary old man (stanza 25), explain that the speaker's tombstone has an inscription (the epitaph) on it.

6.a   Explanation: These lines describe how the end of the day can create a dreamlike beauty.

7.   Sample answer: At night, the speaker feels calm and quiet. The speaker wants to remain outside as long as possible during the night because she enjoys this peaceful feeling. Morning brings with it feelings of confusion and stresses of daily life that make the speaker feel agitated.

8.a   Explanation: Since the horse is chewing the *forage*, it is logical to conclude that *forage* is food.

9.   Sample answer: During the day, the speaker feels disturbed (line 40), while during the night, the speaker feels calm and quiet (line 39).

10.   Sample answer: The speaker describes the coming of the night through these images, creating a dreamlike quality within the poem. The speaker also discusses the emotional impact that the night makes upon her. Both these qualities reflect themes and concerns of the Romantic period.

Questions are classified in these categories:

Comprehension	10 (E)
Interpretation	1 (A), 6 (A)
Literary Analysis	3 (A), 8 (C), 9 (C)
Reading Strategy	4 (E), 5 (A), 7 (A)
Vocabulary	2 (A)

E=Easy, A=Average, C=Challenging

Extended Response

11.   (Easy) Student responses should indicate that the speaker feels sympathy for those people who are buried and forgotten in the churchyard (lines 29–32). He pays tribute to the dead by thinking about them; he imagines what these people were like while they were alive (lines 49–52, 57–60, 73–76).

12.   (Easy) The speaker is concerned that the death of a person causes people to forget about him or her. He feels that the people buried in the churchyard have been forgotten, something that he does not want to happen to himself when he dies. His fear of being forgotten after he dies is so strong that he envisions how he would like his life to be remembered if anyone ever asks about him. Lastly, the speaker's vision of the inscription on his tombstone represents his hopes to avoid the anonymous fate of those buried in the churchyard. The epitaph summarizes the aspects of his life that the speaker wants memorialized.

13.   (Average) The response should indicate that the speaker's description of the natural world, as it makes its transition from day to night, reflects peaceful solitude. Gentle breezes blow, an owl calls in the night, and clouds pass quietly overhead (lines 3, 5, 7). Even the colors of plants are softer; the foxgloves are described as taking on a "paler hue" (line 15). The movement of animals during the night is slow and relaxed, again reinforcing the peaceful atmosphere (lines 29–34).

14.   (Challenging) The punctuation of "A Nocturnal Reverie" gives the impression that we are sharing the speaker's thoughts as they occur to her. The use of commas and semicolons rather than periods to separate ideas encourages the reader to move on to the next phrase rather than come to a full stop before continuing to the next idea. In this way, the many ideas in the poem are linked together rather than separated, much like a person may move from one thought to another through associations.

15.   (Average) In the circle labeled "Elegy Written in a Country Churchyard": Night inspires the speaker to think of the serious issue of death (lines 13–16).

   In the circle labeled "A Nocturnal Reverie": Night inspires a sense of calm introspection for the speaker (lines 41–46).

In section labeled "Both": For both speakers, night is the time when they can privately contemplate serious matters.

Students should use the information they compiled in the Venn diagram as a basis for writing their essay.

Oral Response

16. In their presentations, students should cite specific information from the poems that substantiates their presentations and expands on their earlier responses.

"On Spring"
by Samuel Johnson

from "The Aims of the Spectator"
by Joseph Addison

Open-Book Test (p. 79)

Multiple Choice and Short Answer

1. Sample answer: The story of the man who looks forward to spring sets the tone and purpose for Johnson's essay.

2.a Explanation: People who cannot stand to be alone are either overwhelmed by sorrow, or have nothing to occupy their minds with.

3. Sample answer: Johnson asserts that just as very few people know how to take a walk, very few people know how to derive pleasure from the observation of the natural world.

4. Sample answer: "The spring affords to the mind, so free from the disturbance of cares or passions as to be vacant to calm amusements, almost everything that our present state makes us capable of enjoying."

5. Sample answer: Spring is the season that is associated with youth. In the last paragraph of this essay, Johnson urges young people to take advantage of their youth and acquire the ability and habit of observing nature in the springtime. He states that "their minds may yet be impressed with new images, a love of innocent pleasures, and an ardor for useful knowledge."

6. Sample answer: Addison takes neither his magazine nor his readership seriously. He exaggerates both his purpose for publishing his magazine and the moral condition of his readers.

7. Sample answer: Addison is exaggerating his purpose for publishing *The Spectator*. His exaggeration is evident when he speaks of bringing a serious subject such as philosophy to a tea table, a place known more for lighthearted conversation than philosophical discussion.

8. Sample answer: Addison's humorous attitude is evident when he recommends his magazine to

"everyone that considers the world as a theater and desires to form a right judgment of those who are the actors on it." He pokes fun at those who have the leisure to view life in such an idle manner.

9. Sample answer: Addison asserts that the daily life of a woman is filled with mindless or simple activity. Addison maintains that he hopes that his magazine will be viewed by women as "an innocent if not an improving entertainment, and by that means at least divert the minds of my female readers from greater trifles." By suggesting that reading his magazine is a smaller trifle than the other activities of women, Addison explains that women would be able to read his newspaper for entertainment.

10. Sample answer: necessities

Questions are classified in these categories:
Comprehension   10 (E)
Interpretation   1 (A), 6 (A)
Literary Analysis   3 (A), 8 (C), 9 (C)
Reading Strategy   4 (E), 5 (A), 7 (A)
Vocabulary   2 (A)

E=Easy, A=Average, C=Challenging

Extended Response

11. (Easy) Johnson moves his essay from the general idea of the human condition to the specific idea of how the contemplation of spring serves to rejuvenate the human spirit. First, Johnson first generally explains how an individual is continually engaged in the quest for happiness. He then tells the story of how one man deals with the difficulties in his life by looking forward to spring. This story serves as an example of how looking forward to something as delightful as the coming of spring helps to keep a person's spirits up. Next, Johnson describes how spring has served as an inspiration to poets and as a symbol of renewal. Johnson then distinguishes those persons who would not benefit from the contemplation of spring. Lastly, Johnson explains how the contemplation of nature in the springtime is a valuable means of maintaining a healthy, positive outlook on life, and that such a habit should be cultivated by young people if they are to develop it as a useful habit.

12. (Average) Student responses should indicate that Johnson discusses how the observation of spring may lead to a scientific discovery that may benefit humanity or that may prove lucrative to the individual observer. Helping others to observe the beauties of spring may also improve the health of those people.

13. (Average) Student responses should indicate that Addison employs humor through exaggeration and pokes fun at his readers. Students may cite various examples from the

text to support these ideas. Addison's conversational tone is reflected in the way that he takes the liberty to advise his readers about adopting a morning routine and by such statements as ". . . I recommend this paper to the daily perusal of those gentlemen whom I cannot but consider as my good brothers and allies. . ." Students may cite other examples to support their response.

14. (Average) The responses should indicate that Addison sees his goal as providing information and entertainment. For example, Addison states, "I shall endeavor to enliven morality with wit. . ." Addison underscores the entertainment value of his magazine when he advises his readers that it should be read within the context of such leisurely activities as tea time. The entertainment value of Addison's magazine is also illustrated through Addison's assertion that reading the magazine may help to stimulate conversation.

15. (Challenging) In "On Spring," the tone is thoughtful and serious. Johnson analyzes the value of the contemplation of nature. In "The Aims of the Spectator," the tone is conversational and humorous. Addison reflects on the value of reading his magazine. The tone of each essay reflects how the author attempts to persuade the reader to adopt his stand on the issue that he presents. Students should cite examples from each essay to support their points.

Oral Response

16. In their presentations, students should cite specific information from the essays that substantiates their presentations and expand on earlier responses.

Unit 4: Rebels and Dreamers (1798-1832)

"To a Mouse" and "to a Louse"
by Robert Burns

"Woo'd and Married and A'"
by Joanna Baillie

Open Book Test (p. 82)

Multiple Choice and Short Answer

1. Sample answer: The speaker's plow destroys it.

2.c Explanation: The speaker respects the mouse for having its house destroyed, and that "man's dominion / Has broken Nature's social union . . ."

3. Sample answer: Now you are forced out, for all your trouble / Without house or property, / To withstand the winter's sleety drizzle, / and cold frost.

4. Sample answer: The poet says that compared to humankind, the mouse is blessed because the mouse only knows the present ("The present only toucheth thee . . ."), whereas humans are burdened by dreary ("drear") memories of the past and the fear of what is to come in the future.

5.c Explanation: "Ye" is dialect for "you"; "fit" is dialect for "feet."

6.d Explanation: Vanity and conceit are the poet's objects of scorn. By writing a poem about a louse crawling on a fashionably dressed woman, he is attacking the vanity and conceit of people who believe they are better than others because they dress "better."

7. Sample answer: The louse symbolizes human flaws.

8.a Explanation: The definition of winsome is "having a charming, attractive appearance or manner"; someone or something that is gruff is disagreeable.

9. Sample answer: They are poorly educated Scots.

10. Sample answer: Isn't she very well off?

Questions are classified in these categories:

Comprehension	10 (E)
Interpretation	1 (A), 6 (A)
Literary Analysis	3 (A), 8 (C), 9 (C)
Reading Strategy	4 (E), 5 (A), 7 (A)
Vocabulary	2 (A)

E=Easy, A=Average, C=Challenging

Extended Response

11. (Easy) Students' essays should compare the use of the mouse and the louse in Burns's two poems. The students should recognize and note that the speaker is sympathetic to the mouse but not to the louse. The mouse symbolizes the fragility of life and the impossibility of the predicting the future. The louse symbolizes human flaws that are common to everyone.

12. (Challenging) Students' essays should identify the characteristics that might have made Burns popular with the people of Scotland. For example, they might point out that his use of dialect might have given the Scottish readers the sense that Burns was "one of them" and that he understood the lives of the undereducated workers. Also, the images in his poems—a farmer plowing a field, discovering lice in someone's hair—were images that would have been common to the people of Burns's day. The theme of "To a Louse," that all people are the same, was probably very popular with the masses.

13. (Challenging) Students' essays should identify the use of dialect in the poems by Burns and Baillie, and explain how its use is integral to the subject matter and themes of the poems. For example, the students might discuss how dialect

was commonly used by the masses, to whom the themes of the poems are sympathetic.

14. (Average) Students' essays should analyze the use of dialect in the poems of Burns and Baillie, comparing and contrasting how slang and colloquial speech are used in a work of contemporary poetry, fiction, drama, or music.

15. (Average) Students' graphic organizers and essays should identify the conflict and resolution. For example, the bride is sad because she doesn't have the money to buy nice lace trimmings for her dress, but she is convinced by the bridegroom in the fourth stanza that fancy dress is not important to him and that he loves her more than any well-dressed girl.

Oral Response

16. In their oral responses, students should cite specific information from the poems that substantiates their presentations and expands on their earlier responses.

"The Lamb," "The Tyger," "Infant Sorrow," and "The Chimney Sweeper"
by William Blake

Open-Book Test (p. 85)

Multiple Choice and Short Answers

1.b Explanation: In "The Lamb" the Lamb is also the name that Blake gives the child in the lines, "He is called by thy name, / For he calls himself a Lamb: / He is meek & he is mild, / He became a little child . . ." The child is also a symbol of innocence.

2. Sample answer: The "He" in the poem refers to the Creator.

3.b Explanation: "Serene" is the best word to describe the illustration because it depicts a setting in what looks like a quiet countryside with a child calmly feeding a lamb.

4. Sample answer: The tiger in the illustration seems to be smiling and therefore doesn't seem to possess the "fearful symmetry" depicted in Blake's poem. Nor does the tiger in the illustration seem to have fire in its eyes.

5.c Explanation: "Strive" (which means "to try or struggle hard for") has the closest meaning to "aspire" (which means "to rise high, yearn or seek after").

6. Sample answer: What person could fully understand the immensity of your power?

7. Sample answer: The "swaddling bands" symbolize the confinement that the speaker feels is being placed upon him by his parents and/or society.

8. Sample answer: In the second stanza of "Infant Sorrow," the speaker is sad with the realization of feeling confined.

9. Sample answer: The bags in "The Chimney Sweeper" symbolize the burdens of the world of the living which are left behind when people die.

10. Sample answer: The speaker in the poem is saying that once Tom is old he will realize that what might dirty his body cannot dirty his soul.

Questions are classified in these categories:
Comprehension   2 (A)
Interpretation   6 (C), 8 (E), 10 (A)
Literary Analysis   1 (C), 7 (A), 9 (A)
Reading Strategy   3 (A), 4 (A)
Vocabulary   5 (A)

E=Easy, A=Average, C=Challenging

Extended Response

11. (Easy) Students should first record the similarities and differences between "The Lamb" and "The Tyger" with the Venn diagram, and then interpret and compare the poems. Similarities may include the way the speaker addresses the animals in the poem and the use of the animals to symbolize aspects of human nature. Differences may include the particular aspects of human nature that the lamb and the tiger represent and the setting of the poems. Students should support their interpretation with examples from the text.

12. (Challenging) Students should identify that the speakers in Blake's "The Lamb" and "The Tyger" are addressing animals that are used to represent different aspects of human nature. In Blake's "Infant Sorrow" and "The Chimney Sweeper," the speakers are children, and they are expressing worries about the burdens or hardships of life. Students should support their interpretation with examples from the text.

13. (Easy) Students should identify that "The Chimney Sweeper" addresses the child labor conditions of the Industrial Revolution by depicting a child's dream of liberation from his hard life as a chimney sweep. Students should support their interpretation with examples from the text.

14. (Average) Students should choose any two symbols from the four poems and interpret them using examples from the text. Students may discuss how the lamb is used to symbolize both innocence and the Creator, and how the tiger is used to represent experience and worldliness. Students may discuss how Blake symbolizes paradise with the "green plain" in "The Chimney Sweeper" and confinement with the "swaddling bands" in "Infant Sorrow."

15. (Easy) Students may discuss how the speakers of "Infant Sorrow" and "The Chimney Sweeper" both view life as a struggle. They should analyze how Blake conveys this message with the symbols he uses in the poems. Students should support their interpretation with examples from the text.

Oral Response

16. In their oral responses, students should cite specific information from the poems that substantiates their presentations and expands on their earlier responses.

"The Introduction to *Frankenstein*"
by Mary Wollstonecraft Shelley

Open-Book Test (p. 88)

Multiple Choice and Short Answers

1.d Explanation: During the Romantic period it was uncommon, and perhaps thought strange, for women to write about such shocking subject matter.

2.b Explanation: Stories that lack originality are predictable.

3. Sample answer: She says that he is better skilled at embodying ideas with "brilliant imagery" and "melodious verse" than he is creating the "machinery of a story."

4.a Explanation: She describes the "misery" of writer's block, and the stress she feels when she tries to think of a good story and comes up with nothing.

5. Sample answer: She says she wants to write a story "which would speak to the mysterious fears of our nature and awaken thrilling horror—one to make the reader dread to look round, to curdle the blood, and quicken the beatings of the heart."

6. Sample answer: After Mary Shelley hears Lord Byron and Percy Shelley talking about Darwin's experiment, in which a piece of vermicelli in a glass case begins to move voluntarily, she has a hideous vision of a "phantasm" brought to life by man. She uses this idea to write *Frankenstein*.

7. Sample answer: Students' charts should list the setting as a house in Switzerland; the characters as Mary Shelley, Percy Shelley, Lord Byron, and John William Polidori; situation as Mary Shelley's frustration of trying to think of a ghost story; the resolution as Mary Shelley's dream about the phantasm created by man that gave her the idea for *Frankenstein*.

8. Sample answer: The book is about supernatural events and it is set in a castle, both characteristic of Gothic literature.

9. Sample answer: The use of the supernatural in Gothic literature suggests that not everything can be explained scientifically.

10. Sample answer: Mary Shelley seems to fear the consequences of mankind's attempts to master Nature and to assume the role of Creator.

Questions are classified in these categories:

Comprehension	1 (A), 4 (C), 5 (A)
Interpretation	3 (C), 6 (E), 10 (A)
Literary Analysis	7 (A), 8 (A), 9 (A)
Reading Strategy	
Vocabulary	2 (A)

E=Easy, A=Average, C=Challenging

Extended Response

11. (Easy) Students' essays should explain that Gothic literature explores the supernatural— that which cannot be explained by science—and is characteristically set in castles, monasteries. *Frankenstein* classifies as an example of Gothic literature because it is a story about reanimating the dead—a supernatural feat— which takes place in a classic Gothic setting.

12. (Challenging) Students' essays should include summaries of the plots of both works. Students should indicate, with appropriate examples, that the stories are similar because they both explore the supernatural world. Students should also indicate the stories' differences—that they deal with different types of supernatural events. "The Inconsistent Lover" is about a tale that is set in the distant past and features ghosts, and *Frankenstein* is set in the Romantic period and features a monster that is the product of science.

13. (Average) Students should detail the characteristics that define the Romantic period—that the Romanticists rejected the Age of Reason's claim that everything could be explained by science—and that *Frankenstein*, as a critique of science, is an example of how science can go astray if humankind tries to overcome nature.

14. (Average) Students' essays should include a detailed description of *Frankenstein* and the work of art to which they are comparing it. Essays should also include an analysis of both works and outline how technology and science can be used for the wrong purposes.

15. (Challenging) Students' essays should outline and describe a current ethical issue, along with those ethical issues which Mary Shelley raises in *Frankenstein*, and provide a detailed explanation of how they are similar.

Oral Response

16. In their oral responses, students should cite specific information from the essay that substantiates their presentations and expands on their earlier responses.

"Lines Composed a Few Miles Above Tintern Abbey," "from *The Prelude,* "The World Is Too Much with Us," and "London, 1802"
by William Wordsworth

Open-Book Test (p. 91)

Multiple Choice and Short Answers

1. Sample answer: In the poem, the narrator describes the power of nature and the emotions that nature evokes from him, themes typical of the Romantic period.

2.c Explanation: Wordsworth characterizes himself as a "thoughtless youth" who ran through the woods without stopping to consider his surroundings.

3. Sample answer: The beauty of nature helps the narrator forget his philosophical worries.

4. Sample answer: The narrator says that the world is "unintelligible," which is characteristic of the Romantics, who believed that not everything could be explained by science.

5.d Explanation: After Wordsworth graduated from college, he traveled in France, where he encountered the ideals of the recent French Revolution.

6.b Explanation: "Confounded" means "confused or bewildered." Complex issues can sometimes be confusing or bewildering.

7. Sample answer: In the quote, Wordsworth is describing how he began to question the products of reason ("precepts, judgements, maxims, creeds"), which was a characteristic of the Romantics.

8.b Explanation: In "The World is Too Much with Us," Wordsworth is mourning the loss of awe people once had for nature.

9. Sample answer: Wordsworth wishes he could view the world with the awe and wonder of an age when everything wasn't explained by reason.

10. Sample answer: He says England has lost its life or spirit; that it has become "a fen / Of stagnant waters."

Questions are classified in these categories:

Comprehension	2 (A), 10 (A)
Interpretation	3 (A), 8 (A), 9 (C)
Literary Analysis	1 (A), 4 (C), 7 (C)
Reading Strategy	5 (A)
Vocabulary	6 (E)

E=Easy, A=Average, C=Challenging

Extended Response

11. (Average) Students' essays should explain that Romanticism was a movement that exalted nature and the heart (emotion) over the mind (intellect). In "Lines Composed a Few Miles Above Tintern Abbey," Wordsworth contemplates the power of nature. In "The Prelude," he details his disillusionment with reason. In "The World is Too Much with Us," he mourns the loss of man's awe for the power of nature.

12. (Easy) Answers will vary, but students should choose a specific heroic figure who exhibited virtues (such as Milton did for Wordsworth) that many people in today's society take for granted. Students should give adequate illustrations of these virtuous qualities, and relate them to the contemporary world the way Wordsworth did in his poem.

13. (Average) The Romantics believed that feelings and passions are a most important tool for an artist, and should be emphasized in art over the wit and scholarly rationalism that was becoming increasingly popular during that time. In their essays, students should support this point with lines and passages from Wordsworth's poems.

14. (Challenging) Students should describe the change in the narrator's feelings at Tintern Abbey from the carefree wildness of a young boy to the more sober reflections of a grown man. They should also describe the change in Wordsworth's own feelings regarding the French Revolution—from believing it to be a change for the better to the realization that the new regime was at least as bad as the old. The two works are similar in that they describe changes that come with age and experience, but they are different in that "Tintern Abbey" evokes a more general, universal experience while the selection from *The Prelude* is very specific and personal.

15. (Average) "Wordsworthean" could describe any passages which celebrate nature, or which place the importance of nature above the industrial world or the pursuit of material possessions. "Wordsworthean" could also refer to lines which favor emotion over rationalism and outward elegance. Students should support their definitions of "Wordsworthean" with specific examples from the poems.

Oral Response

16. In their oral responses, students should cite specific information from the poems that substantiates their presentations and expands on their earlier responses.

"The Rime of the Ancient Mariner" and **"Kubla Khan"**
by Samuel Taylor Coleridge

Open-Book Test (p. 94)

Multiple Choice and Short Answer

1.a Explanation: "broad" and "bright" contain repetition of the same sound at the beginning of words in a phrase, and therefore are an example of alliteration.

2. Sample answer: Luck, nature and guilt are some of the qualities that students may say the albatross symbolizes.

3.c Explanation: Students should note that the sanctity of all wild creatures is stressed by the importance of the change in the Mariner—the albatross falls from his neck when he sees the importance in the natural world, and can feel empathy and love for other living creatures.

4. Sample answer: Students should cite the passage at the close of Part IV, where the Albatross falls from the Mariner's neck. This action occurs because the Mariner sees the happiness and beauty of the water snakes, and can therefore now see the sanctity and beauty of all living creatures.

5.a Explanation: "Nostalgia and profound sorrow" best describes the Mariner's tone.

6.b Explanation: "western" and "wave" begin with the same consonant and are therefore examples of alliteration; "wave" and "aflame" contain the same vowel sound (but dissimilar consonant sounds) and are therefore examples of assonance.

7.b Explanation: The poem's last lines shift the focus to the poet as the inspired creator: "I would build that dome in air."

8.a Explanation: the harp is a stringed instrument, like the dulcimer; although a snare drum is played with sticks, similar to the dulcimer, it does not make a melody.

9. Sample answer: The passage can be rearranged to read, "Kubla Khan decreed a stately pleasure dome to be built in Xanadu." Coleridge might have inverted the words of this passage to emphasize certain stresses and rhythms, to set up the rhyme in the poem, and to establish a stately, official-sounding opening tone to the poem.

10.d Explanation: The romantic poets journeyed inwards into the world of imagination, and Coleridge, as shown in "Kubla Khan," often described exotic and faraway dreamworlds to color the themes of his poetry.

Questions are classified in these categories:
Comprehension   5 (A), 10 (A)
Interpretation   3 (E), 4 (C)
Literary Analysis   1 (A), 7 (A), 9 (C)
Reading Strategy   6 (A)
Vocabulary   2 (E), 8 (E)

E=Easy, A=Average, C=Challenging

11. (Average) The Mariner also takes a spiritual journey in the poem. Students' essays should cite passages which illustrate the emotional changes in the Mariner, and analyze the ways he comes to be the sagelike figure that can tell his tale to the Wedding Guest.

12. (Average) Students should give illustrations from "The Rime of the Ancient Mariner" to prove that Coleridge, more than any other Romantic, held strong regard for the power of fantasy and the supernatural. Death and Life-in-Death are two otherworldly characters which serve to lift the poem from regular reality; students might also note how characters and passages like these add an eerie or horrific atmosphere to the poem.

13. (Average) Students should create a chart listing three lines from "The Rime of the Ancient Mariner," the sound devices used, and the effect of this usage. For example, in line 460, Coleridge is using alliteration. He heightens his description of a lush, exotic world, and mirrors the description with the highly musical, murmuring use of alliteration in s sounds, slowing the line down, even making it "flow" like the river he describes.

14. (Easy) Students should give specific examples from both poems to show how Coleridge uses water imagery, for both beauty and horror in "The Rime of the Ancient Mariner," and to illustrate the beauty of his royal world in "Kubla Khan." They should give specific lines from the poems to back up their views.

15. (Challenging) Students should begin by citing Romanticism's fascination with the power of the imagination and relate it to the way Coleridge ends "Kubla Khan" by journeying inward and examining how he created the poem. His love of the exotic is a typical Romantic attribute, and here he revels in the mystery of the unknown as well as celebrates the spirit who assigns him the power to describe something so exotic and mysterious.

Oral Response

16. In their oral responses, students should cite specific information from the poems that substantiates their presentations and expands on their earlier responses.

"She Walks in Beauty," from *Childe Harold's Pilgrimage* and from *Don Juan* by George Gordon, Lord Byron

Open-Book Test (p. 97)

Multiple Choice and Short Answer

1.a Explanation: Only these words correctly describe her.

2. Sample answer: By placing his subject above "all below," the speaker is revering her beauty and virtue above everyone else. Yet she is "at peace" with this, untainted by her status. The lines illustrate the speaker's fondness, even awe, for the woman described.

3.   Sample answer: Here, Byron is using personification—he is assigning human qualities to inanimate subjects (thoughts).

4.d Explanation: Throughout the poem, the speaker reveres the ocean for not only its beauty, but its strength and unchanging power.

5.b Explanation: Since he was a boy, he loved to play in the ocean's waves, despite the ocean's sometimes merciless power.

6.   Sample answer: Monstrous sea creatures, described in the Old Testament. Here the word means giant ships of oak with large wooden beams made by men ("their day creator").

7.   Sample answer: Although the empires were powerful, the speaker notes that the ocean, and the natural world, are more powerful. The ocean, for instance, remains the same, while the "empires" described in stanza five all change, lose power, or disappear. The speaker cannot hold them in the esteem he holds the oceans.

8.c Explanation: The line answers the question saying that he will never again experience the heart's freshness, youth and optimism.

9.b Explanation: The flesh is compared to grass—two apparently unlike things.

10.   Sample answer: "I / Have spent my life, both interest and principal. . ." The speaker is comparing his life to money. Students should adequately explain why they believe this comparison is or is not effective.

Questions are classified in these categories:
Comprehension	1 (E), 5 (A)
Interpretation	2 (A), 4 (A), 7 (C)
Literary Analysis	3 (C), 9 (A), 10 (C)
Reading Strategy	8 (A)
Vocabulary	6 (E)

E=Easy, A=Average, C=Challenging

Extended Response

11. (Easy) Students' essays should use specific quotes from the text to show the tone of praise and awe when describing the sublime beauty of nature in *Childe Harold's Pilgrimage.* They should also cite passages when describing the biting, cynical tone in *Don Juan.*

12. (Average) Students should complete a grid organizer which lists three separate instances of simile, metaphor, or personification in the excerpt from *Childe Harold's Pilgrimage.* They should designate the type of figurative language correctly, and also provide an examination of how Byron makes the description more powerful or effective by the use of figurative language.

13. (Average) Students should explain how Byron's public came to revere him as a heroic figure, like that of the characters in his works, and explain how the audiences during the Romantic period loved the dark and brooding characters

he portrayed in his poems. An example could be the narrator of "Apostrophe to the Ocean," who is solitary and steadfast in his love of nature and passionately celebrates the power and beauty of the ocean. Students should use specific passages from the poems to illustrate their points.

14. (Average) Students should cite examples from the text of *Don Juan* to show how the speaker pokes fun at himself and his society. They might focus on the overall cynical and mocking tone of the poem, or narrow in specifically on the ending of the passage, or show how the speaker associates his life with money, which is easily used and quickly discarded.

15. (Challenging) In their essays, students should examine the admiration the speakers of "She Walks in Beauty" and the excerpt from *Childe Harold's Pilgrimage* both have for their subjects. Although the first speaker is describing a woman, and the second is describing the ocean and natural world, both speakers use figurative language and heightened description to show their joyous and inspired love for their subjects. Students should compare and contrast the usage of language in the poems, noting specific lines and passages from the works to back up their points.

Oral Response

16. In their oral responses, students should cite specific information from the poems that substantiates their presentations and expands on their earlier responses.

"Ozymandias," "Ode to the West Wind," and "To a Skylark"
by Percy Bysshe Shelley

Open-Book Test (p. 100)

Multiple Choice and Short Answer

1.d Explanation: All forms of wealth and power are ultimately impermanent and meaningless. This is shown by the dichotomy between the inscription on the pharaoh's pedestal and the ultimate barren landscape which his kingdom has become.

2.   Sample answer: Responses could list the intense heat, the desert sands, the dry winds, as well as possible things such as tourists, camels, and other sights and sounds and smells.

3.a Explanation: "If I were a dead leaf thou mightest bear" contains the subjunctive—it expresses a wish or condition contrary to fact.

4.b Explanation: Section V contains the poet's plea to the wind to "make me thy lyre," and the final lines of the poem express the wish that his poetry, "words" be scattered "among mankind" like the "trumpet of a prophecy."

5.b   Explanation: dark and destructive. The images throughout the first two stanzas are of violence and destruction and darker colors.

6.a   Explanation: This last direct address to the wind, coming at the end of the poem, is like the climax of the poet's appeal to the wind.

7.   Sample answer: Although the things described are different, Shelley speaks of them with similar exaltation. They are also similar in that they are constantly present and in motion.

8.   Sample answer: "Satiety" means "the state of being filled to excess." Students might apply this word to their everyday lives by describing their feelings after dinner, the satisfaction of finishing work, or so forth.

9.c   Explanation: "Blithe" means cheerful, so it is closest to an antonym of the choice "woebegone."

10.c Explanation: The student might refer to the first five stanzas of the poem or to the lines: "Like a poet hidden / In the light of thought, / Singing hymns unbidden."

Questions are classified in these categories:
Comprehension	5 (A)
Interpretation	1 (A), 4 (A)
Literary Analysis	3 (A), 7 (C), 10 (A)
Reading Strategy	2 (C), 6 (E)
Vocabulary	8 (A), 9 (E)

E=Easy, A=Average, C=Challenging

Extended Response

11.   (Easy) Students should provide three paragraphs detailing Shelley's descriptions and praise of nature in "Ozymandias," "Ode to the West Wind," and "To a Skylark," stressing nature's power over humans with specific passages from the poems.

12.   (Average) Students should provide specific examples of musical references in "Ode to the West Wind" and "To a Skylark" to show how he broadens his depictions and stresses the timeless power of his subjects. They should also cite lines which contain especially musical language in Shelley's poems.

13.   (Average) Students' essays should discuss that Shelley is interested in places existing in the imagination, as well. "Ozymandias" tackles a faraway place as Coleridge might have done, but "Ode to the West Wind," and "To a Skylark" do not. Still, students should note that Shelley still is fascinated with a certain mystery and exoticism in these poems—he consistently focuses on the feelings and emotions generated from the mysterious aspects of his subjects. Students should back up their points with specific examples from Shelley's poems.

14.   (Average) Students' graphic organizers should list three comparisons which Shelley makes between his skylark and other things. After each item, they should give two sentences why the specific comparisons are effective and fitting to describe the Skylark.

15.   (Challenging) Students should focus particularly on the close of "Ode to the West Wind" to show the changes which come in the speaker of the poem. As the Wind scatters leaves, for instance, the speaker wants his "dead thoughts" scattered to generate creativity and productivity. Students should note the ways the speaker addresses the Wind, and use specific examples to show the Wind's effect on him.

Oral Response

16.   In their oral responses, students should cite specific information from the poems that substantiates their presentations and expands on their earlier responses.

Poetry of John Keats
Open-Book Test (p. 103)
Multiple Choice and Short Answer

1.c   Explanation: Students should paraphrase the first few lines of the poem which speak of the amount of reading he has done.

2.   Sample answer: Students should paraphrase the lines with something similar to: "I felt the way an astronomer feels when he discovers a new planet."

3.   Sample answer: The speaker feels very lonely and mournful at the close of the poem, knowing that an untimely death would rob him of his creativity and work and possible love. Students should provide adequate adjectives to describe the speaker's feelings here.

4.b   Explanation: Keats is symbolizing the poems and other works which he, as the artist, will create.

5.   Sample answer: The word is "Forlorn," first word of the last stanza. Students should note that the word echoes an overriding mood or atmosphere of the poem.

6.   Sample answer: Horatian. An Horatian ode contains one type of stanza that is repeated.

7.   Sample answer: "Ode to a Nightingale" is a Horatian ode: it contains only one type of stanza throughout.

8.   Sample answer: Art, through its beauty, has much to teach humans. It is important because it makes beauty immortal, and freezes a certain time for future admirers to see. Students could also note that Keats believed the appreciation of art to be an end in itself, and made the pursuit of beauty the goal of his poetry.

9.b   Explanation: Students should refer to details in the poem to support this choice.

10.d Explanation: Students should refer to lines which emphasize the urns' timelessness.

Questions are classified in these categories:

Comprehension	3 (A), 8 (C)
Interpretation	1 (A), 4 (C), 5 (A)
Literary Analysis	7 (A), 10 (A)
Reading Strategy	2 (E), 9 (E)
Vocabulary	6 (A)

E=Easy, A=Average, C=Challenging

Extended Response

11. (Easy) Students should compare and contrast "Ode to a Nightingale" with "Ode on a Grecian Urn" to show how Keats addresses his subjects, as well as the ways he admires or envies his subjects. They should cite examples from the poems to support their points.

12. (Average) Students should give examples from the texts of at least two of Keats's poems to illustrate his usage of sorrow and melancholy. "When I Have Fears that I May Cease to Be" and "Ode to a Nightingale" might be the two poems on which students choose to focus most; they should also examine how his style and use of language convey the sense of sorrow in the works.

13. (Average) Students should complete the graphic organizer, listing lines from "Ode to a Nightingale" which directly appeal to the sight, sound, taste, touch, and smell. They should then complete a paragraph which concludes what Keats's generous usage of sensory detail does for the overall outcome and theme of the poem.

14. (Average) Students should note that Keats is stating his opinion that beauty in art can be an end in itself; that the beauty as expressed in the Grecian Urn is the ultimate truth in its freezing of the perfect moment. The students may agree or disagree with this point, but should argue their reasons, and should back up their points with specific illustrations from Keats's poems.

15. (Challenging) Students should examine the way Keats feels about the unknown by showing specific examples from his poems. They might note examples from "When I Have Fears that I May Cease to Be," for instance, where Keats does not fear death, but laments it because he may leave the world before he has created his body of work or properly loved. They should then relate their findings from the poems to an opinion about what Keats may have felt regarding his own death.

Oral Response

16. In their oral responses, students should cite specific information from the poems that substantiates their presentations and expands on their earlier responses.

232 Open-Book Test

"Speech to Parliament: In Defense of the Lower Classes"
by George Gordon, Lord Byron

"A Song: 'Men of England'"
by Percy Bysshe Shelley

"On the Passing of the Reform Bill"
by Thomas Babington Macaulay

Open-Book Test (p. 106)

Multiple Choice and Short Answer

1. Sample answer: Students' answers should mention that Byron is making a direct comparison between the destructive weavers and the members of the House of Lords. His purpose was to make the audience feel responsible for the plight of the unemployed weavers.

2.c Explanation: imprison. "Emancipate" means to free from slavery or oppression.

3.a Explanation: Byron exaggerates by suggesting that the Lords could hold executions in every field, and use men's corpses like scarecrows.

4.c Explanation: The anger and power of this question suggests that the only relief from the situation is death. He asks the Lords if they will compel the lower classes with violence into being "tranquil," a sarcastic use of the word.

5. Sample answer: Shelley compares the rich "tyrants" to the drones. He sees them negatively as the type of bees who do not work, therefore unlike the working men of England.

6.d Explanation: The poem is addressed to the working class and discusses their way of life.

7.c Explanation: A crowded city street is the only choice not associated with something "soothing" or "healing."

8.a. Explanation: "It is clear that the Reform Bill must pass, either in this or in another Parliament" contains the correlative conjunctions "either" and "or."

9. Sample answer: Students should note the purpose of a political commentary as simply to express personal opinions on political issues.

10. Sample answer: Students should note that passage of the bill is possible by a margin of a single vote, and its passage is vital to avoid public outrage.

Questions are classified in these categories:

Comprehension	3 (A), 10 (C)
Interpretation	1 (C), 5 (A)
Literary Analysis	4 (C), 9 (A)
Reading Strategy	6 (A), 8 (E)
Vocabulary	2 (E), 7 (A)

E=Easy, A=Average, C=Challenging

Extended Response

11. (Easy) Students should discuss the audiences for whom Byron, Shelley, and Macaulay were writing, noting that Macaulay is addressing one specific person where the others are addressing more, and also noting Shelley's very different form of poetry over prose. The audiences of Byron and Shelley—two respected poets—may have expected something different than the audience of Macaulay. Students should back up these points with specific illustrations from the texts.

12. (Average) Students should first record the similarities and differences between Byron's and Macaulay's works with the Venn diagram, and then interpret and compare the pieces. Similarities may include the address of a group of people in Byron's work, and the more intimate, "letter" form personal address of Macaulay's. Students should examine the effectiveness of each man's individual essay, and then support their interpretations with examples from the text.

13. (Average) Students should refer to past Shelley poems about other topics to make their points about his more political work. Their essays should form a distinct opinion about whether he is as effective when writing poetry with a political message, and they should back up this opinion with specific passages not only from the political poem, but from Shelley's other poems as well.

14. (Average) Students should choose which of the three poems is most effective; answers will vary, but they should support their opinions through specific examples from the texts. They should also decide whose method—Byron's, Shelley's, or Macaulay's—they would follow if making a similar point about a contemporary topic.

15. (Challenging) Students should clearly state their opinions about the relationship between politics and art. They should examine the effectiveness of Byron's and Shelley's usage of politics, and assert whether they think politics has a place in art or poetry. Since Shelley uses a poem to make his points, and Byron does not, students might use this contrast to support their point for or against a specific type of writing (poetry) as effective or not effective in conveying the political message.

Oral Response

16. In their oral responses, students should cite specific information from the selections that substantiates their presentations and expands on their earlier responses.

"On Making an Agreeable Marriage"
by Jane Austen

from *A Vindication of the Rights of Woman*
by Mary Wollstonecraft

Open-Book Test (p. 109)

Multiple Choice and Short Answer

1. Sample answer: Responses should note that Jane Austen wanted Fanny to reconsider the feelings she had written in her recent letter; the purpose was to persuade Fanny to reexamine her suitor's many qualities.

2. Sample answer: In "On Making an Agreeable Marriage," Jane Austen believes that Fanny's suitor is an admirable man of good character, and Fanny should reconsider her feelings.

3.c Explanation: Austen does not say that Mr. J. P. has become increasingly indifferent to Fanny.

4.b Explanation: The opening paragraph specifically cites the "neglected education" of women, and her conviction that this must improve.

5. Sample answer: Students' answers should explain that during the time of Austen and Wollstonecraft, education for women tended to focus on the domestic accomplishments of women—preparing for marriage, household duties, and so forth.

6.a Explanation: *cautiously* is a synonym for *solicitously*.

7.b Explanation: Students should refer to any of the many places in the text that reinforce this theme.

8. Sample answer: In the title, "vindication" means "justification." Wollstonecraft is justifying why women should have equal rights.

9.a Explanation: "Fastidious" means having high and sometimes overly high standards, or difficult to please. Therefore, "easily satisfied" is the opposite.

10. Sample answer: Wollstonecraft compares women's minds to flowers planted in soil that is too rich, where "strength and usefulness are sacrificed to beauty."

Questions are classified in these categories:

Comprehension	3 (E)
Interpretation	2 (A), 5 (C)
Literary Analysis	4 (A), 7 (A), 10 (A)
Reading Strategy	1 (A), 8 (C)
Vocabulary	6 (E), 9 (A)

E=Easy, A=Average, C=Challenging

Extended Response

11. (Easy) Students' responses should focus on how the letter functions as a literary device. They might note the intimacy of having only one person as an audience, as well as Austen's personality, evident in addressing someone she

knew so well. Students should give specific examples to argue whether the letter form helps or hinders the strength of her arguments.

12. (Average) Students should specifically examine the way Austen judges human character in "On Making an Agreeable Marriage." They should point to the qualities she finds most valuable in Fanny's suitor, and agree or disagree with Austen's points by using specific references from the letter. Finally, they should imagine themselves as the recipient of the letter, deciding whether or not they would agree with the way Austen judges the suitor's character and human nature in general.

13. (Average) Students should cite specific examples from Austen's letter and Wollstonecraft's essay to show which of the authors' points they find most and least effective.

14. (Average) In their charts, students should cite examples from both texts to show how women were treated and regarded during that time. They should compare and contrast these points with examples from today's society. In their paragraphs, students should base their arguments on the examples from the chart to explain whether or not the treatment of women in today's society has changed for the better, changed for the worse, or stayed the same.

15. (Challenging) Students should examine the directness of Wollstonecraft's style in *A Vindication of the Rights of Woman.* People of the time were not accustomed to this sort of bluntness in women writers, and certainly would have reacted strongly. While students may or may not agree that this kind of style would be as direct and blunt by today's standards, they should nonetheless support their opinions with specific examples from Wollstonecraft's essay.

Oral Response

16. In their oral responses, students should cite specific information from the selections that substantiates their presentations and expands on their earlier responses.

from "In Memoriam, A.H.H.," "The Lady of Shalott," "Ulysses," and from *The Princess*: "Tears, Idle Tears" by Alfred, Lord Tennyson

Open-Book Test (p. 112)

Multiple Choice and Short Answers

1. Sample answer: "Far off thou art, but nigh; I have thee still, and I rejoice;" These lines tell us that the poet has decided that his friend is still with him even though he has died, and this conclusion makes him rejoice. Students may choose other lines and support their positions.

2. The poet suggests that great love can bring grief, but grief is worth the risk when the love is strong. Sudents' personal experiences and judgments will vary. Be sure that students rely on a clear understanding of the poet's message, as well as on specific experiences and observations from their own life.

3.a Explanation: Tennyson's poem is a testament to the memories of his dead friend that remain with him.

4. Sample answer: "Who is this? And what is here?" The people at Camelot say this line. It places the reader in the crowd at Camelot, bringing him closer to the action.

5. Sample answer: She believes that knights are loyal and true, which is the traditional view.

6.d *Waning* implies a gradual fading of light rather than one that occurs suddenly.

7. Sample answer: The speaker of the poem is Ulysses; the use of the pronoun "I" indicates a first-person point of view and references to travel; the sea, roaming, and battling in Troy allude to "The Odyssey." His conflict is that he has grown old and no longer has the challenge of his adventures.

8. Sample answer: He feels that his life has been based on the adventures that he has had and they have become part of who he is; without adventuring further, the opportunities of the world are fading as he ages.

9.b Explanation: Line 5: "And think of the days that are no more."

10. Sample answer: The poet portrays the happiness and freshness of young love and then contrasts it with the nostalgia of days that are no more, His language evokes longing for the past. Students' judgments will vary. Be sure that students rely on a clear understanding of the poet's message, as well as on specific experiences and observations from their own lives.

Questions are classified in these categories:

Comprehension	1 (A), 8 (A)
Interpretation	3 (A)
Literary Analysis	4 (C), 5 (A), 7 (A), 9 (E)
Reading Strategy	2 (A), 10 (A)
Vocabulary	6 (E)

E=Easy, A=Average, C=Challenging

Extended Response

11. (Easy) Students should recognize and address Tennyson's struggle over coming to terms with his friend's death and cite examples from the poem that illustrate the conflict, such as "a hand that can be clasped no more," "I wage not any feud with Death," and "Nor blame I Death."

12. (Average) The Lay floats away in a boat in a storm and freezes to death. Students should cite

details from Part IV of the poem which indicate the Lady's fate.

13. (Challenging) Students' essays should note Ulysses' nostalgic references to his travels and adventures and recognize that the adventure he now faces is that of going to his death.

14. (Challenging) Students' charts and essays should note the speaker of "In Memoriam, A.H.H.," is Tennyson himself and the subject is understanding his friend's death; the speaker of "The Lady of Shalott" is an omnipresent narrator about the Lady and how she represents the loneliness of being an artist; the speaker of "Ulysses" is Ulysses pondering his own impending death; and "Tears, Idle Tears" is the Princess who is nostalgic about growing old. Students should note the speakers' attitudes as being personally involved or impassioned about their subjects.

15. (Challenging) Students will probably note the sadness and nostalgia associated with death, dying, and growing old that is present in all of the poems. They should cite appropriate examples.

Oral Response

16. In their oral responses, students should cite specific information from the poems that substantiates their presentations and expands on their earlier responses.

"My Last Duchess," "Life in a Love," and "Love Among the Ruins"
by Robert Browning

Sonnet 43
by Elizabeth Barrett Browning

Open-Book Test (p. 115)

Multiple Choice and Short Answers

1.b Explanation: The poem's introduction explains that the Duke is addressing an agent; lines 49–51 address the listener, saying "The Count your master" and referencing the employer's daughter's dowry.

2. Sample answer: His family name is old and respected and he considers it very valuable.

3. Sample answer: Browning has the Duke speak of the expression on the face of his late wife's portrait in order to reveal his inner feelings. "She smiled, no doubt, When'er I passed her; but who passed without / Much the same smile?"

4. Sample answer: Love that is not reciprocated is a strain but consumes the speaker's life.

5. Sample answer: "My life is a fault at last, I fear." The speaker feels that love is unattainable, and continues to seek it, letting it take up his life.

6. Sample answer: Examples of people include: men who had ordinary feelings, royalty and their attendants, charioteers, and soldiers; activities include buy and selling, games, building the structures, and fighting battles; structures include a palace with spires, a wide wall, temples, causeways, bridges, and aqueducts. Students should recognize that the city was developed and sophisticated.

7.d Explanation: "With their triumphs and their glories and the rest!/Love is best."

8.b Explanation: With all bits or traces gone, nothing would be left.

9.c Explanation: The ideas of the poem suggest that true love lasts forever.

10. Sample answer: The comparison of innumerable ways of loving suggests that the love is boundless.

Questions are classified in these categories:

Comprehension	2 (A), 4 (A), 9 (E)
Interpretation	6 (A), 10 (C)
Literary Analysis	1 (E), 3 (C), 5 (A)
Reading Strategy	7 (A)
Vocabulary	8 (E)

E=Easy, A=Average, C=Challenging

Extended Response

11. (Easy) Students' essays should show an understanding of the Duke's jealousy and possessiveness, based on his attitude that his name demands the Duchess', full attention and devotion.

12. (Average) Students should offer their own ideas about the images and descriptions; their essays should be well-supported with examples that they explain in the context of their essays.

13. (Challenging) Students' Venn diagrams and essays should acknowledge that "Love Among the Ruins" uses a magnificent comparison to love while Sonnet 43 uses uncountable comparisons; both indicate a great love.

14. (Average) Students' essays should address the messages or theme of the two poems they select and then support their theses with examples of comparisons and contrasts in the poems.

15. (Average) Students should recognize that the Brownings' personal love is reflected in their poetry and should cite examples of modern-day songs or poems that address the topic of "true love."

Oral Response

16. In their oral responses, students should cite specific information from the poems that substantiates their presentations and expands on their earlier responses.

from *Hard Times*
by Charles Dickens

from *Jane Eyre*
by Charlotte Brontë

Open-Book Test (p. 118)

Multiple Choice and Short Answers

1.a Explanation: The excerpt addresses the issues of being a student and a teacher and touches on the topic of economics, but the main focus is education.

2. Sample answer: Students diagrams may include the following types of responses: ideas—education, teaching, fact-based teaching and learning; choice of characters' names—Gradgrind, Sissy Jupe, Bitzer, M'Choakumchild; attitudes toward characters—disgust, sarcasm, scorn, absurdity; outcome of events—Sissy Jupe is humiliated, Gradgrind and the third gentleman can't get past the facts, and M'Choakumchild knows too much to teach. Dickens is pointing out the absurdity and impracticality of only teaching facts without context.

3. Sample answer: Gradgrind has a hard-nosed, unforgiving approach to teaching students; he wants to elicit facts at whatever cost to understanding. Students' examples may be drawn from any of the interactions that Gradgrind has with Sissy Jupe or Bitzer.

4. Sample answer: The focus of the teaching that is portrayed in the excerpt is completely on facts with no allowance for understanding, application, or creativity.

5.b Explanation: An adversary is an opponent or an enemy. In this case, the adversary is M'Choakumchild.

6.a Explanation: Jane has observed the harsh treatment that Helen has received from Miss Scatcherd and she want to know why Helen does not rebel against the way she is treated.

7. Sample answer: Helen feels that she must endure severity in order to overcome her faults; Jane feels that she should not ever have to tolerate cruel or unjust treatment, even from a teacher.

8. Sample answer: *Obscure* in this context means not readily seen or to go unnoticed. Miss Scatcherd keeps calling on and addressing Burns, making it impossible for her to go unnoticed.

9. Sample answer: Students' responses should be a paraphrase or interpretation of Helen's explanation that ". . . Miss Temple has generally something to say which is newer to me than my own reflections: her language is singularly agreeable to me, and the information she communicates is often just what I wished to gain."

10.b Explanation: The classroom situation at a boarding school is depicted, discussed, and analyzed.

Questions are classified in these categories:

Comprehension	9 (A), 10 (E)
Interpretation	4 C), 6 (A), 7 (C)
Literary Analysis	1 (A), 3 (A)
Reading Strategy	2 (E)
Vocabulary	5(A), 8 (A)

E=Easy, A=Average, C=Challenging

Extended Response

11. (Easy) Students' essays should include similarities such as school settings and harsh teachers; differences may include the exaggerated tone of *Hard Times* which is used to make the author's points and the discussion that the characters have in *Jane Eyre* which explores the author's ideas in depth. Students' writing should expand upon the similarities, differences and points of contrast that they gathered in their Comparison-and-Contrast notes.

12. (Average) Students' essays should provide examples from the excerpt in which the characters they chose are portrayed, exploring how the characters represent two different elements of the author's views on the topic, offering a multi-faceted social commentary.

13. (Challenging) Students' essays should address the harsh, unrelenting style of Miss Scatcherd and the positive, encouraging nature of Miss Temple and explain that Helen feels that she needs to be reminded of her faults so that she can correct them; students' opinions about the better teaching style should be supported.

14. (Average) Students may prefer either of the two teachers, but may tend toward Gradgrind because of the farcical description of him. With either choice, students should support their ideas with examples from the novel excerpts.

15. (Challenging) Students' summaries of the education situations presented in *Hard Times* and *Jane Eyre* should be accurate and concise; their essays should compare and contrast what they have described to a modern situation that they adequately explain.

Oral Response

16. In their oral responses, students should cite specific information from the novel excerpts that substantiates their presentations and expands on their earlier responses.

"Dover Beach"
by Matthew Arnold

"Recessional" and **"The Widow at Windsor"**
by Rudyard Kipling

Open-Book Test (p. 120)

Multiple Choice and Short Answers

1.b   Explanation: The poet uses phrases such as the following: "sea is calm;" "moon lies fair;" "tranquil bay;" "sweet is the night air."

2.   Sample answer: Students should recognize that the speaker appreciates the range of the sea and respects its power and impressions and the impact it has on people.

3.   Sample answer: The world is varied and beautiful, but also confusing with conflict and struggle; we must trust in one another because there is no other help or certainty.

4.   Sample answer: The poem is specifically addressed to God, but the larger audience is the people of the British Empire.

5.c   Explanation: Kipling sets a mood that portrays the greatness of the British Empire, but warns of the follies of humanness.

6.   Sample answer: Kipling seems to admire and respect the British Empire, but recognizes its fallibility based on the fates of other great civilizations, recognizing that people who boast may forget what they are about.

7.d   Explanation: Negative behavior is cause for repentance or atonement. Kipling cautions the English people against excessive pride, "Lest we forget."

8.   Sample answer: References to her sons and all that she has indicate that the "Widow at Windsor" is Queen Victoria.

9.   Sample answer: Mood details may include: pays poor beggars in red; barbarous wars; 'alf of Creation she owns/we've salted it down with our bones; they'll never see 'ome. Theme: The commoners do not profit from the power and wealth of the Queen.

10.   Sample answer: Examples may include the dropped "h" sound and the repeated reference to poor beggars. The cockney accent represents the perspective of the commoners, reinforcing their plight.

Questions are classified in these categories:

Comprehension	4 (A), 8 (E)
Interpretation	3 (A), 6 (C), 10 (C)
Literary Analysis	1 (E), 5 (A), 9 (A)
Reading Strategy	2 (A)
Vocabulary	7 (E)

E=Easy, A=Average, C=Challenging

Extended Response

11.   (Easy) Students' essays should note the mood of sadness, struggle, and lack of joy and hope that Arnold portrays. Their statements of the theme should reflect this mood.

12.   (Average) Students should note the tranquil literal sea that is described, yet the turmoil which is the "Sea of Faith." Their conclusions should recognize and address this dichotomy.

13.   (Challenging) Students' lists and essays should note the formal tone of "Recessional" and the commoner's attitude in "The Widow at Windsor," but recognize that both poems question the Victorian Age British Empire and what it stands for.

14.   (Average) Students may note the historical plight of commoners that went along with the progress of the Victorian Age and explore this relationship as it is presented in Kipling's poems.

15.   (Challenging) Students' essays should note that both Arnold and Kipling have a dimmer view of the gilded age of Queen Victoria than it was touted and portrayed to the rest of the world.

Oral Response

16.   In their oral responses, students should cite specific information from the poems that substantiates their presentations and expands on their earlier responses.

"Condition of Ireland"
by *The Illustrated London News*

"Progress in Personal Comfort"
by Sydney Smith

Open-Book Test (p. 123)

Multiple Choice and Short Answers

1.d   Explanation: The essay thoroughly describes the conditions of the Irish poor people in the 1800s.

2.   Sample answer: "The present condition of the Irish, we have no hesitation in saying, has been mainly brought on by ignorant and vicious legislation." The essay blames the legislators.

3.a   Explanation: The quotation presents facts about the potential productivity of the land.

4.   Sample answer: The article is based on the event of the Great Famine, and addresses the trend of the British government to deal with the situation from a theoretical and idealistic perspective rather than to practically deal with the hungry people.

5.d   Explanation: A person who is *indolent* is lazy or idle, so their accomplishments would be limited, not great, productive, or memorable.

6. Sample answer: *The Illustrated London News* suggests that the obvious solution is to allow the Irish farmers to cultivate the land.

7. Sample answer: Student's answers should include some of the eighteen changes. Smith wrote the essay, using examples, to help the current generation to be thankful for modern comforts. The examples help to illustrate predecessors of those comforts.

8.b Explanation: The changes made his life easier, saved him time or money, or replaced "miseries" he didn't know he had endured.

9. Sample answer: Examples of denotative language may include the specific amounts of time it took to travel between destinations; the reference to thousands of contusions and Macadam being born are connotative, because they imply how Smith feels about the conditions of travel.

10. Sample answer: The essay addresses a variety of "changes," and uses them to build a unique story about Smith's perspective on progress, making it a journalistic essay.

Questions are classified in these categories:

Comprehension	8 (E)
Interpretation	2 (C), 6 (C), 7 (A)
Literary Analysis	1 (E), 4 (E), 10 (A)
Reading Strategy	3 (A), 9 (A)
Vocabulary	5 (A)

E=Easy, A=Average, C=Challenging

Extended Response

11. (Easy) Students' writing should cover the main points of the essays that they choose and accurately describe the reasons the pieces of writing are journalistic essays.

12. (Average) Students' Venn diagrams and essays should address the fact that both essays look at life in the 1800s, but "Progress in Personal Comfort" is a personal, anecdotal account of specific changes in lifestyle, using a tone that is light, almost humorous; "Condition of Ireland" addresses the issues of a broad group of people from a political standpoint with a serious, almost grim tone.

13. (Challenging) Students should recognize that both essays use both connotative and denotative language. Both essays use denotative language to present the facts of the topics they are addressing; *The Illustrated London News* article uses connotative language to illustrate the misery of the hungry people; Smith uses connotative language to highlight the comfort factors of the changes he is describing.

14. (Average) Students should note three examples from the essay and give reasons for their choices.

15. (Challenging) Students may note that *The Illustrated London News* article takes a cynical approach to what the government considers to be progress and points out how the laws that are supposed to bring about change bring misery instead, citing a more practical approach that would feed hungry people, even if it wasn't progressive. Smith's essay measures progress in terms of innovative changes to day-to-day life's needs and leaves less room for disagreement, but doesn't present anything that has a tremendous impact on survival. Students may agree or disagree, but they should support their opinions.

Oral Response

16. In their oral responses, students should cite specific information from the essays that substantiates their presentations and expands on their earlier responses.

"Remembrance"
by Emily Brontë

"The Darkling Thrush" and "Ah, Are You Digging on My Grave?"
by Thomas Hardy

Open-Book Test (p. 126)

Multiple Choice and Short Answers

1.d Explanation: Because the speaker has lost love, he or she has determined that it is best to live without it in the future.

2. Sample answer: 15 years; the third stanza includes the phrase "fifteen wild Decembers."

3. Sample answer: Students may note patterns such as the first and third stanzas which begin "Cold in the earth, . . ."; the first, third, and last stanzas that end with questions; or the nouns that are capitalized—Time, World, Despair, and Memory. The patterns emphasize ideas and feelings that the speaker is expressing, and set the reader up for the final thought of the poem.

4.b Explanation: Lines 7–8: "And all mankind that haunted nigh/Had sought their household fires."

5. Sample answer: Students may suggest that the speaker perceives Winter as dreary, based on words and phrases such as "Frost was specter-gray;" "dregs made desolate;" shrunken hard and dry;" "fervorless," and "bleak."

6. Sample answer: ababcdcd; The poem's repetitive rhyme strongly suggests the sameness of the bleak winter mood so that the introduction of the thrush in the third stanza is a surprise to readers.

7.c Explanation: Twigs is the only possible answer because it is the only thing that relates to the earth.

8.b Explanation: In the fourth stanza, the digger responds, saying it is "Your little dog," and the last stanza supports the response with an explanation for the digging.

9. Sample answer: Stanza 1: the speaker wonders if the digger is her loved one; Stanza 2: the speaker wonders if the digger is one of her kin; Stanza 3: the speaker wonders if the digger is an enemy; Stanza 4: the speaker discovers that the digger is her dog; Stanza 5: the speaker rejoices at the fidelity of her pet; Stanza 6: the speaker discovers that the dog was simply burying a bone. The irony is that the digger is not acknowledging the speaker; like everyone else, the dog is going about its daily business with no thought for the deceased speaker.

10. Sample answer: The speaker wants to be remembered and wants to know who is acknowledging her grave.

Questions are classified in these categories:

Comprehension	4 (A), 8 (E)
Interpretation	1 (A), 5 (A), 10 (C)
Literary Analysis	3 (C), 6 (C), 9 (A)
Reading Strategy	2 (E)
Vocabulary	7 (A)

E=Easy, A=Average, C=Challenging

Extended Response

11. (Easy) Students' cubes should include examples of settings, human behavior, and the thrush's behavior. Their answers should suggest that Hardy wanted readers to remember that good things happen even when things seem bleak.

12. (Average) Students should note the descriptions of the speaker's detachment process in each of the stanzas, followed by the final resolution to no longer seek an empty world.

13. (Challenging) Students' essays should address the effect created by the individual stanzas leading up to the later stanzas that introduce irony; they should include specific examples from the poem that they selected to analyze.

14. (Average) Students may explore the despair of "Remembrance," the optimism of "The Darkling Thrush," or the irony of "Ah, Are You Digging on My Grave?"

15. (Challenging) Students should address the literal and symbolic aspects of the titles in relation to the meanings of the poems.

Oral Response

16. In their oral responses, students should cite specific information from the poems that substantiates their presentations and expands on their earlier responses.

"God's Grandeur" and "Spring and Fall: To a Young Child" by Gerard Manley Hopkins

"To an Athlete Dying Young" and "When I Was One-and-Twenty" by A.E. Housman

Open-Book Test (p. 129)

Multiple Choice and Short Answers

1.b Explanation: Of the answer choices, the reference to the Holy Ghost is the strongest indication of Hopkin's religious background.

2.d Explanation: The sunrise is an example of the grandeur that Hopkins describes in his poem.

3. Sample answer: Students may cite the grandeur of the world, the freshness of nature, or the sunset or sunrise described in lines 11–12.

4. Sample answer: Hopkins wants all of the feet of the poem to begin with a stressed syllable, creating sprung rhythm.

5. Sample answer: Spring and fall and their contrast are symbolic of childhood and adulthood and the contrast between those times in life.

6.a Explanation: The athlete's death will memorialize the glory of winning a race; if he aged after winning the race, others would undoubtedly surpass his achievement or replace him in the townsmen's minds.

7.c Explanation: There are four feet per line. Lines 3, 6, and 8 are trochaic.

8. Sample answer: Students' diagrams may explore the issue of an athlete who dies young and doesn't have opportunities to excel further, have more of an impression on others, and his or her life and experiences are cut short. Housman's poems reflect the loss of his mother at a young age without opportunities to spend time with her being cut short.

9. Sample answer: The word "given" must be treated as one syllable in order to follow the established iambic trimeter rhythm.

10. Sample answer: In the first stanza the speaker is told not to give away his or her heart; in the second stanza the speaker is told not to be sorry about having given away his or her heart—it is never a vain act.

Questions are classified in these categories:

Comprehension	10 (A)
Interpretation	3 (C), 5 (C), 6 (A)
Literary Analysis	4 (A), 7 (A), 9 (A)
Reading Strategy	1 (E), 8 (C)
Vocabulary	2 (E)

E=Easy, A=Average, C=Challenging

Extended Response

11. (Easy) Students' charts and writing should include examples of Hopkins's references to nature from the poems and relate to Hopkins's respect and love of nature and the world.

12. (Average) Students should recognize the emphasis that the rhythm places on ideas and how the unpredictability of the rhythm reflects the unpredictability of nature and the world.

13. (Challenging) Students' essays should address the topics of each poem and identify the potential audiences as those with less experience or understanding of the topics.

14. (Average) Students should recognize that Housman's poems have literal meanings; but with more thought and reflection, there is deeper meaning that explores the topic in a more serious and involved manner.

15. (Challenging) Students' personal levels of connection to the poem's meaning will determine their responses; their essay should be supported with examples from the poem.

Oral Response

16. In their oral responses, students should cite specific information from the poems that substantiates their presentations and expands on their earlier responses.

Unit 6: A Time of Rapid Change (1901–Present)

"When You Are Old," "The Lake Isle of Innisfree," "The Wild Swans at Coole," "The Second Coming," and "Sailing to Byzantium"
by William Butler Yeats

Open-Book Test (p. 132)

Multiple Choice and Short Answer

1.b Explanation: The speaker declares that as the woman reads the book, she will remember what she used to look like and how men fell in love with her (lines 4–6).

2. Sample answer: This man loved the "pilgrim soul" in the woman (line 7), meaning that he loved her for her inner beauty, not for her good looks.

3.a Explanation: The fact that love is described as running away and hiding from her implies that the woman is unable to find a love that she once had.

4. Sample answer: The diagonal lines of the herringbone organizer should indicate that Innisfree is described as natural (lines 3–4), secluded (lines 5–6), peaceful (line 5), and calm (lines 9–10). Line numbers in parentheses indicate the proof from the poem that should have been written on the horizontal lines of the organizer.

5. Sample answer: This place represents a haven from the travails of the modern world. Stanza three supports this idea.

6.a Explanation: The speaker states that his heart is "sore" when he looks at them during this moment (line 14).

7.d Explanation: The speaker is describing how noisy the swans are when they fly away from the water.

8. Sample answer: The speaker views his world as anarchic and violent (lines 4–6).

9. Sample answer: Here, Yeats describes the coming destruction of the world, symbolized by the beast. The rebirth of the world is symbolized by the city of Bethlehem, the city where Christians believe their savior was born.

10.d Explanation: In this line the speaker seeks immortality by becoming a work of Greek art.

Questions are classified in the following categories:

Comprehension	3 (A), 8 (A)
Interpretation	2 (A), 4 (A), 6 (A)
Literary Analysis	1 (A), 5 (C), 10 (C)
Reading Strategy	9 (C)
Vocabulary	7 (E)

E=Easy, A=Average, C=Challenging

Extended Response

11. (Easy) Yeats may be telling Maude that she will regret her decision not to return his affection (lines 9–10). Yeats may be the "one man" (line 7–8) who truly loved Maude.

12. (Average) "Lake Isle of Innisfree," with its natural setting, represents a haven from the modern world for the speaker in this poem (lines 11–12), while "Sailing to Byzantium" represents a symbolic journey to the world of art. Both poems represent sanctuaries to their speakers.

13. (Easy) Responses should indicate that the swans represent the transient beauty of nature to the speaker (lines 25–30).

14. (Average) The speaker sees the end of this cycle as a violent period that needs to end (lines 3–6). The speaker expresses his hope that the Second Coming will begin a new cycle of rebirth (lines 21–22) and thus end the violence and degeneration of the present era (lines 10–17).

15. (Challenging) Responses should indicate that the speaker in this poem sees his former country as a symbol of mortality (lines 1–3, 6) and the city of Byzantium as a symbol of immortality through art (stanza III).

Oral Response

16. Student's responses should cite specific information from the poems that substantiates their presentations and expands on their earlier responses.

"Preludes," "Journey of the Magi," and "The Hollow Men"
by T. S. Eliot

Open-Book Test (p. 134)

Multiple Choice and Short Answer

1. Sample answer: City life is portrayed as bleak and difficult. Students may cite various lines from these stanzas to support this response.

2.b Explanation: The speaker views his subject as a wretched person.

3. Sample answer: The speaker has a pessimistic view of the world, as evidenced by the comparison of something as large and grand as the world to the sordid life of the women in the lots.

4.a Explanation: The speaker states that they had a hard time (line 16), but that he would do it again (line 33).

5. Sample answer: Eliot's view of the world is a depressing one. He feels that people cling to false hopes and ideas (lines 40–43) much to their detriment, and that death is preferable to such a narrow-minded existence.

6. Sample answer: The birth represents the clear vision of the world and how to live in it; the death represents the shedding of old, dangerous ideas about the world. Shedding these ideas is difficult, for as the speaker says, he is among only a few people who have done so, which makes living among the people who cling to these ideas depressing and difficult.

7.b Explanation: The words on these lines create a vision of hopelessness. Vermin such as rats walk over something that is destroyed— the broken glass. Even speaking is described as "meaningless" in these lines.

8. Sample answer: The eyes represent those people who are able to see the way in which to live their lives successfully and well. On lines 62–67, the eyes are likened to a guiding star in the sky, which the hollow men hope will lead them out of their bleak existence.

9. Sample answer: The Shadow is the area of uncertainty that lies between a process and a result—for example, the shadow lies between conception, the process by which life begins, and creation, the result of conception.

10.a Explanation: Tumid describes the destructive condition of the river, which is part of the landscape of destruction in "The Hollow Men."

Questions are classified in the following categories
Comprehension   7 (A)
Interpretation   4 (A), 6 (A), 8 (A)
Literary Analysis   1 (E), 3 (C), 5 (C)
Reading Strategy   2 (A), 9 (A)
Vocabulary   10 (E)

E=Easy, A=Average, C=Challenging

Extended Response

11. (Average) The response should indicate that the images that Eliot includes in "Preludes" are examples of the bleak existence of the working person in the industrialized age. Students may cite various examples from all parts of the poem.

12. (Easy) Responses should indicate that such conversational language creates a feeling of immediacy to the ancient story of the magi. In this way, Eliot reminds the reader that questions of faith and one's ability to navigate this world are age-old questions with which each generation of people grapples. Students may cite examples from lines 35–43 to support these ideas.

13. (Average) The hollow men represent the people who have no direction in life and who do not know how to lead anything but a "broken," destructive existence. Students may cite lines 3–7, 11–12, 15–17 to support these ideas, though other lines may be used for support as well.

14. (Average) Responses should indicate that while "Preludes" portrays a bleak picture of life in the modern age, "Journey of the Magi" offers some hope to finding a meaningful existence through struggle. Students may cite various lines from each poem to support these ideas.

15. (Average) Venn diagram: Circle labeled "Preludes": this poem criticizes the environment that people live in during the modern age. Examples cited should emphasize how Eliot criticized places and their effects on people more than people themselves. Circle labeled "The Hollow Men": this poem criticizes the results that the modern age has on people—they have become directionless and corrupt. Examples cited from the poem should support this idea. Area labeled "Both": Each poem paints a bleak picture of this era. In both poems, the speaker asserts that nothing positive will result from this period in time.

Oral Response

16. Student's responses should cite specific information from the poems that substantiates their presentations and expands on their earlier responses.

"In Memory of W. B. Yeats"
and **"Musée des Beaux Arts"**
by W. H. Auden

"Carrick Revisited"
by Louis MacNeice

"Not Palaces"
by Stephen Spender

Open-Book Test (p. 138)

Multiple Choice and Short Answer

1.c Explanation: The speaker emphasizes that while Yeats has died, his poetry will live on.

2. Sample answer: Yeats' poetry is read all over the world; as such, Yeats lives in the memories of the people who read his poetry.

3. Sample answer: Like farming, writing a verse of poetry requires care in its development.

4.c Explanation: People's indifference to the suffering of others is captured in this line. Icarus is depicted as falling into the sea, and no one bothers to rescue him.

5. Sample answer: Icarus' fall into the sea has nothing to do with the ploughman's work in the field, so the ploughman doesn't bother to investigate the noise he may have heard.

6. Sample answer: The length of time that has passed since the speaker last visited Carrick alters the speaker's perception of his experiences there.

7. Sample answer: Many factors that were out of the control of the speaker contributed to who he now is. Students may cite from lines 21–25 or lines 26–30 to support this idea.

8.b Explanation: *Schemes* are a type of secret thought. One can conclude that *intrigues* means schemes.

9.c Explanation: The poet believes that poetry should exude energy of the present, not wax nostalgic about past experiences and memories (lines 6–8).

10. Sample answer: Spender believes that poetry should function as an agent of social change (lines 21–23).

Questions are classified in these categories:

Comprehension	3 (A), 5 (A), 6 (A)
Interpretation	2 (A), 9 (A)
Literary Analysis	4 (C), 7 (A), 10 (A)
Reading Strategy	1 (A)
Vocabulary	8 (E)

Extended Response

11. (Easy) Yeats's poetry has had a lasting effect on the world. Yeats will continue to be read after his death by people all over the world because people can relate to the message behind his poetry (lines 32–41).

12. (Average) Auden contrasts the tragedy of Icarus' fall into the ocean (a familiar Greek myth) to the indifference of the people who are nearby and may have rescued him— a ploughman who may have heard the fall, the ship whose sailors may have seen something. Auden also illustrates this callousness by likening it to the inability of children to appreciate the greatness associated with the "miraculous birth" (line 6).

13. (Average) The speaker asserts that forces beyond his control have worked to form his identity. He cites boarding school as one example (lines 21–25).

14. (Challenging) Spender dismisses the traditional celebratory use of poetry as useless (lines 6–8), and urges to his readers that poetry should deal with making people aware of the need to change society (lines 19–24).

15. (Average) Venn Diagram: Circle labeled "In Memory of W. B. Yeats": Time does move on, but the passage of time will enhance rather than diminish Yeats's reputation as a poet; his poetry will survive the passage of time. Circle labeled "Carrick Revisited": Time's passage cannot be controlled; in fact the passage of time affects one's view of the past. Area labeled "Both": Time's passage cannot be controlled by the speakers in either poem. The essay should develop these ideas, citing various lines from the poems to support these points.

Oral Response

16. Student's responses should cite specific information from the poems that substantiates their presentations and expands on their earlier responses.

"Shooting an Elephant"
by George Orwell

Open-Book Test (p. 141)

Multiple Choice and Short Answer

1. Sample answer: Orwell's position of authority as a police officer earned him the resentment of the Burmese, whom he managed within the scope of his duties.

2.a Explanation: Orwell hated his job because he was able to see first hand how the Empire oppressed the Burmese people.

3. Sample answer: One would normally ask officials for information about state functions since they are public servants. Orwell ridicules this function of state officials by implying that this answer isn't readily available from state officials.

4.b Explanation: The description of this neighborhood suggests it is an incredibly poor area of the city where life is difficult. Since *squalid* is used to describe it, it is logical to conclude that a synonym for it is *wretched*.

5. Sample answer: Orwell contradicts himself and shoots the elephant in order to save his reputation among the Burmese people, not because the elephant posed any threat to him.

6. Sample answer: Orwell resents the Burmese. While he sympathizes with their plight as members of the British empire, he resents the fact that he feels pressured by them to shoot the elephant.

7.a Explanation: The flow of the elephants' blood as a result of a bullet wound is likened to the drape of a luxurious fabric, a shocking contrast in images.

8. Sample answer: Life under British rule was one of desperation. The Burmese see the dead elephant as a source of food and income (the tusks could be sold for money).

9.d Explanation: The death of the Indian assuaged Orwell's guilt over shooting the elephant.

10.c Explanation: Orwell needs to seek the approval of others in order to feel better about his decision to shoot the elephant.

Questions are classified in the following categories:

Comprehension	1 (E), 9 (A)
Interpretation	8 (A), 10 (A)
Literary Analysis	3 (C), 5 (A), 7 (C)
Reading Strategy	2 (A), 6 (A)
Vocabulary	4 (E)

E=Easy, A=Average, C=Challenging

Extended Response

11. (Easy) While Orwell sympathizes with the plight of the Burmese and Empire's harsh treatment of them, he is also exasperated by them because they make his job so difficult. The decision to shoot the elephant is one example of how the Burmese complicated Orwell's job.

12. (Average) Diagonal lines of the organizer may contain the following qualities: indecisive, confused, sensitive, guilt-ridden. Essays should expand on the qualities compiled in the organizer, using evidence from the story to support statements made about Orwell's personality.

13. (Average) Responses should indicate that both groups of people suffered. The Burmese suffered economic, social, and political hardships, while the British colonizers suffered from crises of identity and guilt over their role in the oppression of the Burmese. Examples from throughout the story may be cited to support these points.

14. (Average) Even though the elephant has killed one person, Orwell sees that it has passed through the dangerous "must" stage and now

poses no threat. The elephant is an important economic asset to its owner, so shooting it would produce a considerable hardship on him. At the same time, Orwell's desire to win the approval and respect of the Burmese (thus reinforcing his authority over them) is also important to Orwell, and it is this desire that ultimately wins out.

15. (Challenging) The response should indicate that Orwell's use of irony serves to emphasize the brutality involved killing the elephant and in oppressing the Burmese. Other examples of irony may be cited to support these points.

Oral Response

16. Student's responses should cite specific information from the essay that substantiates their presentations and expands on their earlier responses.

"The Demon Lover"
by Elizabeth Bowen

Open-Book Test (p. 144)

Multiple Choice and Short Answer

1.d Explanation: The notion of death and stillness in the house contributes to the eerie atmosphere of the story.

2. Sample answer: Bowen heightens the idea that the house is empty and deserted by describing the stains left on the furniture and the marks on the wallpaper— marks Mrs. Drover never noticed when the house was full of people and furniture.

3. Sample answer: We learn that Mrs. Drover is forty-four years old and is a worrier who is able to maintain a calm demeanor.

4.c Explanation: It is odd that Mrs. Dover is unable to remember the face of the man she was supposed to marry. The only aspect of her fiance that she does remember clearly is the pain he caused her by his touch.

5. Sample answer: The fiancé seems to have a dominating personality. He intimidates Mrs. Drover by not kissing her, drawing away from her, and staring at her. He also vows that he shall be with her "sooner or later."

6.d Explanation: Mrs. Drover thought the promise that she was forced to make was unnatural, and it caused her to be separated from the rest of humanity.

7.a Explanation: Mrs. Drover fails to make connections with other men after her fiancé leaves for the war. *Dislocation* is the condition of feeling out of place; *connection* means the opposite of *dislocation*.

8. Some students may feel vulnerable and alone

themselves, or identify with those feelings in Mrs. Drover. They also may recognize the way she sits against the wall to make herself feel less vulnerable. The author probably intended this for readers to identify with Mrs. Drover's feelings, as almost everyone has times of vulnerability and fear.

9. Sample answer: The narrator describes the house as hollow and empty. The letter has made Mrs. Drover feel alone and vulnerable in the house. She tries to imagine that it doesn't exist in order to drive this feeling away.

10. Sample answer: The taxi driver seems to know what Mrs. Drover wants before she asks for it. The taxi appears to be "alertly waiting for her." The driver turns his cab around to meet her without looking around. The taxi driver also turns left before Mrs. Drover tells him to.

Comprehension	3 (A), 6(E)
Interpretation	2 (A), 5(A)
Literary Analysis	1 (A), 4(C), 9 (A), 10 (C)
Reading Strategy	8 (C)
Vocabulary	7 (E)

E=Easy, A=Average, C=Challenging

Extended Response

11. (Average) Student's essays should focus on how Bowen develops the supernatural atmosphere of her story through description of the setting and Mrs. Drover's reaction to it. Students should cite examples.

12. (Average) The diagonal lines of the herringbone organizer should include the following qualities of Mrs. Drover: confused, passive, sensitive to her environment, nervous. Students may cite examples from throughout the story to support these qualities. Essays should explain how these aspects of her personality work to make her react so fearfully to the letter.

13. (Challenging) Responses should indicate that the fiancé controlled the relationship through fear and intimidation. Students should cite examples to support this idea.

14. (Easy) Responses should indicate how Mrs. Drover's recollections, vague though they may be, haunt her and fill her with fear, just as demons or ghosts in nightmares might haunt a person who dreams of them or who believes in them. Though she tries to convince herself that her fiancé must have been killed in the war, Mrs. Drover is haunted by the possibility that he will come back to claim her. Students should cite examples to support these assertions.

15. (Easy) Responses should indicate that Bowen builds suspense through the lonely, empty atmosphere of the house and its effect on Mrs. Drover's emotions; Mrs. Drover's desperate attempt to recall her fiancé's face and the time that they were supposed to meet, and the way in which the taxi driver seems to know what Mrs. Drover Wants before she does. Students should cite examples from throughout the story to support these ideas.

Oral Response

16. Student's responses should cite specific information from the story that substantiates their presentations and expands on their earlier responses.

"The Soldier"
by Rupert Brooke

"Wirers"
by Siegfried Sassoon

"Anthem for Doomed Youth"
by Wilfred Owen

"Birds on the Western Front"
by Saki (H. H. Munro)

Open-Book Test (p. 147)

Multiple Choice and Short Answer

1.b Explanation: The speaker presents only positive images about England and his connection to England (lines 5–8).

2. Sample answer: The speaker's spirit will reflect, for eternity, all of the wonderful images of England (lines 11–12).

3. Sample answer: The wires of the front line are repaired at night by soldiers who work quietly and quickly in the dark.

4. Sample answer: This image reinforced the haunting, unreal quality of the images of the soldiers who are working at night to repair the wire. This image may also be read to foreshadow the certain doom of those soldiers who are sent to repair this wire (lines 7–8, 11).

5. Sample answer: The speaker is bitter. He resents the fact that one of his comrades was killed for what he sees as a pointless exercise in repairing the wire.

6.a Explanation: This line reflect the brutal and inhuman way that the soldiers were killed during the war.

7.d Explanation: The sounds reflected by actual prayers or bells during formal funeral services are ridiculed here, because the noise of war is the last sound that the soldiers will hear before they die.

8. Sample answer: Owen focuses on the sound produced by these weapons and compares them to sounds of a solemn ceremony (lines 3–4, 7–8).

9.a Explanation: Saki seeks to convey the terrible toll that war has taken on humanity by illustrating its effect on birds—no one would stop to think about the toll the war has taken on such a small animal. In this way, Saki is exhorting people to contemplate the effects of war on people.

10. The air war is compared to the mid-air, territorial fights between birds. Saki implies that such warfare is animalistic in nature.

Questions are classified in the following categories
Comprehension   8 (A)
Interpretation   2 (A), 4 (E), 10 (A)
Literary Analysis   5 (A), 6 (C), 9 (C)
Reading Strategy   1 (A), 3 (A)
Vocabulary   7 (A)

E=Easy, A=Average, C=Challenging

Extended Response

11. (Easy) The speaker sees dying in war as a means to fulfill his duty to his country, England. Lines that may be cited to support this idea include lines, 1–3 and 9–11, but students may cite other lines to support their responses.

12. (Challenging) Responses should indicate that the speaker suggests the difficulty of keeping such a noisy affair a secret from the enemy (lines 3–4), and the confusion and danger that result from being discovered (lines 6–8).

13. (Average) Stanza 1 focuses on the violence of war and the terrible way that the soldiers died by contrasting the gruesome way that the soldiers died with formal funeral rites; Stanza 2 functions as a response to the violence presented in Stanza 1, describing how these dead soldiers will be remembered through the acts and expressions of the loved ones they left behind. Various lines from the poem can be used to support these ideas.

14. (Easy) While Saki describes the widespread destruction of the birds to be pronounced, he marvels as the ability of the birds to make the best of their situations.

15. (Average) The graphic organizer should contain the following information: Owls: ability to find food to survive; crows and rooks: soldiers, including deserters of the army; magpies: ability of people to make a home among the destruction; larks: coping with injuries received from the war. Essays should indicate how each of these birds represents a behavior exhibited by people during war.

Oral Response

16. Student's responses should cite specific information from the selections that substantiates their presentations and expands on their earlier responses.

"Wartime Speech"
by Winston Churchill

"Defending Nonviolent Resistance"
by Mohandas K. Gandhi

Open-Book Test (p. 150)

Multiple Choice and Short Answer

1. Sample answer: Churchill describes the war as a "tremendous battle raging in France" and the presence of armored vehicles "in unexpected places behind our lines." Students may list other examples to answer this question.

2. Sample answer: The main idea of paragraph three is that the seriousness of the war must be carefully weighed by military leaders so that proper defensive action will be taken. Churchill opens the paragraph by stating "It would be foolish, however, to disguise the gravity of the hour."

3. Sample answer: Churchill presents the information about the French and English armies' progress in a positive manner. He states that "the relative balance of the British and German Air Forces is now considerably more favorable to us than at the beginning of the battle." Churchill also describes the French army as having a "genius for recovery."

4.d Explanation: Churchill expresses his confidence in the ability of the British people to fight the Germans.

5. Sample answer: The reference to Trinity Sunday serves as a reminder to the British people of the importance of their duty to defend Britain against the Germans. It also serves to remind them that their national sovereignty is at stake in this war.

6.c Explanation: Gandhi has spoken out against what he sees as the injustice of the British regime, even though it may have the outward appearance of being a just one.

7. Sample answer: Rather than fight the court's inevitable decision to sentence him to a term in prison, Gandhi uses this opportunity to express his belief that peaceful resistance, which he accomplishes through his speeches to the Indian people, will result in India's independence.

8.a Explanation: Evidence supporting the fact that these acts and reforms have oppressed the Indians is found in the seventh paragraph of the speech.

9.b Explanation: This example shows how British control and exploitation of India has prevented the Indian people from being able to feed themselves.

10. Sample answer: Gandhi is offering himself as an example to his followers. By putting him in jail for merely speaking against the government, the

British government will prove to the Indians how unjust their legal system is, and many more of them will join Gandhi in the fight for Indian independence.

Questions are classified in these categories:

Comprehension	1 (E)
Interpretation	3 (A), 4 (A), 7 (C)
Literary Analysis	2 (A), 8 (A), 9 (C)
Reading Strategy	5 (C)
Vocabulary	6 (E)

E=Easy, A=Average, C=Challenging

Extended Response

11. (Easy) Churchill reassures his listeners about a British victory over Germany, despite the fact that Germany is at this time winning the battle. He also expresses confidence that the British people will make whatever sacrifices are necessary to win this war Students may select various comments by Churchill to support these points.

12. (Easy) Even though the French army is currently losing the battle against Germany, Churchill describes the French army's efforts in a positive way and suggests that now that the French have dealt with their initial surprise over Germany's invasion, they have now regrouped and will turn the tide of the war to their advantage.

13. (Average) Qualities listed in the herringbone organizer should include the following: courage; intelligence; compassion; honesty; leadership. Examples supporting these qualities are located on the pages cited in parentheses. Essay should elaborate and explain the information compiled in the herringbone organizer.

14. (Challenging) Parts of the speech that may be cited include Gandhi's explanation of his experiences with British rule, explaining why he is qualified to lead this rebellion; analysis of the effect of British laws on the Indian people, proving that there is a basis for the rebellion; and his request that he be sentenced the maximum penalty for his acts if the judge believes that such sentence is warranted, revealing how unjust the British legal system is.

15. (Average) Churchill advocates active, violent resistance to the German army; he does so because at any moment the Germans may invade and control England and subject her people to the same violence that other captured nations have suffered. Churchill rallies his people around a cause that requires immediate, active attention. Gandhi, on the other hand, advocates nonviolent resistance to the British rule of India, so that everyone involved may understand the devastating effects that British rule has had on Indian society. In this way, Gandhi hopes to gain the support of all people

concerned and win India's independence from Britain.

Oral Response

16. Student's responses should cite specific information from the speeches that substantiates their presentations and expands their earlier responses.

"The Fiddle"
by Alan Sillitoe

Open-Book Test (p. 153)

Multiple Choice and Short Answer

1. Sample answer: The description of the cottages on Harrison's Row introduces the bleak mood that is later reinforced by the description of the difficult lives that the people of the neighborhood, such as Jeff Bignal, led.

2.a Explanation: The narrator tells us that "Harrison's Row was the last of Nottingham where it met the countryside."

3. Sample answer: Harrison's Row is set in an isolated area just near the river and the farms.

4.c Explanation: Jeff's fiddle playing has a hypnotic effect on his neighbors. They stop whatever they are doing to listen to it.

5. Sample answer: Column labeled "Details of Setting": Harrison's Row is composed of run-down cottages, and is located on the edge of the city. It is isolated from the rest of Nottingham because of its location. Column labeled "Effect on Jeff Bignal": Jeff is frustrated at this isolation. He yearns for freedom ("Jeff played for the breeze against his arm, for the soft hiss of the flowing Leen and the end of the garden, and maybe for the horse in the field.") Column labeled "Reaction of Jeff Bignal": Jeff finally decides to sell his fiddle and buy a butcher shop, located farther up from Harrison's Row on Denman Street.

6. Sample answer: When Jeff plays his fiddle, the troubles of the members of the community disappear temporarily, and a mood of relaxation settles over Harrison's Row.

7.d Explanation: Blonk is described as being *harried* by his wife and children to work in the pit in order to make some money, something that he is unwilling to do. Thus, he must be *harassed* by them before he decides to work at the pit.

8. Sample answer: Improving his lot in life means more to Jeff than playing his fiddle in order to escape the hardships of it. He is sick and tired of the difficult and dangerous work he performs in the coal pit.

9. Sample answer: The fiddle represents the hope that life may get better for the people of Harrison's Row. Each time Jeff plays the fiddle,

they can forget about their troubles and concentrate on the pleasure that the music of the fiddle brings them.

10.a Explanation: The narrator asserts that no matter where these people are, they will survive because of their shared experiences on Harrison's Row.

Questions are classified in the following categories:

Comprehension	2 (A)
Interpretation	4 (A), 8 (A), 9 (A)
Literary Analysis	1 (A), 3 (E), 6 (A), 10 (A)
Reading Strategy	5 (C)
Vocabulary	7 (E)

E=Easy, A=Average, C=Challenging

Extended Response

11. (Average) Responses should indicate that the flooding of the River Leen, the description of its color as a "menacing gun-metal blue," the visions of crocodiles in it, and the account of the drowning of a young boy all contribute to the depressing mood at the beginning of the story because all of these images suggest that the river can be threatening and deadly.

12. (Average) Qualities that students may discuss include Jeff's work ethic and his determination to improve his life. Various examples from the story may be used to support these qualities.

13. (Easy) Responses should indicate that the description of the houses, the odd jobs that people took in order to make ends meet, the inability of the rent man to collect all the rents from the people, the difficult conditions of working in the mine, as well as Jeff's decision to sell his precious fiddle in order to open a butcher shop (though "no one could say that he prospered" at it) all work together to establish that the people of Harrison's Row were poor.

14. (Average) Jeff is happiest during the long summer months, when he can play his fiddle outdoors in the evenings. Jeff becomes depressed during the winter because he spends the daylight hours at work. He spent Sunday in bed as well.

15. (Challenging) The narrator explains that the unemployed husbands are not bitter or puzzled about their decision to leave the farm to find work in the city; they may be envious of those who work outdoors, but they accept their decision. The narrator also admires how, despite the hardships they face, the people of Harrison's Row are still able to find pleasure in Jeff's fiddle-playing. Finally, in the last paragraph of the story, the narrator respects the fact that, no matter where these people may find themselves, they will never forget where they came from.

Oral Response

16. Student's responses should cite specific information from the story which substantiates their presentations and expands their earlier responses.

"The Distant Past"
by William Trevor

Open-Book Test (p. 156)

Multiple Choice and Short Answer

1.b Explanation: Evidence to support this statement is found in the second paragraph of the selection.

2. Sample answer: The decay of the house may also represent the deterioration of the Middletons' associations with the townspeople. It is described as having "reflected in its glory and decay the fortunes of the family." Just as the estate was situated three miles outside of town, the Middletons' relationship with the people of the town is a distant one.

3. Sample answer: The conflict between the British and the Irish over who should rule Ireland is referred to here. Ireland eventually won its independence from Britain; even so the Middeltons maintain their ties to Britain, which controlled Ireland in the "past."

4.b Explanation: The Middeltons maintain their nostalgia for the past when Ireland was under British rule. That position has no place in the independent Ireland.

5. Sample answer: The town's prosperity increased. More tourists came to the town, and employment opportunities increased.

6. Sample answer: This linen cloth represents how Britain (represented by St. George) once controlled Ireland (represented by the linen cloth).

7. Sample answer: Miss Middleton means that because her political sympathies represent the opinion of the minority in town, she must be very tactful about how she responds to comments such as Fat Driscoll's, or she risks alienation from these people.

8.a Explanation: When the British invaded Northern Ireland, "the town's prosperity ebbed." The people were reminded of the last time that the British occupied Ireland; since the Middletons never made a secret of their British sympathies, they have come to represent what the people see as British oppression of them.

9. Sample answer: Since the Middletons are regarded as outcasts by the townspeople, putting away these family objects represents the Middletons' loss of the townspeople's tolerance and respect.

10.d Explanation: Miss Middleton derived a sense of dignity from this peaceful coexistence, and she appreciated that.

Questions are classified in the following categories:

Comprehension	8 (A)
Interpretation	2 (A), 7 (A), 9 (A), 10 (A)
Literary Analysis	3 (A), 5 (C), 6 (A)
Reading Strategy	1 (E)
Vocabulary	4 (E)

E=Easy, A=Average, C=Challenging

Extended Response

11. (Easy) Responses should indicate that while the town prospered after Irish independence form British rule, relations with the Middletons were positive. After the British invaded Northern Ireland, the town suffered, and so did the townspeople's relations with the Middletons.

12. (Easy) The response should indicate that it is the Middletons' historic and familial ties to Britain that dictate how they will be received by the townspeople. Thus, since the Middletons are unable and unwilling to shed these ties, they must constantly deal with the effects of these ties.

13. (Average) The response should indicate that while the Middletons' friendships with the townspeople are never very close, there exists a mutual caring and concern. The Middletons appreciate their neighbors' tolerance for their ties to England. However, the townspeople turn against the Middletons when the political and economic climate changes. Thus, the value of such friendships to the Middletons is questionable, since these relationships were unable to survive during the time of the Middletons' greatest need for them.

14. (Average) Qualities listed on the diagonal line may include the following: loyal, tactful, courageous, peaceful. The essay should elaborate on how these personalities are presented in the story, and how a judicious balance of them enables the Middletons to live peacefully among their neighbors without compromising their beliefs.

15. (Challenging) Responses should indicate that respect plays no role in the harmonious existence between the Middletons and the townspeople; rather it is the Middeltons' tolerance of the townspeople's sometimes callous remarks to them and the people's indulgence of the Middletons' customs that enables everyone to live in peace.

Oral Response

16. Student's responses should cite specific information from the story that substantiates their presentations and expands on their earlier responses.

"Follower" and "Two Lorries"
by Seamus Heaney

"Outside History"
by Eavan Boland

Open-Book Test (p. 159)

Multiple Choice and Short Answer

1.a Explanation: The speaker suggests that he wants to become a farmer like his father when he grows up (stanza 5).

2. Sample answer: The son watches his father assemble the plow and use it to make the furrows in the field without breaking it.

3. Sample answer: Heaney selects "earthy" action words and phrases to emphasize the speaker's desire to grow up to be like his father. Examples include "plow," "close my eye," and "stiffen my arm." These actions are what the speaker thinks a good farmer, like his father, engages in.

4. Sample answer: Now, it is the speaker who guides the father through his old age.

5. Sample answer: The speaker is suspicious of the coalman's motive for asking his mother to the movies (lines 12, 13).

6.c Explanation: These lines explain that the explosion occurred "in a time beyond her time" (line 34); thus his mother was never involved in the explosion.

7. Sample answer: The speaker reveals his horror of violence in these stanzas (See lines 21–24 as the speaker describes with increasing horror the explosion of the lorry and his vision of his mother being killed in it).

8.a Explanation: All of the words in this answer suggest a fantastic or movie-like quality about the speaker's vision.

9.a Explanation: support for this answer is found in lines 13–15.

10.a Explanation: Lines 16–19 describe what the speaker witnesses when she decides to become an active shaper of history.

Questions are classified in the following categories:

Comprehension	4 (A), 6 (A)
Interpretation	1 (E), 5 (A), 7 (C)
Literary Analysis	3 (C), 8 (C), 9 (C)
Reading Strategy	2 (A), 10 (A)
Vocabulary	

E=Easy, A=Average, C=Challenging

Extended Response

11. (Average) Farming represents the nurturing of the son by his father. Responses should indicate that the son's appreciation for the father's mastery of the difficulties of farming forms the basis for their relationship. The son's respect for his father is rooted in his admiration for his father's abilities as a farmer (line 5), because the

son has no such ability (stanza 4).

12. (Easy) The response should indicate that Heaney first presents the lorry in its conventional form—as a means for delivering coal to houses. Heaney strives to make the reader aware of the possibility that violence can erupt during seemingly ordinary situations. The boy's distrust of the coalman in the first three stanzas is amplified and distorted into the boy's horror that his mother may have been killed by an exploding lorry in the final stanzas of the poem.

13. (Challenging) Heaney recycles the coalman, the silk-white ashes, the town of Magherafelt, the lorry and his mother in the sestinas of the poem. Recycling these images help Heaney to tell his story about how sinister intentions may lie beneath the most ordinary objects and people.

14. (Average) Circle labeled "Abstract Images": Boland's references to stars being outside history are abstract. The stars are personified, and the speaker explains that no connection can be made with them. At this point in the poem, the speaker is detached from the ordeal of life. In circle labeled "Concrete Images"- these images include the fields, rivers, and roads that are filed with dead people. The speaker describes how she is too late to help these people. These images are more concrete because the speaker has made the decision to deal with the difficulties that life may bring her. Essays should elaborate on these ideas and cite specific lines from the poem to substantiate them.

15. (Challenging) Responses should indicate how as the speaker chooses to become involved in the "ordeal of history" (line 14), the lines of the poem seem to run into each other, as if mimicking the speaker's rush to help people. In contrast to the first half of the poem, where the speaker maintained her distance from history, the second half of the poem uses less punctuation within and between the lines.

Oral Response

16. Students' responses should cite specific information from the poems that substantiates their presentations and expands their earlier responses.

"No Witchcraft for Sale"
by Doris Lessing

Open-Book Test (p. 162)

Multiple Choice and Short Answer

1. Sample answer: Gideon plays with Teddy and helps him learn to walk. Teddy values Gideon's affection, as evidenced by his efforts to win back Gideon's favor after the incident with Gideon's son.

2.c Explanation: Teddy says that Gideon's son is "'only a black boy,'" implying that the boy is inferior to Teddy.

3.d Explanation: Gideon knows through his own experiences that black people are unable to rise beyond the status of a servant in British-controlled Africa.

4. Sample answer: Circle labeled "Mrs. Farquar": She feels helpless but tries to treat her son by bathing his eyes in a special solution, to no avail. She allows Gideon to treat Teddy. Circle labeled "Gideon": Gideon immediately went to get a special plant to treat Teddy's injury. He prepares it expertly and confidently to Teddy's eyes, and the child is cured. Area labeled "Both": Both characters react with great concern over Teddy's injury.

5. Sample answer: Gideon refuses to take the scientist to where the plant is located because he views this knowledge as something that is special to his people; since the British have taken away their land and their liberty, he refuses to voluntarily relinquish his knowledge about the plant.

6. Sample answer: The scientist is not surprised that Gideon refuses to take him to the plant. He is skeptical that Gideon's brand of medicine has any value at all.

7.a Explanation: The phrase "as if he could not believe his old friends could so betray him" assists the reader in determining that incredulously means "to do something in a doubting manner."

8.a Explanation: Gideon feels betrayed by the Farquars, especially since they order him to reveal the location of the plant.

9. Sample answer: Gideon's laughter is described as "polite," which implies that a distance has grown between Gideon and Teddy over the years. Gideon also calls Teddy "Little Yello Head," and he speaks of all that Teddy will be able to have when he grows up, suggesting that it is because he is white that Teddy is entitled to these privileges.

10. Sample answer: Teddy treats Gideon informally, and acts as if there is a greater intimacy between them than there really is. He calls Gideon an "old rascal" and speaks to Gideon about an incident which hurt and upset him.

Questions are classified in the following categories:

Comprehension	1 (E)
Interpretation	3 (A), 9 (C), 10 (C)
Literary Analysis	2 (A), 5 (A), 6(A), 8 (A)
Reading Strategy	4 (A)
Vocabulary	7 (E)

E=Easy, A=Average, C=Challenging

Extended Response

11. (Easy) Responses should indicate that the conflict over the plant illustrates how the Farquars exerted their authority over Gideon by ordering him to reveal its location. Gideon, however, rebels, and presents the Farquars and the scientist with the wrong plant.

12. (Average) Teddy represents the callous, superior attitudes of the British colonists in this essay. He does not hide his contempt for the native Africans, and Gideon, because his livelihood depends on staying in the Farquars' good graces, has no choice but to accept it. Gideon's distant politeness to Teddy represents how the native Africans tried to deal with the colonial rulers.

13. (Average) Responses should indicate that this peaceful coexistence is partly due to Gideon's ability to forgive the Farquars for their occasional mistreatment of him and the Farquars' gratitude for Gideon's kindness to them.

14. (Easy) Responses may indicate that Gideon has a forgiving and generous nature, or that he is stubborn, or that he is unafraid to stand up for his beliefs. Various examples from the story any be used to support these characteristics.

15. (Challenging) The scientist's attitude reflects the purpose of the British presence in Africa. His skepticism about the value of Gideon's medicine reflects British feeling that the native Africans are inferior to themselves. Examples from the selection should be used to support these ideas.

Oral Response

16. Students' responses should cite specific information from the story that substantiates their presentations and expands their earlier responses.

"The Lagoon"
by Joseph Conrad

"Araby"
by James Joyce

Open-Book Test (p. 165)

Multiple Choice and Short Answer

1. Sample answer: The description of this clearing suggests that it is an isolated spot which the oarsmen believe is haunted. This description prepares the reader for Arsat's haunting narrative about how Diamelen came to this place.

2. Sample answer: The oarsmen dislike Arsat. He is a stranger to them and they are uncomfortable staying with a man who is "not afraid to live amongst the spirits that haunt the places abandoned by mankind."

3.d Explanation: One can reach the conclusion that Arsat feels guilty about abandoning his brother because he insists that he loves his brother, even though he abandoned him.

4. Sample answer: Arsat will go back to receive his punishment for kidnapping Diamelen. Now that she is dead, he has nothing to live for.

5.a Explanation: Diamelen has blocked Arsat's thoughts of anyone or anything else.

6. Sample answer: The white man's silence spurs Arsat on to tell his story and to express his feelings about what he has done. For example, after Arsat tells Tuan about the death of his brother, Tuan's silence and subsequent remark "We all love our brothers" encourages Arsat to express his feelings about his brother's death and to rationalize his actions.

7.c Explanation: Houses cannot show emotions.

8. Sample answer: The narrator watches the girl leave her house every day from the floor of his front parlor, so that he may observe her actions without her knowledge. He looks forward to watching her leave every morning.

9. Sample answer: The narrator is distracted by his promise to the girl. He cannot concentrate on his schoolwork and is restless at home.

10.a Explanation: The narrator realizes that a mere gift will not win the affections of this girl and his romantic visions of her make him feel frustrated.

Question are classified in the following categories:

Comprehension	2 (A)
Interpretation	5 A), 9 (A)
Literary Analysis	1 (A), 6 (A), 10 (C)
Reading Strategy	3 (A), 4 (C), 8 (A)
Vocabulary	7 (E)

E=Easy, A=Average, C=Challenging

Extended Response

11. (Average) In the beginning of the story Arsat is in control of his feelings when he greets Tuan. As he begins to tell his story, Arsat reveals his anguish over Diamelen's impending death and his guilt over the death of this brother. Arsat has difficulty controlling his feelings for Diamelen, since he has allowed these strong emotions to guide his decisions to kidnap her and to refuse to help his brother when he was attacked by the Ruler's men.

12. (Easy) Responses should indicate that Arsat must give his own account of the story; otherwise, the reader will never discover the complex emotions that lay behind Arsat's decisions.

13. (Easy) Aspects of Arsat's personality which may be listed in the organizer include obsessiveness, bravery, and devotion. Various examples from the story may be used to support these qualities. Essays should examine these qualities and explain that Arsat may be considered admirable because he is willing to sacrifice his life for love and is willing to accept the consequences of his actions, as exemplified by the fact that he plans to return to the Ruler, now that Diamelen is dead.

14. (Average) The narrator dreams that he and the girl share a walk through the market and that he is a hero of sorts to her. His desire for the girl makes him emotionally vulnerable, which is why he offered to buy the girl something from the bazaar. When he was unable to purchase the gift, he realizes the futility of his daydreams, because they were turned into a reality.

15. (Challenging) Responses should indicate that the setting is a cold and poorly lit neighborhood. The grayness of the neighborhood contrasts directly with the passionate feeling that the narrator has for the girl. The darkness of the empty bazaar at the end of the story reflects the narrator's anger at how foolishly he behaved for an unrequited love.

Oral Response

16. Students' responses should cite specific information from the stories that substantiates their presentations and expands their earlier responses.

"The Lady in the Looking Glass: A Reflection"
by Virginia Woolf

"The First Year of My Life"
by Muriel Spark

Open-Book Test (p. 168)

Multiple Choice and Short Answer

1. Sample answer: Like the naturalist described in the story, the narrator is concealed from Isabella and is able to watch her normal movements unseen.

2. b Explanation: The narrator states that "she suggested the fantastic and the tremulous convolvulus rather than the upright aster."

3. a Explanation: The answer is supported by information in the text.

4. Sample answer: The narrator does not appear to know Isabella very well. She says her speculations about the flowers can come between her eyes and "the truth"— but what that truth about Isabella is, the narrator cannot say.

5. Sample answer: The narrator's perceptions about Isabella contrast with what she is really like. The last paragraph of the story contains various examples to support this answer.

6. b Explanation: The narrator realizes that there is a difference between her sleeping and her waking moments.

7. Sample answer: The narrator tells the reader about a new school of psychology that explains that babies are omniscient.

8. Sample answer: This type of account serves to emphasize the extreme youth of the narrator; while she is omniscient, her ability to judge people still needs to be developed.

9. a Explanation: At each point that the poems appear, the baby describes some aspect of her healthy, normal life.

10. Sample answer: The baby recognizes that Asquith's remark signals a new beginning for the world, and after all of the devastation she has witnessed, this makes her happy.

Question are classified in the following categories:

Comprehension	1 (E), 2 (A), 7 (A)
Interpretation	3 (A), 9 (C),
Literary Analysis	4 (C), 5 (C), 8 (A)
Reading Strategy	10 (A)
Vocabulary	6 (E)

E= Easy, A= Average, C= Challenging

Extended Response

11. (Easy) The mirror represents the impressions, or reflections that the narrator formulates about Isabella, based on what she observes of Isabella. Students should cite examples from the selection to support this idea.

12. (Challenging) Woolf's use of the stream-of-conscious technique is evident when the narrator first associates Isabella with various types of flowers, but then asserts that "such comparison are worse than idle and superficial." She then tells the reader that the truth about Isabella is hard to determine. Later, the narrator, after speculating about the facts surrounding Isabella's life, realizes she is entirely wrong when Isabella walks into the room. This technique serves to emphasize Woolf's point about the gulf that separates speculation from truth.

13. (Average) Response should indicate that the health and growth of the baby is used to contrast with the destruction of war, as the narrator provides the reader with accounts of both simultaneously. Various examples from the story may be cited to support this idea.

14. (Average) The narrator's actions reflect the public's attitudes about the war. For example, the narrator scowls after she learns of the German Offensive, thus suggesting to the reader the struggle involved in the war. When the armistice is signed, the baby pulls herself up to signal her approval of it.

15. (Challenging) Circle with "Lady in the Looking Glass: A Reflection": the narrator establishes her unreliability by the way that she indulges in detailed, though unproven, speculations about Isabella's personality. Circle with "The First Year of My Life": The narrator is difficult to believe because she is a baby, even though she tries to explain a scientific basis for her omniscient ability. Area labeled "Both"—Each of the narrators eventually gives the reader the truth about their subject. The essay should use the information from the diagram to evaluate the reliabilities of each narrator. Responses will vary about which narrator is more reliable, but students should support their answer with proof from the stories.

Oral Response

16. In their oral responses, students should cite specific information from the stories that substantiates their presentations and expands their earlier responses.

"The Rocking-Horse Winner"
by D. H. Lawrence

"A Shocking Accident"
by Graham Greene

Open-Book Test (p. 171)

Multiple Choice and Short Answer

1. Sample answer: The mother married a man for love, but the love left the marriage. The mother is always short of money, no matter how hard she works to raise it.

2. Sample answer: The toys were purchased with money that the family doesn't have, in order to keep up appearances. Making the toys hear this whisper emphasizes that these purchases were foolish.

3.d Explanation: This answer is correct because Paul insists that when he goes to the place where luck is, he discovers the names of the winning racehorses.

4. Sample answer: The rocking horse represents the desperate measures which people will take to achieve material success. Paul dies for money, and his uncle comments that maybe he is better off dead if that is all he lives for.

5.a Explanation: These descriptions emphasize how the mother has no real attachment to her son; she is more concerned with getting luck and money.

6. Sample answer: This remark emphasizes the futility of Paul's death. The mother will always want more money than she will have, but she has lost her son forever.

7. Sample answer: The housemaster is trying not to laugh while he tells Jerome this news.

8. Sample answer: Rather than ask for more information about his father, Jerome instead concentrates on the pig. Greene is mocking Jerome's supposed idealization of his father.

9.b. Explanation: The sentence suggests that the aunt is setting out on a long endeavor—telling the story of his father's death.

10.a Explanation: Jerome wants to add some dignity to the story of his father's death so that people will not laugh when he tells it.

Question are classified in the following categories:

Comprehension	1 (E), 10 (A)
Interpretation	2 (A), 7 (A), 3 (C)
Literary Analysis	4 (A), 6 (A), 8 (C)
Reading Strategy	5 (A)
Vocabulary	9 (E)

E=Easy, A=Average, C=Challenging

Extended Response

11. (Easy) The response should indicate that the family members do not share any close emotional ties. Paul and his mother are bound by their desire to find luck and as a result, money. Students should cite examples from the text to support their answer.

12. (Average) The response should indicate that the theme is the futility of finding happiness and contentment in money. Students should cite examples from the text to support this idea.

13. (Average) The response should indicate that Paul would define luck as the place where he can go to find a way to get money. Various examples from throughout the story may be cited to support this idea.

14. (Easy) The accident that befalls Jerome's father is not shocking, but ridiculous. While most people would express shock or disbelief at a serious accident, the characters have difficulty containing their laughter when they hear about how Jerome's father died.

15. (Challenging) Information listed in the organizer may include Jerome's concern about the pig, his efforts to develop two ways to tell the story of his father's death, and his joy at Sally's reaction to the true story of his father's death. The essay should utilize the information compiled in the organizer to emphasize how Greene used the character of Jerome to illustrate how absurdly people may react in the most serious circumstances.

Oral Response

16. In their oral responses, students should cite specific information from the stories that substantiates their response and expands their earlier responses.

"Do Not Go Gentle into That Good Night" and "Fern Hill"
by Dylan Thomas

"The Horses" and "The Rain Horse"
by Ted Hughes

Open-Book Test (p. 174)

Multiple Choice and Short Answer

1.a Explanation: line 10 is an example of how the phrases run into each other; the hard consonant sounds, such as -g and –b, as well as the -r sound, imply the frustration of the speaker and are examples of the way that Thomas uses alliteration.

2. Sample answer: The speaker encourages his father to fight his impending death and to indicate his success by either cursing or blessing the speaker.

3. Sample answer: The speaker uses images of green grass to indicate happiness, and indicates his carefree mood through the descriptions of what he does on the farm. Various examples from this stanza can be cited to support these ideas.

4.d Explanation: Lines 4, 13, and 53 support this statement.

5.b Explanation: While the speaker's memories of his youth are happy (lines 10), he tells us that Time holds him and he is dying.

6. Sample answer: Stanza 4 prepares the setting for the speaker's sighting of the horses. His description adds to the intensity of his vision, expressed in a simple, non-descriptive statement: "And I saw the horses."

7. Sample answer: The solidity of the horses is emphasized by their gray color. The other colors serve to provide an emotional contrast which mirrors the speaker's emotions at seeing them (lines 18–19).

8. Sample answer: The memory of the horses amid the bustle of modern life is a calm reminder of the peace that he had found during his walk through the woods.

9.a Explanation: The man expected to undergo some sort of change after he reached his destination.

10. Sample answer: Hughes creates vivid visual images ("the dark mud of the lower fields inching up against his trousers") and sounds ("there was a raw, flapping wetness in the air"). The careful selection of words suggests how miserable the man feels.

Question are classified in the following categories:

Comprehension	4 (C)
Interpretation	2 (A), 3 (A), 5 (A), 7 (A)
Literary Analysis	1 (A), 6 (C), 10 (A)
Reading Strategy	8 (A)
Vocabulary	5 (E)

E=Easy, A=Average, C=Challenging

Extended Response

11. (Easy) The response should indicate that the speaker tries to persuade his father to fight for his life by providing examples of other men who have engaged in such a struggle. Various examples may be cited from the poem to support this statement.

12. (Average) The speaker at first is unconcerned about the passage of time (stanzas 1–3); he grows sad at the thought that Time controls the course of his life and death (stanza 6).

13. (Challenging) The response should indicate that Hughes's comparison of the horses to great statues (lines 9–10), and the way the descriptions of the horses are grouped to emphasize their amazing stillness (lines 9–15), reflects Hughes's awe of these horses.

14. (Average) Responses on the diagonal lines should indicate that the man deals with these issues with anger and frustration. The essay should use this information to explain that the man's feelings about the attack of the horse represents his frustration at his disconnection with the land. Examples supporting these ideas should be cited from the text.

15. (Challenging) "Fern Hill" contemplates nature to explore a person's inability to control the passage of time, while "The Horses" examines the healing properties that nature can have on a person's soul. Various examples from the poems may be cited to support these points.

Oral Response

16. In their oral responses, students should cite specific information from the poetry and the story that substantiates their presentations and expands their earlier responses.

"An Arundel Tomb" and "The Explosion"
by Philip Larkin

"On the Patio"
by Peter Redgrove

"Not Waving but Drowning"
by Stevie Smith

Open-Book Test (p.177)

Multiple Choice and Short Answer

1.a Explanation: The speaker emphasizes how typical this sculpture is by remarking on the blurred faces and *that* faintly absurd inclusion of the dogs on the tomb—the word *that* suggests such a motif was commonly found on tombs.

2. Sample answer: The variation in the rhythm in lines 11–12 emphasizes the surprise felt by the speaker when he sees the couple is depicted as holding hands.

3. Sample answer: The speaker feels that the image of the earl and countess as a loving couple is a lie that will be interpreted as a truth because it is carved in the stone of the tomb.

4.a Explanation: The miners are described as laughing (line 11). Their carefree behavior is exhibited when one miner chased after rabbits (line 7).

5. Sample answer: The variation in rhythm in lines 13–14 of the poem reflects the suddenness of the explosion that resulted in the miners' deaths.

6. Sample answer: The images of the miners in happier, carefree days is how their wives will remember them; this image is emphasized in the last line of the stanza, which reminds the reader of those days through the image of the unbroken eggs.

7.a Explanation: The speaker contrasts this idea earlier in the poem with examples of the destructive ability of the rain (lines 5–7).

8. Sample answer: The length of the lines in the poem emphasizes its torrential aspect (line 5).

9. Sample answer: The title might represent the speaker's disconnection from his society (line 11).

10.c Explanation: Observers or society note that the drowning man always liked kidding around. Outsiders think this may have cost him his life.

Question are classified in the following categories:

Comprehension	7 (A)
Interpretation	1 (A), 3 (A), 4 (A)
Literary Analysis	2 (C), 5 (A), 8 (A), 9 (C)
Reading Strategy	6 (A)
Vocabulary	10 (E)

E=Easy, A=Average, C=Challenging

Extended Response

11. (Easy) The response should indicates that while the sculpture of the tomb creates a romantic image of the earl and countess, the speaker believes that this image is untrue. He thinks this false image has been created because people do not carefully examine the couple's relationship as it is presented in this sculpture on the tomb (line 24). Various lines from the poem may be cited to support these ideas.

12. (Challenging) The response should indicate the happy carefree mood of the first four stanzas, the religious, reverential mood of stanzas 4-8, and the spiritual beauty suggested by the last line.

13. (Average) The response should indicate that the rain is portrayed as a powerful force in the poem (lines 3–9), but the speaker challenges this power by drinking from the glass (lines 15-17).

14. (Challenging) The alternation of long and short lines of the poem emphasizes how the speaker floats on the edge of his society as well as how he floats in the water, drowning, because no one realizes that he is not waving, but asking for help.

15. (Challenging) In circle labeled "An Arundel Tomb": the lives of the earl and countess were interpreted to be happy and romantic, based on the appearance of the sculpture. In circle labeled "Not Waving but Drowning": the drowning person is thought to be larking, not asking for help. In area labeled "Both": In both poems, people are mistaken about the subjects of the poem because they take these subjects at face value. Students should elaborate these ideas in an essay and cite examples from the poems to support them.

Oral Response

16. In their oral responses, students should cite specific information from the poems that substantiates their presentations and expands their earlier responses.

"B. Wordsworth"
by V.S. Naipul

Open-Book Test (p. 180)

Multiple Choice and Short Answer

1. Sample answer: The narrator contrasts B. Wordsworth with the other beggars. He is neatly dressed and speaks English well. The narrator is surprised that B. Wordsworth appears to call at his house for alms.

2. Sample answer: When the narrator related what he said during this experience, he uses the language that he spoke as a youth. This language is contrasted with the more formal language of his narration.

3.d Explanation: After Wordsworth tells the narrator that he is a poet, he explains how he is like the "White Wordsworth"—a famous poet.

4. Sample answer: The narrator describes how Wordsworth helps him to cope with the difficulties of his life by speaking to him and consoling him after he is beaten by his mother. The narrator tells the reader that the world became more exciting as a result of his friendship with this man.

5.b Explanation: Wordsworth is training the narrator to observe and react to nature.

6.c Explanation: The narrator tells us that Wordsworth acts carefully, as if he were doing everything for the first time.

7. Sample answer: The childlike admiration of the narrator serves to idealize Wordsworth in the reader's eyes. The narrator tells the reader that his experiences with Wordsworth filled him with wonder.

8. Sample answer: The narrator is concerned about Wordsworth. He realizes that Wordsworth's sadness is due to his memories of the past and his failure to complete the poem.

9.a Explanation: One can conclude that *keenly* means *sharply* because the word is clarified by the narrator's description of feeling as if he had been slapped by his mother.

10. Sample answer: Wordsworth realizes that the life of the poet is a painful one, and he is trying to direct the boy away from this life. One gets the impression that Wordsworth cares a great deal about the boy's welfare.

Question are classified in the following categories:
Comprehension	3 (A)
Interpretation	5 (A), 6 (C), 8 (A)
Literary Analysis	2 (C), 4 (A), 7 (A)
Reading Strategy	1 (E), 10 (A)
Vocabulary	9 (E)

E=Easy, A=Average, C=Challenging

Extended Response

11. (Average) This poem represents Wordsworth's life. He writes it in order to give meaning to his existence, now that his wife and child have died. Students should cite and explain examples from the text to support this point.

12. (Challenging) Examples of how Wordsworth teaches the boy about the value of observation are found throughout the story. The boy's description of the street demonstrates that he can see objects before him in a clear-eyed manner, and then distill his impression about what he has seen into a powerful statement (much like the lines from Wordsworth's poem): "it was as though Wordsworth had never existed."

13. (Easy) Qualities that may be listed in the left-hand column include Wordsworth's powers of observation, his compassion, his commitment to poetry, his careful actions. In the right-hand column, include various examples from story to illustrate these qualities. The student should discuss these qualities in the essay and conclude that the boy admired Wordsworth because he worked to instill these same qualities in the boy in order to make him a poet.

14. (Challenging) The response may indicate that the boy is in need of someone to guide him through life or that he is sensitive. Students should conclude that the boy found a teacher in Wordsworth who showed him how to harness his sensitivity and create poetry.

15. (Average) Wordsworth may be looking for two things: an apprentice poet (He later tells the boy that he has been waiting for him), or inspiration to write a poem.

Oral Response

16. In their oral responses, students should cite specific information from the story that substantiates their presentations and expands on their earlier responses.

"The Train from Rhodesia"
by Nadine Gordimer

Open-Book Test (p. 183)

Multiple Choice and Short Answer

1. Sample answer: The lifestyles of these people are bleak and filled with poverty. Dogs are described as bony, and the people live in mud huts.

2. Sample answer: The man is smiling only in the hopes that this friendly expression will encourage the woman to buy the wooden lion.

3. Sample answer: The separation between blacks and whites is evident from the way that the whites undergo an emotional separation from their contact with the black people outside the train station.

4.a Explanation: The wife is furious that her husband bargained such a low price for the wooden lion. She has just realized how unjustly the old man is treated by the white people in Africa.

5. Sample answer: While the wooden figurines symbolize the former pride and power of the black people, the begging children illustrate their present, desperate condition.

6.b Explanation: The glass of the train is the physical barrier that represents the social and political barrier that exists between blacks and whites.

7. Sample answer: Until this trip, the woman has never been faced with the inequality that exists between black and whites in Rhodesia.

8.d Explanation: The repetition of this phrase underscores her indignation at her husband's unnecessarily hard-nosed bargaining with the old man, and at the shocking poverty level of the black people.

9.c Explanation: A slackening of the hands' grip can be likened to a deterioration of some sort.

10. Sample answer: The trains represents the oppression of black people that the British colonists instituted in Africa. There is no answer to the train's call because the black people at the station have no hope that the train will bring them freedom and equality.

Question are classified in the following categories:
Comprehension	5 (C), 7 (E)
Interpretation	1 (E), 8 (A), 10 (A)
Literary Analysis	3 C), 4 (A), 6 (A)
Reading Strategy	2 (A)
Vocabulary	9 (E)

E=Easy, A=Average, C=Challenging

Extended Response

11. (Average) The train, in both its physical description and the positioning of the white passengers on it, represents British oppression of the native population. The glass window of the train separated the whites from the black people outside. The movement of the train represents how the British have established their racist system in the areas of Africa that are under their jurisdiction. The "blind end" of the train represents the refusal of the British to see how their policies have caused the local population to suffer.

12. (Challenging) The examples compiled in the organizer should include that the train is described as a resting beast, it has a segmented body, it has a blind end, and it casts the station like a skin. Students should explain that giving the train the qualities of a snake–like organism represents the predatory qualities of the British colonial empire.

13. (Easy) The response should indicate that the woman's encounter with the old man has made her aware of the differences between blacks and whites in Africa. Various examples may be cited to support this statement.

14. (Average) The wooden lion represents the former glory and independence of the black people. Students may cite examples the text to support this response.

15. (Challenging) The response should indicate that the placement of the wife behind a screen represents the separation between blacks and whites; her stillness represents the resignation to the fact that whites now dominate African society; the sheep carcass may represent all that remains of African society after the British have colonized Africa.

Oral Response

16. In their oral responses, students should cite specific information from the story that substantiates their presentations and expands their earlier responses.

from "Midsummer XXIII" and from "Omeros" from "Chapter XXVIII"
by Derek Walcott

"From Lucy: Englan' Lady"
by James Berry

Open-Book Test (p. 186)

Multiple Choice and Short Answer

1.d Explanation: This comparison is stated in lines 2–3 of the poem.

2. Sample answer: Walcott wants to emphasize the oppressive actions that the police took to subdue the rioters. He likens it to the brutal effects of the apartheid regime in South Africa.

3. Sample answer: Walcott suggests that a reader can find situations and dialogue similar to those of the Brixton riots in Shakespeare's Sonnets or his play Othello ("the Moor's eclipse" or fall). Walcott also suggests how ironic the racism is of those people who say "blacks can't do Shakespeare," when clearly their experience of racial conflict in England is similar to themes which Shakespeare addresses in his word.

4. Sample answer: The speaker expresses his anger over the way that the rioters were treated. (lines 18-21).

5.a Explanation: Since *rancor* refers to the hatred of the black people because of the brutal way in which they were treated, the antonym is *love*.

6. Sample answer: Walcott states that little has changed; the black people of the Caribbean are still enslaved (lines 20–24).

7. Sample answer: These elements represent the slaves' connection to Africa, their homeland (line 16–18).

8. Sample answer: Walcott illustrates how native Africans were scattered in various directions by using the phrase "one way" and the word "another." As a result, the individuals from these tribes are torn away from their tribes and families and are alone in the world (line 33).

9.a Explanation: Line 20 supports this answer.

10. Sample answer: Lucy must have led a simple life in Jamaica. She is impressed with the business of the city and the way that the Queen handles people's expectations of her.

Question are classified in the following categories:

Comprehension	1 (E), 8 (A)
Interpretation	4 (E), 7 (C), 10 (C)
Literary Analysis	3 (A), 6 (A), 9 (A)
Reading Strategy	2 (A)
Vocabulary	5 (E)

E=Easy, A=Average, C=Challenging

Extended Response

11. (Average) The response should indicate that like the leaves racing to extinction with the advent of fall, the rioters of Brixton are being killed by the police as they free themselves from the oppressive "tree" of English society (lines 6–7). "Midsummer" represents the mid-point between two seasons and the coming change of fall; Walcott suggests it is "Midsummer" for England and its colonial history. The tide is turning with the riots.

12. (Challenging) The response should indicate that Walcott has a great familiarity with, and love of English literature. But after the Brixton riots, he can no longer think of Britain in fairy tale terms (line 9). The paradox of the racism implied in line 13 hurts him. As a black caribbean poet/ playwright, he sees the rioters as a modern-day

Calibans, a reference to a character from Shakespeare's play *The Tempest*. In the play, Caliban, a (black) native of an island, is enslaved by Prospero, a magician. Walcott sees the modern-day Calibans rising up to finally throw off the British empire's long history of oppression.

13. (Average) Walcott believes that slavery has left an indelible mark on the peoples of the Caribbean. Not only are they still oppressed in society (lines 20–24), but they have lost their African identities (lines 31–33).

14. (Average) The conversational tone of the speaker reveals her naive pleasure at the business of London (lines 11–17). The speaker's language also enables her to make an insight about the difficulty that the Queen must have in keeping up a regal appearance (lines 21–27).

15. (Challenging) In the circle labeled *"Midsummer, XXIII,"* the speaker describes his anger at the oppressive way in which blacks are treated in England. He analyzes this treatment through an account of the Brixton riots. In the circle labeled "From Lucy: Englan' Lady," the speaker is excited to be living in London; it contrasts sharply with the rural lifestyle that she left behind in Jamaica. In area labeled "Both," both poems describe their situations from the point of view of outsiders. Students should write an essay and elaborate on these points, citing examples from each poem to support their response.

Oral Response

16. In their oral responses, students should cite specific information from the poems that substantiates their presentations and expands their earlier responses.

"A Devoted Son"
by Anita Desai
Open-Book Test (p. 189)

Multiple Choice and Short Answer

1.a Explanation: Rakesh's behavior so impresses some of the women that they weep.

2. Sample answer: Rakesh's father is proud of how his son does not let his achievements get in the way of upholding tradition.

3.b Explanation: The sentence reveals that Rakesh was noticed by prestigious hospitals and his family was proud his accomplishments. Since he was not a student anymore, he did not need to win scholarships, and no specific award is mentioned. He was already working at a hospital, so he did not win an offer of a job. Thus, *encomiums* must mean *praise*.

4. Sample answer: From his humble roots, Rakesh has gone to medical school and has established a successful medical practice. These outward examples of progress may serve to indicate that Rakesh's character has changed as well.

5. Sample answer: The neighbors are somewhat envious of Rakesh, but they eventually accept his success.

6. Sample answer: Varma seeks attention by complaining of imaginary illnesses and faking his death.

7. Sample answer: Varma views Rakesh's efforts as an attempt to control him; Rakesh views his efforts as another example of the way in which he is a dutiful son.

8.a Explanation: Bhatia remarks, "Is it possible, even in this evil age, for a son to refuse his father food?" This comment is an indication that Rakesh has, in the men's opinion, flouted tradition.

9.d Explanation: Varma misses his favorite foods and bemoans the disrespectful attitude of his daughter-in-law and his grandchildren.

10. Sample answer: Varma no longer views Rakesh as a devoted son. He sees him as heartless and controlling, which is why he refuses the medicine that his son gives him and instead asks to be left alone.

Question are classified in the following categories:

Comprehension	1 (E)
Interpretation	2 (A), 5 (A), 7 (A), 8 (C)
Literary Analysis	4 (A), 6 (A), 10 (C)
Reading Strategy	9 (C)
Vocabulary	3 (E)

E=Easy, A=Average, C=Challenging

Extended Response

11. (Easy) The response should indicate that while Rakesh thinks that his behavior toward his father is respectful and loving, it only makes Varma resentful and sick. Examples may be cited from various sections of the story.

12. (Average) While Rakesh has become wealthier and more educated, his attitude toward his father remains the same throughout the story—although his father's personality changed. Students may locate examples from the selection to support this idea.

13. (Challenging) The response may include the following qualities of Varma: independent, traditional, hardworking, strong-willed attention-seeking. Students may cite various examples from the story to support these qualities. In the essay, students may conclude that Varma's retirement, coupled with his wife's death and his son's success, caused his personality to change from an independent man to one who is controlled by his son.

14. (Average) Rakesh interprets the tradition of caring for one's parents in the strictest possible sense. He notion of caring for his father's health is transformed into controlling his father's health (and ultimately his father's actions) through medicine, diet, and prescribed rest periods.

15. (Average) The response may indicate that Rakesh speaks in a patronizing manner to his father. He also refuses to take Varma's wishes into consideration when he fulfills his duty to his father.

Oral Response

16. In their oral responses, students should cite specific information from the story that substantiates their presentations and expands their earlier responses.

from "We'll Never Conquer Space"
by Arthur C. Clarke

Open-Book Test (p. 192)

Multiple Choice and Short Answer

1.a Explanation: Clarke feels man's current progress in space exploration has made people unnecessarily optimistic.

2.d Explanation: For example, Clarke compares space exploration to an analogy of island people who sail to discover new islands.

3. Sample answer: There are limits to man's ability create technology that is advanced enough to explore space.

4. Sample answer: Clarke feels confident that this event will occur.

5. Sample answer: Clarke believes that the massive size of space will make it scientifically impossible to control it.

6.a Explanation: Clarke confidently predicts that people will settle on "star-borne colonies."

7. Sample answer: Clarke is saddened by this thought. He appears to value the bonds that exist among human beings. Colonization of the galaxy will occur, but the comfort of human connections on earth will be cut.

8. Sample answer: *Conquered* means that distance is controlled by man. He implies this through his comments about earth. "Because we have. . . remote places on earth."

9.d Explanation: Clarke advises the reader to gaze upward at the sky and look at the stars. This advice implies that the reader must look to this highest point in the sky.

10. Sample answer: While Clarke feels that people will set up space colonies, he is saddened by the idea that these colonies will have no ability to communicate to people on earth. This inability to communicate across distances is why Clarke feels that we will never conquer space.

Question are classified in the following categories:

Comprehension	1 (E), 7 (A)
Interpretation	2 (A), 4 (A), 8 (A)
Literary Analysis	3 (A), 6 (A), 10 (C)
Reading Strategy	5 (C)
Vocabulary	9 (E)

E=Easy, A=Average, C=Challenging

Extended Response

11. (Easy) Clarke feels that the human race is inventive, intelligent, and tenacious. It is because of these qualities that Clarke knows that humans will continue to strive for what he believes is the impossible goal: conquering space. Students may cite examples from various areas of the essay.

12. (Challenging) Responses in the sunburst organizer may include the following: the definition (through example) of the word *conquer*; the use of analogy to clarify difficult points; the analysis of hypothetical situations ; hypothesizing about situations; and the appeal to the readers' emotions. Students' essays should analyze how Clarke uses these techniques to persuade the reader to agree with his point. Conclusions about Clarke's effectiveness in persuading the reader will vary, but the students should support their conclusions with proof from the text.

13. (Average) These debatable statements include the following:

"Man will never conquer space."

"One day, it may be in this century. . .we shall discover a really efficient means of propelling our space vehicles."

"All the star-borne colonies of the future will be independent, whether they wish it or not." Answers to this question will vary, depending on which statements the students select.

14. (Average) The response should indicate that Clarke firmly believes that man will discover the means to explore and settle space. However, Clarke feels that the price that will be paid for such an achievement will be the strain on human relationships because the communications between the people of the colonies and the people of earth will be nonexistent. Various examples from the essay may be cited to support these ideas.

15. (Average) Clarke asserts that humans value their connection to each other the most. He says people will sacrifice this value when they set out to colonize space. Students may cite examples from the selection to support this idea.

Oral Response

16. In their oral responses, students should cite specific information from the essay that substantiates their presentations and expands their earlier responses.